kosher by design
cooking coach

Recipes, tips,
and techniques
to make anyone
a better cook

By **Susie Fishbein**

Photography by John Uher

Published by ARTSCROLL / SHAAR PRESS
4401 Second Avenue / Brooklyn, NY 11232 / (718) 921-9000
www.artscroll.com • www.kosherbydesign.com

Distributed in Israel by SIFRIATI / A. GITLER
6 Hayarkon Street / Bnei Brak 51127 / Israel

Distributed in Europe by LEHMANNS
Unit E, Viking Business Park, Rolling Mill Road
Jarrow, Tyne and Wear, NE32 3DP / England

Distributed in Australia and New Zealand by GOLDS WORLD OF JUDAICA
3-13 William Street / Balaclava, Melbourne 3183, Victoria / Australia

Distributed in South Africa by KOLLEL BOOKSHOP
Northfield Centre / 17 Northfield Avenue / Glenhazel 2192 / Johannesburg, South Africa

ISBN-10: 1-4226-1309-7 / ISBN-13: 978-1-4226-1309-2

Printed in the USA by Noble Book Press

This book is dedicated to **KAREN AND STEVEN FINKELSTEIN**
who **coach** by example on how to live a rich, grateful, and meaningful life.
I am blessed to have you in mine.

and to **MARISA STADTMAUER**
who walks me through and laughs me through all of life's joys and challenges.

To my family: **KALMAN**, you are my home sweet home. And to my children: **KATE, DANI, JODI,** and **ELI**. You are an endless source of pleasure and pride. As Grandma Linda says, "You are my diamonds."

To **JOHN UHER, MELANIE DUBBERLEY, MAX LAU,** and **MARIANNE ZANZARELLA**: You make work feel like play. You never cease to amaze me with your patience and talent.

To **DEVORAH BLOCH**: You were the rookie on this book. Thank you for putting your heart into this project.

To **TZINI FRUCHTHANDLER**: My heroine. Is there anything you can't enhance, sharpen, or elevate?

To **ELI KROEN**: Your creativity and style are much appreciated on every project.

To **FELICE EISNER**: You make me giggle, you make me hungry, and you make my work better.

To **ELISA GREENBAUM, KAREN FINKELSTEIN, TOVA OVITS,** and **ELIZABETH PARSON**: Even short deadlines couldn't scare you off. Thanks for your incredible attention to detail and for catching all the things that slipped through the cracks.

To **GEDALIAH ZLOTOWITZ**: Who would have thought when we did our first book, in our early years, that this series would see us into middle age? I hope to still be working with you at 120.

To **GAVRIEL SANDERS**: You make every project better just by being on it.

To **MICHAEL KANE** of **PARK EAST KOSHER BUTCHERS & FINE FOOD**: Thank you for being a most generous and outstanding man, and to your butcher, **JOSE LLIGUCOTA**, for the private butchering class.

To **LAUREN EPSTEIN**: You are a rising star — a name to look for in the world of PR and social marketing.

To **ARI HEINEMAN** of **POMEGRANATE SUPERMARKET** and **BRENT DELMAN** of **THE CHEESE GUY**: Thank you for your counsel and advice.

To **GLADYS ESTRADA**: *Gracias por tu ayuda*. No matter how messy I got, you always had a smile.

and of course, to **THE ONE ABOVE**: Who makes all things possible.

It has been over 10 years since I started giving cooking classes. I have traveled extensively and on average have given, somewhere in this world, one class a week, with audiences ranging from 30-300 people.

When I first started, my goal was to teach 3 new recipes to the guests and have them feel comfortable enough to try them successfully at home. Once my nerves settled, a few months into the classes, I started thinking about my previous life as a teacher and realized that my goal at these cooking classes was misdirected. What I really wanted for my cooking class "students" was to free them from cookbooks, whether mine or other people's. My real job was to give my students tips, techniques, advice, and information that would make them more knowledgeable and capable in the kitchen. My new goals were: my readers would be able to create a meal using ingredients they had on hand, ingredients that they liked; they would to be able to realize that parts of recipes could be used in other way, thereby reducing work for a future meal. I wanted to give them encouragement to become more comfortable in the kitchen, to recognize techniques, and to think about other ways to apply them. I wanted to help develop instincts about cooking. Once you have those, you are able to work confidently, using visual cues, smells, textures, and feel. You can then focus less on written cooking times and exact instructions.

The game plans at the start of each section are meant to help teach the fundamental principles of cooking. They provide techniques, advice, and information to guide you so that you will have more success in the kitchen. If you can think your way through a recipe, you can rely on core concepts and intuition.

The playbook section is a guide to help you be your most resourceful in the kitchen. Be it actual leftovers from last night's dinner or extra ingredients that were used in a recipe, this section shares creative and money-saving ideas, concepts, and in some cases, a whole new recipe, breathing life into your tired leftovers. Think of the money and time you will save — and talk about getting your creative juices going!

All this — a decade's worth of guidance and instruction — is what you will find in this book. Although I trust that you will always turn to my books and recipes, my true hope is that after working with this one for awhile, you will feel empowered to trust your own ability. I hope it provides you with the license to create and cook and to truly enjoy your time in the kitchen.

Susie Fishbein

CONTENTS

GAME PLAN

GEAR

KNIVES

Your most important pieces of equipment are your knives. Buy them once, buy them well, and learn how to keep them sharp. A knife purchase is a personal decision. It should feel good in your hand. The grip should feel secure. Go to a store with a variety of brands and hold them. There are two basic styles:

JAPANESE These are typically made from very hard steel so the blades are thinner and sharper and the knife is lighter overall.

EUROPEAN These are made from softer steels and tend to have thicker and heavier blades.

Buy your knives à la carte, not in a set, so that you spend the money only on what you truly need. I can make any recipe that I have ever written with a simple and basic set of 3 knives:

1. **A CHEF'S KNIFE** This is the workhorse in the kitchen. It can be a 7-10-inch heavy blade, a lighter Japanese version, a cleaver-looking knife like I use, or a Santuko blade, which I avoid. These "hollow-ground" knives have indents in the blades that I find difficult to sharpen but many people do like them; again it's a personal choice. This chef's knife will do most of your cutting, chopping, dicing, and prep work.

    Notice where the blade eases into the handle. Check that your blade has a full tang. The "tang" is

» *If you cook a lot of fish that you want to remove from the skin, then you may want to include a thin, flexible knife.*

» *Don't let the high price tag of a good knife scare you. Buy a good one once, learn to care for it, and it will last you for generations.*

» *Care: Don't leave your knife at the bottom of a full sink where you can't see it. Always wash your knife with warm soapy water and dry with a soft cloth, from back to front.*

» *Never put good knives in a dishwasher or leave them banging around in a cutlery drawer. I keep mine in a case. A magnetic strip or knife block works well too.*

Paring Knives   *Serrated Knives*   *Chef's Knives*

the part of the blade that forms the handle. A full tang runs the full length of the handle rather than ending part way through. This feature provides strength and balance.

2. **A SERRATED BLADE** Although a serrated knife can be as small as a paring knife or as large as a bread knife, I prefer the larger size. Use this for slicing bread, sponge cakes, meats, tomatoes, and melons. The longer blade will mean fewer strokes.

3. **A PARING KNIFE** 2-4 inches in length, a paring knife is used for small jobs like crowning a tomato or dicing a shallot.

SHARPENING KNIVES Learn how to sharpen your knives, as all knives dull and nothing is more dangerous or less effective than working with a dull knife.

A honing steel, or sharpening steel, does not sharpen a knife, it just realigns the "teeth" or the molecules and straightens the blade. Every time you use your knife, you create minor dings and bends in your blade on a microscopic level. Any one imperfection doesn't add up to much, but use your knife regularly for a week or two and you'll start to notice the dullness. A honing steel, used frequently, can help reset or straighten these imperfections and help keep your knife sharp, but it does not actually sharpen your knife.

Sharpening consists of re-building a new edge on a worn blade. This involves removing a bit of the metal edge to uncover a new, sharper one. There are three ways to do this: using an electric knife sharpener, utilizing a whetstone, or taking it to a professional to sharpen. I use a combination of all three.

STEP 1 *Hold the steel with your left hand and the knife with your right (lefties simply do the opposite), with the tip of the steel on your cutting board.*

STEP 2 *Put the knife at 90°, then tilt it to 45°, half of that will be about 23°.*

STEP 3 *Drag it across the steel at that 23°, making sure to get the whole length of the blade. Start at the heel and go all the way to the tip.*

STEP 4 *Repeat this process 6-8 times.*

» *Never stroke the same side more than once in succession.*

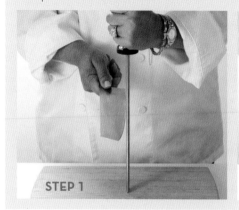

STEP 1

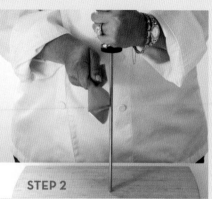

STEP 2

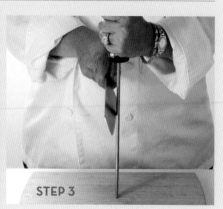

STEP 3

ELECTRIC SHARPENER

High-quality electric sharpeners get the job done and are convenient and easy to use. If you've never sharpened your knives, you'll certainly improve your edges by using a good electric sharpener. I use a Chef's Choice sharpener once every 10 days. I break out my whetstone a few times a year and have my knives professionally sharpened 2-3 times a year.

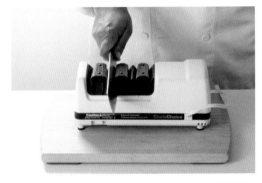

WHETSTONE

Whetstones are for people who take their knives seriously. They are blocks that are available in various coarseness levels — or grit sizes — depending on how much work the knife actually needs. They must be soaked in water for 15 minutes before use and anchored to your work surface with a towel. When you buy a whetstone, learn proper technique, angle, and amount of pressure. You can even purchase a guide to attach to your knife that will keep your knife at the proper angle (20°) This will result in the best-quality edge once you've refined your technique. Move the blade back and forth at the correct angle, using gentle pressure. Start at the tip of the blade, continue with the middle section, and finish at the end of the blade. Repeat the process on the other side of the blade. Turn the stone over and repeat the procedure, this time using the fine grit of the stone.

After using a sharpener or a steel, make sure you give your knife a quick wipe with a paper towel because it will have some very fine metal shavings on it.

BASIC CUTS Consistent cutting technique not only enhances the visual appeal of your finished dishes, it ensures your food is cooked to a uniform degree of doneness. Large pieces of vegetables take longer to cook than smaller ones. So if you're sautéing a vegetable that is cut to different sizes and shapes, you'll either overcook the smaller pieces by the time the bigger ones are done, or you'll cook the smaller pieces properly but leave the bigger ones undercooked. Keep this in mind when you are in a rush; cutting things smaller will mean they cook faster, just make sure they are cut evenly.

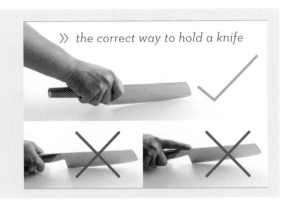

» *the correct way to hold a knife*

When working with a rounded vegetable like a sweet potato, potato, or zucchini, take a little slice off one of the long ends to create a flat surface that the potato can rest on without it rolling over. Cut slices, or planks; the thickness will vary based on the size dice you are looking to make. Stack some of the slices and make sticks, thin for sticks called julienne, wider for making french fry-sized shapes. Then turn them and cut again to make even dice.

Mincing can be used for any vegetable but is most often used for garlic or fresh herbs. Put some rough cuts of the vegetable, garlic, or herb on your board in a pile. It's all about the motion. Place the tip of the chef's knife on the board over the herbs or vegetables, holding it steady with your hand that is not on the handle, and use a rocking motion until you get very small minced pieces.

To make a chiffonade, stack leaves, mint, basil, or lettuce. Roll into a tight cylinder. Run your knife over the roll to make thin ribbons. You can use them as is or mince for a finer result.

TO DICE AN ONION

STEP 1 Start with a peeled onion that you have cut in half from stem end to root end. Place one of the halves cut-side-down on the cutting board with one hand pressing down on the onion, with fingers out of the way. Make a series of horizontal cuts through the onion. By leaving more or less space between the cuts, you control how big your dice will be. **STEP 2** Turn the onion and make a series of vertical cuts, following the natural lines of the onion, keeping your fingers in a claw position for safety, again, leaving more or less space between these cuts to control the size of the dice. **STEP 3** Turn it the original way and cut down, the dice will fall off, perfectly sized.

chiffonade cut

STEP 1 **STEP 2** **STEP 3**

CUTTING BOARDS

I like having a variety of cutting boards at my disposal. Small ones for small items, ones with a trench for capturing juices, and most the right size to fit in my dishwasher. If yours don't, clean with a solution of a teaspoon of bleach in a quart of water. I mostly use heavy poly or thick plastic boards but I do have one bamboo cutting board. These are the choice of many environmentalists. As a hard grass, it is a sustainable, renewable resource. They do absorb less liquid than wooden boards, so many believe they are as sanitary or more sanitary than wood boards. Wood, bamboo, and plastic are all soft on knives, which is good. Avoid glass and acrylic, and use marble only for rolling dough, not for cutting on. Hard surfaces will kill your knives. Anchor your cutting board to your work surface with a damp cloth or paper towel to keep it from sliding around.

PREVENT CROSS-CONTAMINATION When you're preparing fresh or thawed meat, chicken, or seafood, it's important to prevent bacteria from spreading to ready-to-eat food. Take these steps to avoid cross-contamination between raw and cooked foods: Wash hands thoroughly with soap and warm water before and after handling any raw food. Wash your cutting board as described above, in the dishwasher or with a bleach solution. Inspect your cutting boards from time to time and make sure they are free of cracks and crevices. Smooth surfaces can be cleaned more easily and thoroughly.

FOOD PROCESSOR

I use mine constantly for slicing; chopping nuts; making pestos, chummos, breadcrumbs, sauces, pastry doughs, and more. Food processors, as opposed to blenders, allow you to retain texture. A good model for a home kitchen is an 11 or 14 cup size.

STAND MIXER

A heavy-duty stand mixer is the baking workhorse. It allows for hands-free mixing. Use it for batters and doughs. Be sure you have at least a 4½-quart bowl to allow for double batches of recipes. Buy a strong one with a large horsepower motor if you plan on using

Stand Mixer

Blender

Food Processor

it for bread doughs. I use the paddle, whisk, and dough hook on my mixer. If a stand mixer is not in your budget, a powerful hand mixer and good mixing bowl can step in for most jobs.

BLENDER

Milkshakes and smoothies are popular uses for blenders, but I find the most valuable use is in liquefying foods or puréeing hot soups to a velvety texture. Just remember that when working with hot items, fill the blender only halfway so that the mixture doesn't expand over the top of the blending jar.

IMMERSION BLENDER

An immersion blender is a great little machine that can emulsify mayonnaise, whip up salad dressings and pestos, and purée hot soups right in the pot. Immersion blenders are simple to use and easy to clean. Immersion blend in the tall narrow mixing cups that they come with or in quart-sized plastic containers to prevent splashing and to keep the food close to the blade to work more effectively. The best way to clean an immersion blender is to put hot soapy water in one of these containers and run the motor.

OVENS

Always preheat your oven to the desired temperature before starting to cook. Keep a thermometer in the oven to check for accuracy. Note any differences between correct temperature and desired temperature and adjust accordingly. If your temperature is more than 25°F off or the hinges are loose, allowing cool air in, it's time for a service call.

Some ovens have a convection mode. In standard mode, heat comes from above or below. In convection mode, air circulates via fan so the food cooks more evenly and faster. If using convection mode, preheat as usual but reduce standard baking temperatures by 25°F and watch the time, because things may cook more quickly. I don't write recipes utilizing convection mode, but in my real life I use it often to roast vegetables in a hurry.

NECESSARY OBJECTS

》 *Unhook a few sets of measuring spoons and keep them handy in a mug. Look for ones that have easy-to-read numbers and bowls that are narrow enough to fit into spice bottles.*

》 *I keep a crock of utensils within an arm's reach of my stovetop so anything I need is right there and no rifling though drawers is necessary. It includes: a whisk, a selection of silicone spatulas, fish turner, ladle, slotted spoon, wooden spoon, metal tongs, small strainer, microplane, basting spoon, spider, silicone pastry brush, olive wood spatula, and a small metal offset spatula.*

THERMOMETER

These inexpensive pieces of equipment are vital to the quality and safety of your food. You can pick them up at any supermarket. I keep 2-3 in various areas of my fridge to make sure I am in the safe temperature zone. You want your refrigerator to be cold, but not so cold that things freeze. The preferred temperature is somewhere between 35° and 38°F. Your freezer should be at 0 degrees. I keep 2 of these oven thermometers in different parts of my oven, since ovens have hot spots.

Deep Frying Thermometer

Instant Read Thermometer

Meat Thermometer

Candy Thermometer

Digital Meat Thermometer

Oven Thermometer

Refrigerator-Freezer Thermometer

》 *Calibrate your thermometers. When your thermometer stands in ice water, it should register 32°F and in boiling water it should register 212°F. Adjust it if possible or note the difference when you cook.*

FREEZER

Anyone who has taken a class with me knows I am freezer-phobic and freeze almost no cooked foods. That is a bit extreme and the pace of some people's life makes freezing a must. So, understanding that almost everything loses a bit of taste and texture when frozen, follow these rules:

Make sure you label all foods that are going into the freezer and date them too; you may not recognize them once they are frozen.

You can freeze most things as long as they don't contain: mayonnaise, gelatin, cream, milk, egg whites, potatoes, mushrooms, leafy greens, or raw vegetables. Stews, braised meats, and soups freeze well.

》 *Double wrap anything being frozen to protect from freezer burn.*

KITCHEN ESSENTIALS

When buying pots and pans, buy the best you can afford. I am an All-Clad girl. They make heavy-duty 18-gauge stainless steel pots and pans that are nonreactive, cook evenly, and retain heat well. They will last a lifetime. Don't be tempted to buy a set of pots and pans. Very often they include pieces that may not be practical — and lids count as pieces. I prefer open stock so I can get just the pieces I need.

POTS

The most useful pieces that I own include:

A small **SAUCE PAN** with lid for making rice or couscous and steaming vegetables.

A large **SOUP POT** with lid for making stews, soups, chilis, and pasta. A good heavy pot will allow you to braise on the heat for long stewing periods without burning. Brands like All-Clad can also do double duty by starting on the stove and finishing in the oven, since there are no plastic knobs.

If budget and space allow, I recommend a very large soup pot so you can make big batches of soup, chili, or meatballs, and freeze a batch for a rainy day.

12-Quart Soup/Stock Pot

6-Quart Saucepan

8-Quart Soup Pot

10-Inch Nonstick Frying Pan

2-Quart Saucepan

14-Inch Frying Pan

4-Quart Sauté Pan

10-Inch Frying Pan

Nonstick Grill Pan

A 3-4-quart **SAUTÉ PAN** has straight sides, making it good for dishes that have a lot of sauce or liquid.

A **SKILLET** or **FRYING PAN** has sloped sides to help moisture evaporate. I like a 10-inch pan for smaller jobs. If you cook small amount of foods in too large a pan, a lot of the juices will evaporate. I find a 14-inch skillet invaluable. I can cook 5-6 chicken cutlets at a time instead of having to make multiple batches. It also allows plenty of breathing room, so food is not crowded into the pan, which will make it steam. If you can, having an additional 14-inch nonstick pan is a nice luxury as well. To avoid wrecking a nonstick skillet, always lubricate it with a paper towel sprayed or dipped in canola oil or butter. Don't use metal utensils or steel wool; they can pierce the coating.

A nonstick **GRILL PAN** is wonderful for indoor grilling and will give you a great sear and grill marks on your burgers and steaks. Allow these to preheat very well.

Although they are heavy to maneuver, an enameled cast iron **DUTCH OVEN** is a fabulous addition to a set of pots. It is non-reactive, doesn't need to be seasoned like regular cast iron, is beautiful enough to leave out, and is easy to clean. It is wonderful for braises and long-simmering stews and great for browning. Le Crueset and Staub make gorgeous ones.

Although many people use disposable roasting pans for foods like turkey and brisket, I really urge you to get a heavy-duty stainless steel **ROASTER WITH A RACK**. From a safety point of view, these pans will not warp or twist. They allow for even heat distribution and you can deglaze and make a pan sauce right in them for roasted meats and turkeys. Roasts can even be started in them by searing on the range and then finished in the oven. Measure your oven before you buy one to make sure of the size that will fit, including the handles. Make sure the handles are thick and riveted for when you are carrying a hot, heavy load from the oven, and choose a rectangular shape with rounded corners so a whisk can reach in easily.

>> *If your stainless steel pots have baked-on residue, pour in vinegar to cover the bottom. Add some baking soda and bring to a boil. Boil for 20-30 minutes; using a wooden spoon, loosen the bits every few minutes. Pour out the dirty liquid. Sprinkle with fresh baking soda and scrub. Rinse well. Repeat as necessary.*

Roasting pan with rack

Dutch Oven

COLANDERS VS. STRAINERS

COLANDERS are useful for straining pasta or washing vegetables, basically separating liquids from solids. **MESH STRAINERS** are useful for straining out finer particles, seeds, lumps in sauces or soups, and for sifting dry ingredients. **FINE MESH STRAINERS** are great for sifting confectioner's sugar or cocoa.

Colander

Strainer

Fine Mesh Strainer

SCALE

A kitchen scale is an important tool in cooking, in baking, and in preparing healthy portions of food. For instance, it makes dividing a chunk of chopped meat into equal portions for burgers a breeze. When preparing pasta, I weigh out 4 ounces for each person. Without the scale, I always made way oversized portions.

When making challah, I divide the dough and weigh the pieces so they are all the same size. When chopping chocolate, the scale is a great tool to know when I have the 4 ounces I need for a given recipe.

The **DIGITAL MODEL** has a feature that allows you to put a bowl or tray on the scale, zero out the bowl, and then weigh the contents in the bowl, thus weighing the true weight of the contents and not the weight of the bowl. This also allows you to keep zeroing out as you add more than one ingredient to the bowl.

>> *When using an analog scale to weigh a large amount of an item, place a bowl on the scale. Adjust the knob to turn the indicator back to zero so that the weight of the bowl is not counted. Then add the ingredients to the bowl on the scale for an accurate reading.*

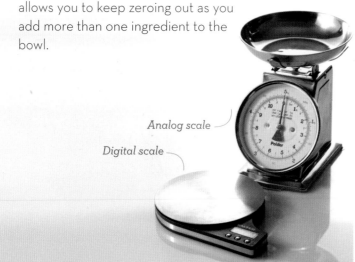

Analog scale

Digital scale

STOCKING YOUR KITCHEN

With good ingredients at your disposal, you can whip up a great quick meal any time. Keep good ingredients on hand:

IN MY REFRIGERATOR

>> *fresh eggs*
>> *butter*
>> *margarine*
>> *milk*
>> *fresh fruit*
>> *Parmesan cheese*
>> *fresh peeled garlic cloves*
>> *phyllo dough*
>> *lemons*
>> *herbs*
>> *scallions*
>> *shallots*
>> *carrots*
>> *celery*
>> *tortillas*
>> *lettuces*
>> *cheese*
>> *unsweetened soy milk*

OUT OF THE FRIDGE

>> *tomatoes*
>> *red and white onions*

IN MY FREEZER

>> *peas*
>> *spinach*
>> *sausages*
>> *pie crust*
>> *nondairy whipped topping*
>> *nuts*
>> *edamame*
>> *chicken bones*
>> *chicken parts and cutlets*
>> *homemade soups*

IN A DRAWER

>> *plastic wrap*
>> *parchment paper*
>> *disposable latex gloves*
>> *nonstick aluminum foil*
>> *heavy-duty aluminum foil*

IN MY CUPBOARD

>> *canned tomatoes*
>> *tomato paste*
>> *chick peas*
>> *black beans*
>> *kidney beans*
>> *white beans*
>> *coconut milk*
>> *chicken, beef, and vegetable stock*
>> *red and white wines*
>> *mirin*
>> *brandy*
>> *sherry*
>> *olive oil*
>> *canola oil*
>> *toasted sesame oil*
>> *balsamic vinegar*
>> *red wine vinegar*
>> *rice vinegar*
>> *Worcestershire sauce*
>> *olives*
>> *salsa*
>> *rices*
>> *grains*
>> *quinoa*
>> *pasta*
>> *panko*
>> *soy sauce*
>> *teriyaki sauce*
>> *sriracha*
>> *chili garlic sauce*
>> *honey*
>> *honey mustard*
>> *Dijon mustard*
>> *sun-dried tomatoes*
>> *capers*
>> *black olives*
>> *ketchup*
>> *barbecue sauce*
>> *nonstick cooking spray*

IN MY BAKING CABINET

>> *all-purpose flour*
>> *bread flour*
>> *cake flour*
>> *fine sea salt*
>> *coarse sea salt*
>> *kosher salt*
>> *sugar*
>> *confectioner's sugar*
>> *superfine sugar*
>> *dark and light brown sugar*
>> *vanilla, almond, and lemon extracts*
>> *Dutch-process cocoa*
>> *regular cocoa powder*

>> *baking powder*
>> *baking soda*
>> *espresso powder*
>> *yeast*
>> *old-fashioned oats*
>> *milk chocolate bars*
>> *semisweet chocolate bars*
>> *white chocolate bars*
>> *chocolate chips*
>> *apricot preserves*
>> *currant jelly*
>> *canned pumpkin*
>> *nonstick baking spray*
>> *raisins*

SPICES

Buy spices in small amounts, as they lose flavor after 6 months. Date them on their lids so you can keep track. Keep them away from light and heat in airtight containers. Dried herbs such as thyme and oregano should be crumbled in your palm to release their aroma before being added to a dish. I keep some spice blends on hand as well: a barbecue blend, Cajun blend, blackening spice, za'atar, hawaij, and schwarma spice.

Barbecue

Cajun

Za'atar

Hawaij

Blackening Spice

Schwarma

GAME PLANNING

When planning for a special meal or a Shabbos or a holiday, give yourself plenty of time to create and enjoy it. Organize your recipes and read them. Make your shopping lists carefully. Include amounts so you know exactly how many eggs or onions you will need in total to avoid multiple trips to the store. If you need 1 teaspoon of Dijon mustard, you will know not to buy a gallon. Read through all the recipes again, focusing on what steps can be broken down into parts that can be done in advance and just do the finishing work right before serving.

Don't be too ambitious. When planning a menu, think about the amounts of food you are served at a fine restaurant: a small appetizer to whet your appetite, a soup, and maybe a salad. You are then served one main course, so at home you may chose to make two main dishes to satisfy the taste of various guests. One vegetable and one side round out the plate. Dessert is a single decadent selection; a home meal need not include a buffet of desserts. Break that mindset and your work load will lighten significantly.

Time management is key when planning for a holiday meal. Divide recipes into things that need the oven and things for the stove so you can work at two recipes simultaneously. While things bake, do your chopping and washing, making the most of your waiting-around time. When you are ready to cook, glance over the recipes again. Look for preheating oven temperatures, pan size, how to prep the pan. Get your ingredients out and measured, and make sure to clean as you go so you are not overwhelmed in your space and don't face a disaster of a kitchen when you are done.

Follow the French phrase "mise en place" (everything in its place) and cook like a pro! This important term, which should become your mantra, includes preheating your oven, pans, or grills that you will be cooking on, steps that make a big difference in final results. Have your ingredients prepped to their final form. If a recipe calls for a carrot peeled and cut into ¹/₂-inch dice, do that and put the carrots into a bowl before you start cooking. If it calls for 2 tablespoons chopped parsley, have that ready to go. Then once you are ready to start cooking, it is a snap to just toss things in at their proper time. No waiting around halfway through a recipe to peel and chop that onion that you forgot about or for discovering that you are missing a needed ingredient.

» *Salad dressings, soups, spice rubs, and marinades can be made to completion days in advance.*

» *I have even been known to set my table a week in advance for major parties or holidays.*

» *A bowl for garbage and scraps comes in handy too, to keep your space tidy.*

» PLAYBOOK

My family, like many, is anti-leftovers. Few like to see the same dish, slightly more overcooked each time, come out to the table night after night after night. However, from a time management aspect as well as from an economical standpoint, being able to re-use leftovers or leftover ingredients that you have already purchased, in a whole other way can be magical. I like to call this reincarnated food. Nothing makes me happier than being able to recycle dishes or even from the outset, double just a part of a recipe to use it in a totally altered dish. One shop, one cleanup, and efficiency all around — music to my ears.

The placement of this section is right up front so that you can keep the Playbook concept in your mind as you are planning your menus for the day or the week. Right from the outset, you'll be prepared to double parts of a recipe or know exactly what you are doing with the leftovers.

Where this section is a little tricky, and the part that makes me most excited, is that I can't know how much of a dish you will have left over, so on some of these Playbook plays, you will have to fulfill my goals of this book for you. You will have to free yourself from an actual cookbook and use your senses and judgment to decide how much of this and that of the suggested ingredients to use. If just a little bit of a main dish is left over, it often can't become a second main dish but may reincarnate into a fantastic hors d'oeuvre, side, or even a soup. Do not overcook your food on the first go around or it will not be tasty when reused and re-cooked in its second form; cook just to the point of being done as per each recipe.

 This symbol on a recipe indicates that the recipe is included in the Playbook on the page specified.

From a kosher perspective, try to preplan how you will use the leftovers so that you can cook them in a parve pot, if necessary, from the outset.

34 » BEEF TOSTADOS

Use any leftover **TOMATO SALSA** or make a double batch of it at the start: Mix the salsa with 1-2 fresh minced garlic cloves and enough extra-virgin olive oil so that it is moist. Spoon over turkey burgers, hamburgers, grilled chicken, or chummos on pita bread triangles. You can also brush slices of Italian bread with olive oil and grill on a hot grill pan to toast. Then, pile on the salsa to make a **BRUSCHETTA**.

36 » VEGETABLE STUFFED CABBAGE

CABBAGE SOUP is warm, filling, and healthy — and a great way to use up leftover Vegetable Stuffed Cabbage: In a large soup pot, heat 2 tablespoons canola oil. Sear 2 strips of flanken on both sides. Remove the flanken; set aside. Add 4 cups beef broth, 2 cups tomato juice, $1/4$ cup lemon juice, $14^{1}/2$-ounce can diced tomatoes, 1 tablespoon brown sugar, 1 teaspoon chili powder, and $1/4$ teaspoon red pepper flakes. Bring to a boil, stirring and scraping the bottom of the pot. Turn down to a simmer, return flanken to the pot, and cook, covered, for $1^{1}/2$ hours. Thinly slice leftover Vegetable Stuffed Cabbage rolls and add to the pot. You may need more beef broth to maintain a soupy consistency. Cook until the cabbage and filling are heated through.

40 » TOMATO TARTE TATIN

When roasting the tomatoes and shallots, make extra of both. The uses are endless. **OVEN-ROASTED TOMATOES** are great in salads, omelets, any pasta dish, or cut up into cooked brown rice or wheatberries mixed with a little store-bought pesto. I love adding them to grilled cheese sandwiches and tuna sandwiches. You can toss them in the food processor with fresh thyme and 1-2 cloves of garlic; process to make a **PESTO** that goes with grilled chicken or fish. You can add them to an **ANTIPASTO PLATTER** or make cute **HORS D'OEUVRES** by alternating roasted tomatoes with small marinated fresh mozzarella balls and fresh basil leaves on a toothpick.

ROASTED SHALLOTS are a great ingredient to add to your homemade **VINAIGRETTES**; use an immersion blender to blend them in. I squeeze roasted shallots out into a pan and sauté in a little olive oil as the **BASE FOR A RED WINE SAUCE** for a steak. You can sauté them in olive oil in a pan and then add baby spinach and a tablespoon of balsamic or red wine vinegar; cook until the spinach is wilted and you have a great **SIDE DISH**. You can even just squeeze them out onto a good roll as the ultimate condiment for a **GRILLED STEAK SANDWICH**.

FAUX CRAB CAKES 42

Leftover faux crab cakes are great as the next day's **LUNCH** on a toasted English muffin with melted cheese – a spin on a tuna melt. Alternatively, make **STUFFED MUSHROOMS**: Finely chop the cakes and mix with $^1/_4$ cup shredded mozzarella cheese. Stuff into cremini mushrooms, drizzle with olive oil, and bake at 400°F for 10-15 minutes until they are hot and melty and the mushrooms release their juices.

SCALLION PANCAKES 44

When making the **DIPPING SAUCE**, prepare a double batch to use as a sauce for dipping baby lamb chops, dumplings, sesame-crusted tuna, or grilled chicken. It is also great as a dipping sauce for these **ASIAN CHICKEN MEATBALLS**: Preheat oven to 400°F. Heat 1 tablespoon olive oil in a medium skillet; sauté 1 small finely chopped onion, and 1 minced garlic clove over medium heat until shiny and fragrant, 4-5 minutes. Set aside. In a medium bowl, lightly beat 1 large egg. Add 1 pound ground chicken (I like a mix of white and dark), 1 tablespoon roasted sesame oil, 1 tablespoon chopped fresh parsley, 1 finely chopped scallion, $^3/_4$ cup panko breadcrumbs, $^1/_4$ cup hot water, and the sautéed onion/garlic. Form into 12 meatballs. Place into a lightly oiled 9 x 13-inch roasting pan. Mix 1 tablespoon hoisin sauce with 1 tablespoon roasted sesame oil and brush onto the tops of the meatballs. Bake 15-20 minutes until cooked through. Serve with the dipping sauce.

HELENE'S TURKEY TACO EGGROLLS 46

Make a double batch of the filling. It freezes beautifully up to a month. When you are ready to use, defrost it and mix with $^1/_4$ cup jarred marinara sauce to make **STUFFED PORTOBELLO MUSHROOM CAPS**. Bake at 350°F until the mushrooms are soft and the filling is warmed, about 20 minutes. You can also add an additional $^1/_2$ cup of marinara and serve over freshly cooked **PASTA**.

FLORENTINE MEATLOAVES 50

Chop up any leftover meatloaves and serve over **BROWN RICE** or cut into large chunks and serve in a **SUB SANDWICH** with your favorite jarred marinara sauce.

65 ⟫ LENTIL AND SAUSAGE SOUP

Drain the liquid from leftover soup and serve the lentils and sausage over steamed kale or steamed spinach the next night as a **SIDE DISH**. You can also toss it with pasta and a little marinara sauce for a kid-friendly side.

74 ⟫ CHICKEN POT PIE SOUP

For an easy **APPETIZER**, bake Pepperidge Farm Puff Pastry Shells, according to package directions. Heat any leftover chicken pot pie soup, adding in some frozen green beans. Once the soup is warmed through, remove the top layer of the pastry and spoon the soup into the pastry shells, using a slotted spoon to leave some of the liquid behind. Top with the pastry "tops," if desired.

76 ⟫ YEMENITE BEEF SOUP

YEMENITE RICE is a fabulous **SIDE DISH** for grilled chicken or steak. Heat any leftover soup on low to warm. Over medium heat, sauté 1 finely chopped onion and 4 cloves chopped garlic in 3 tablespoons canola oil in a medium pot for 4-5 minutes until shiny and fragrant. Add 2 teaspoons cumin, 1 teaspoon turmeric, $1/2$ teaspoon black pepper, $1/4$ teaspoon salt and stir until the spices are fragrant and start to toast. Stir in 2 cups long grain white rice, like basmati, and coat with the spices. Add 4 cups liquid made up of any soup that you can strain out and add chicken stock to make up the 4 cups. Raise heat, bring to a boil, turn down to a simmer and cook, covered, for 18 minutes. Do not remove lid and allow to stand for 10 minutes. Fluff with a fork and top with chopped beef and carrots from the leftover soup.

78 ⟫ YELLOW SQUASH AND CORN SOUP

For a second shot at this soup, make a double batch at the outset. You can freeze the second batch or use it right away to turn into a thick **WHOLE-GRAIN SOUP** with the texture of a mushroom-barley soup. Heat the second batch of soup (defrosted if it had been frozen). Add an additional 4-5 cups chicken or vegetable stock to make it very thin. Add 1 cup semi-pearled farro and simmer it in the soup, with the lid half covering the pot, for 20-30 minutes, until tender but not mushy. Stir with a wooden spoon occasionally to scrape the bottom of the pot. If the soup is too thick, add more broth to thin it. Don't let it boil vigorously or the liquid will cook out.

3-BEAN CHILI SOUP 86

Heat leftovers of this soup in the pot, uncovered, over medium heat until the liquid is all cooked out. Serve the beans over cooked short-grain brown rice for a filling **SIDE DISH** or **VEGETARIAN MAIN**, depending on how much you had left over. Trader Joe's sells pre-cooked brown rice that you store in your freezer and quickly microwave. This makes preparation for many of dishes, such as this one or the Edamame Slaw Playbook idea (p. 23), a snap.

SALAD

COWBOY CHICKEN SALAD 96

The leftovers of this salad are perfect to wrap in a flour **BURRITO** for lunch the next day. Make sure to add some fresh chopped Romaine lettuce and drizzle with sriracha sauce before rolling up the wrap.

CHICK PEA AND FENNEL SALAD 98

Place the leftover salad into the bowl of a food processor fitted with a metal "S" blade. Pulse until it is smooth but not runny. Spread the dip on toasted sourdough or Italian bread slices for a fabulous **APPETIZER**, **SNACK**, or **HORS D'OEUVRE**.

STRAWBERRY-GOAT CHEESE SALAD 100

This salad lends itself well to a **BURRITO** wrap that should include tuna salad and goat cheese. Before rolling up, drizzle with thickened balsamic such as Bartenura's Blaze Balsamic Glaze.

BUFFALO CHICKEN SALAD 104

Another great candidate for a wrapped **BURRITO** lunch using these leftovers.

SLOW-ROASTED SHIITAKE ASPARAGUS SALAD 108

Pick out and discard any of the dressed, wilted lettuce and turn the leftovers into a great **STIR FRY**. Heat 2 tablespoons olive oil in a medium skillet. Sear boneless skinless chicken breasts on both sides; lower heat and cook until almost cooked through. Brush both sides with Dijon mustard. Add $^1/_2$ cup white wine to the pan and allow it to simmer until the wine cooks out. Add remaining salad ingredients to the pan and heat through. Serve chicken topped with the shiitakes and asparagus. This can also be made with quick-cooking steaks such as rib steaks or minute steak fillet.

110 >> ISRAELI EGGPLANT PEPPER SALAD

Serve the leftovers as a **CHUNKY PASTA SAUCE** for rotini pasta or spooned over prepared short-grain brown rice for a great side dish.

114 >> LENTIL AND BEET SALAD

Crazy hot pink, healthier than healthy — try these **VEGAN VEGGIE BURGERS**: In the bowl of a food processor fitted with a metal "S" blade, pulse 1 cup cooked lentils, 1 cup cooked brown rice, 1 cup beet chunks (about $1^1/_2$ leftover beets), 2 cloves fresh garlic, $^1/_2$ peeled onion cut in chunks, $^1/_2$ teaspoon salt, $^1/_2$ teaspoon black pepper, 1 teaspoon dried thyme, 1 teaspoon dry mustard, $^1/_4$ teaspoon ground fennel, and $^1/_4$ teaspoon oregano. Pulse until the mixture looks like ground beef, leaving some texture. Add in 2 tablespoons tahini paste and pulse again. Transfer to a medium bowl and mix with $^1/_2$ cup breadcrumbs. Form into patties. Heat a thin layer of canola oil in a skillet over medium-high heat. Add the patties and cook 5-6 minutes per side until cooked through and somewhat charred.

Serve in buns with a thick dollop of store-bought chummos, shredded lettuce, and sliced avocado.

118 >> EDAMAME SLAW

Empty the container of slaw into a strainer to drain out the liquid. Use one chicken cutlet per cup of packed slaw. Thinly slice chicken on the diagonal. Heat 2 teaspoons canola oil in a large skillet over medium heat. Sear chicken strips on both sides in the skillet. When almost cooked through, add the drained salad and 2 teaspoons roasted sesame oil. Serve this **STIR FRY** as is or over prepared brown rice.

132 >> HOT AND CRISPY CHICKEN WITH MANGO SLAW

POULTRY

Leftover slaw makes a **TOPPING** for hot dogs, beef or turkey burgers, and fish tacos.

CHICKEN SCARPIELLO WITH RED SAUCE 128

When preparing this recipe make a double batch of sauce or use leftover sauce as a **TOPPING** for grilled hot Italian beef sausages for a reincarnated meal. If you only have a little bit left, you can even place the grilled sausage into a hot dog bun and use the sauce as a relish.

BALSAMIC ONION CHICKEN 140

Use the mounds of delicious **CARAMELIZED ONIONS** as **TOPPING** for grilled steak or burgers. They are also great mixed into a **SALAD**.

LEMON GARLIC SPATCHCOCKED CHICKEN 142

For great **PASTA SALAD**, cook 8 ounces farfalle pasta in boiling salted water until al dente. Drain. Return the pasta to the pot, off the heat. Remove any leftover chicken meat from the bones, chop it into bite-sized pieces and add it to the pasta. Drizzle with 2 tablespoons extra-virgin olive oil and $1/4$ cup white wine. Set aside. In the bowl of a food processor fitted with a metal "S" blade, process 2 cups fresh basil leaves, 2 cloves fresh garlic, 3 tablespoons pine nuts, $1/2$ teaspoon fine sea salt, and $1/2$ cup extra-virgin olive oil. Pulse until a **PESTO** forms. Scrape into the farfalle pasta; warm through over medium heat.

Another option is to make **GREEK AVGOLEMONO**, a lemony chicken soup with rice. Heat 8 cups chicken stock. Add 2/3 cup arborio rice. Bring to boil over high heat, then turn down to a simmer and cook until the rice is al dente, about 30 minutes. Add the leftover chicken meat to the pot, adding more stock if necessary. In a medium bowl, whisk 2 eggs and $1/3$ cup fresh lemon juice. Whisking continuously, pour 2 cups of hot broth slowly into the bowl of egg and lemon, to temper the eggs. Once all the broth is incorporated, add the mixture into the pot of soup, off the heat. Return to heat but do not allow soup to boil or the eggs will curdle. Stir to blend thoroughly. Season with salt and pepper. Serve hot.

CURRIED SUNFLOWER CHICKEN 144

Even a fancy schnitzel can find a new form in a **CHICKEN CROQUETTE**: In a small skillet, sauté 1 small finely chopped red onion in 2 tablespoons canola oil until translucent, 4-5 minutes. Finely chop enough leftover cutlets to make $1^{1}/2$ cups chopped chicken for every 2 croquettes. Add 2 eggs, 2 tablespoons matzo meal, 1 tablepoon finely chopped fresh parsley, $1/4$ teaspoon salt and $1/4$ teaspoon black pepper. Add the sautéed onion. Mix well, form into croquettes. Size will depend on if you are using it as an **APPETIZER**, **HORS D'OEUVRE**, or **MAIN**. Fry in 3 tablespoons hot canola oil. Serve with mayonnaise seasoned with curry powder to taste or in a pita with store-bought chummos.

148 ⟫⟩ LATIN CHICKEN

Leftover Latin Chicken makes for a fabulous **SALAD**. Amounts will vary based on how much chicken you are using. Use a mandolin to thinly slice red radishes. Add drained and rinsed canned black beans, drained canned corn, chopped fresh tomatoes, diced avocado, and diced leftover Latin Chicken at room temperature. Make dressing: In a quart container, shake or whisk $1/4$ cup lime juice, $1/4$ cup extra-virgin olive oil, 2 tablespoons honey, 2 tablespoons chopped cilantro, 1 clove fresh minced garlic, $1/8$ teaspoon cayenne. Dress the salad with some of the dressing.

152 ⟫⟩ ROAST TURKEY WITH MAPLE-MUSTARD GLAZE

For a fabulous **CURRIED TURKEY SALAD**, chop leftover turkey meat into bite-sized pieces. For each 1-1$1/2$ cups chopped turkey: Mix 1 rib celery, chopped, $1/2$ unpeeled Granny Smith apple chopped, $1/4$ cup dried cranberries, and $1/4$ cup cashews. In a small bowl whisk $1/4$ cup mayonnaise, 1 tablespoon white wine, $1/2$ teaspoon curry powder, $1/8$ teaspoon cayenne, $1/8$ teaspoon salt, and $1/8$ teaspoon black pepper. Combine the salad with the dressing. Serve in Boston lettuce leaf cups.

Once all the meat and skin is off the carcass, make **TURKEY SOUP**. If you have any leftover dark meat, shred and reserve it. Place the carcass into a very large soup pot, breaking the carcass as needed to fit into the pot. Add 8 cups chicken stock, 2 cups water, 1 peeled whole onion, 2 peeled carrots, 2 ribs celery, 1 large peeled sweet potato, cut into chunks, and a bouquet garni of fresh sage, parsley and bay leaves. Bring to a boil over high heat. Turn down to a simmer and cook, with the lid half covering the pot, for 1$1/2$ hours. Strain the soup to catch any small bones. Discard the bouquet garni, onion, and the turkey carcass. Return the soup to the pot. Add in the dark meat turkey, slice the vegetables and heat through.

156 ⟫⟩ MOROCCAN CHICKEN

Tonight's Moroccan Chicken can be tomorrow's **MOROCCAN COUSCOUS**! Heat 4 tablespoons olive oil in a large sauté pan. Add 3 chopped shallots and sauté for 3 minutes over medium heat. Add $1/4$ cup chopped kalamata olives. Toss in any of the leftover chicken, chopped into pieces, as well as any of the vegetables from the chicken. Add 3 cups chicken stock and $1/2$ teaspoon black pepper. Raise the heat to high and bring the stock to a boil. Remove from heat and add $1\,1/2$ cups couscous. Cover the pan and let it sit for 10 minutes. Fluff with a fork. Sprinkle in 1 tablespoon each fresh chopped mint and fresh chopped cilantro. Drizzle with extra-virgin olive oil, juice of $1/2$ lemon, $1/4$ cup orange juice, and pinch of cayenne. Mix well.

MEAT   MOJO BEEF AND POTATOES 172

Make **BEEF KEBOBS**! Chop red onion into 2-inch dice. Thread onto metal skewers and brush with olive oil. Grill for 5 minutes, rotating to cook on all sides. Thread on cubes of leftover Mojo Beef and Potatoes as well as cherry tomatoes. Grill until heated through. Brush with any leftover juices from the pan.

CRUSTLESS MEAT AND ONION PIE 176

Slice any leftovers to make a great **TAKE-ALONG SANDWICH**. For another option, make a **SHEPHERD'S PIE**: Slice the pie. Move the onion crust onto the cut side of the slice, top with mashed potatoes. Heat in a 350°F oven for 10 minutes until warmed through. Finish under the broiler to brown the potatoes.

VIETNAMESE BURGERS WITH PEANUT SAUCE 178

Serve leftover burgers for lunch the next day over a flavorful **SALAD**: Combine $1\,1/2$ cups julienned daikon radish, $1\,1/2$ cup shredded carrot, $1/2$ cup rice vinegar, $1/2$ cup sugar, 1 thinly sliced jalapeño pepper (see *p. 260*). Marinate for 1 hour. Stir in $1/2$ cup mayonnaise, 2 scallions thinly sliced on the diagonal, 1 tablespoon sriracha chili sauce, and 2 tablespoons chopped fresh cilantro. Stir well. Serve salad with room-temperature burgers whole or chopped into large chunks.

LAMB COUSCOUS 182

Heat 2 tablespoons olive oil in a large skillet. Add the leftover lamb couscous along with some chopped sundried tomatoes, chopped kalamata olives, pine nuts, fresh chopped cilantro, and lime juice. Warm through. Serve in a **PITA** with chummos or techina.

184 » BULGOGI

Make a tasty **ASIAN BEEF SOUP** with your leftovers: In a soup pot, heat 1 tablespoon canola oil. Add 1 sliced onion, 10 sliced shiitake mushrooms, and 2 teaspoons fresh grated ginger. Sauté until the mushrooms and onions are wilted. Add 6 cups chicken stock, $1/4$ cup shredded carrots, a handful of pea pods, and 1 thinly sliced stalk bok choy. Bring to a simmer; cook for 10 minutes. Mix in 1 tablespoon soy sauce, $1/2$ teaspoon roasted sesame oil, and 1 teaspoon sriracha chili sauce. Chop the leftover bulgogi and add to the pot along with 2 scallions thinly sliced on the diagonal.

200 » FALL HARVEST SILVER TIP ROAST

Roast beef can be thinly sliced and served the next day on a **HOAGIE ROLL** with horseradish mayonnaise. Alternatively, turn it into an exotic but simple **THAI BEEF SALAD**: Cut leftover roast beef into tiny cubes. Place into a bowl. Add the juice of 2 limes, $1 1/2$ tablespoons roasted sesame oil, $1/2$ minced jalapeño pepper (*see p. 260*), 3 tablespoons rice vinegar, 1 clove minced fresh garlic, $1 1/2$ tablespoons soy sauce, 2 pinches cayenne, and 2 tablespoons olive oil. Toss well. Serve in cucumber cups or over a bed of chopped lettuce and cucumber.

204 » CHILI BURGERS

SLOPPY JOES are a great way to use up these burgers. Heat 1 tablespoon canola oil in a medium skillet. Crumble leftover burgers into the pan. Immediately cover with bottled taco sauce or Manwich sauce. Cook until the sauce is bubbly. Serve in prepared taco shells. Top with shredded lettuce.

210 » SOY-POACHED SALMON WITH CHIVE OIL   FISH

An **ASIAN RICE BOWL** is a healthy pack-and-take lunch. Using a fork, separate the salmon into large chunks. Mix it with prepared brown rice and a handful of snap peas sliced on the diagonal. In a small bowl, whisk together 2 tablespoons lemon juice, 2 teaspoons soy sauce, $1/2$ teaspoon sugar, $1/4$ teaspoon salt, and 2 tablespoons extra-virgin olive oil. Drizzle over salad and toss to coat.

CHILEAN SEA BASS WITH COCONUT-MANGO SALSA 216

This salsa is great with **FISH TACOS**, but for a different spin, place it into a blender with coconut milk. Purée until a smooth sauce forms. Dip thinly sliced and pounded chicken strips into beaten eggs and then breadcrumbs mixed with shredded coconut and panko. Pan sear until cooked through. Thread onto skewers. Serve this purée as a **DIPPING SAUCE**.

SALMON NIÇOISE BURGERS 220

Give your salmon burgers a round two in a **SALAD NIÇOISE**: Quarter baby red potatoes and boil them in a pot of salted water until tender but not falling apart, about 15 minutes. Drain and cool. Boil green beans in boiling salted water until bright green, about 6 minutes; blanch in cold water. Arrange the potatoes, green beans, quartered hard-cooked eggs, cherry tomatoes, and niçoise olives on a platter. Slice leftover salmon burgers and add to plate. In a quart container, whisk 2 tablespoons fresh lemon juice, $1/2$ cup extra-virgin olive oil, $1/2$ teaspoon Dijon mustard, 1 clove minced fresh garlic, $1/2$ teaspoon coarse sea salt, and $1/8$ teaspoon black pepper. Drizzle over the salad. Extra dressing can be used as a marinade for asparagus spears, which can then be sautéed or roasted.

TANDOORI SALMON 228

Make extra yogurt-spice mixture and mix it into canned tuna instead of mayonnaise for a great **TUNA SALAD**. Serve on toast.

PASTA/EGGS

ROTINI WITH EGGPLANT CAPONATA 236

This caponata can do double duty spooned over **GRILLED CHICKEN**. I like to serve little crocks of it at each person's place setting as a **SPREAD** for challah on Shabbos or with crackers on a weeknight.

POACHED EGGS WITH HOLLANDAISE 244

Serve extra hollandaise as a **DRESSING** for blanched asparagus or Brussels sprouts.

SHAKSHOUKA 248

Make extra shakshouka base and serve it in small ramekins as a **DIP** for Shabbos challah.

261 ⟫ CAJUN QUINOA

If your quinoa was made in a parve pot, try these fantastic **QUINOA BURGERS**: Mix 2 cups leftover Cajun quinoa with 3 beaten eggs, $\frac{1}{4}$ cup Parmesan, $\frac{3}{4}$ cup breadcrumbs, and 3 ounces crumbled goat cheese. Form into 4 burgers. Heat 2 tablespoons olive oil in a skillet and sear the burgers 2-3 minutes per side.

264 ⟫ MISO-GLAZED EGGPLANT

Leftover miso glaze is fantastic as a **MARINADE** for cod or salmon. Marinate the fish in the miso glaze for 1 hour. Bake at 375°F for 5-6 minutes, then broil until the glaze starts to caramelize. Garnish with sliced scallions.

266 ⟫ SILAN-ROASTED SWEET POTATOES AND LEEKS

Side dish tonight ... **SWEET POTATO LEEK SOUP** tomorrow! Put the leftover sweet potatoes and leeks into a soup pot. Add chicken stock to cover by 2 inches. Bring to a simmer. Pull out and discard any sweet potato skins. Transfer to a blender and purée. Add more stock as needed to thin. Add salt and pepper to taste.

268 ⟫ MUSHROOMS ARRABIATTA OVER SQUASH

Use leftover mushrooms as a **TOPPING** for baked potatoes, tossed with pasta shells or brown rice, or even spooned over thin fish fillets like tilapia.

272 ⟫ GREEN BEAN AND ASPARAGUS FRIES

Make extra dipping sauce. It is a fantastic **SHMEAR** on a burger or schnitzel sandwich or as a **DIPPING SAUCE** for chicken fingers.

274 ⟫ HERB-ROASTED BABY PEPPERS

You can chop them up and serve as a **TOPPING** on burgers, hot dogs, and sausages, or mix them into salads. My kids add them to tuna or goat cheese **WRAPS**; the possibilities are endless.

CHEESY GIGANTE BEANS ◀◀ 276

The original Cheesy Gigante Beans and its after-life partner, **WHITE BEAN BRUSCHETTA**, based on a recipe from *Fine Cooking* magazine, will make you a bean junkie! Pour 1 cup extra-virgin olive oil into a small pot with 5 cloves fresh garlic and 2 sprigs fresh rosemary. Heat the oil on medium for 3-4 minutes, until the garlic starts to sizzle and release its fragrance. Turn off the heat, pour the oil though a strainer and discard the garlic and rosemary. Warm 2 cups of the leftover Cheesy Gigante beans. Place them in bowl of a food processor and add $^1/_2$ cup of the garlic oil, $^1/_3$ cup grated parmesan, juice of $^1/_2$ lemon, 4 leaves fresh mint, leaves from 1 sprig rosemary, $^1/_2$ teaspoon salt, $^1/_2$ teaspoon black pepper. Pulse until it is puréed. Chop 2-3 large heirloom tomatoes. Place into a bowl and toss with $^1/_4$ cup garlic oil. Sprinkle with a little salt and black pepper.

Slice Italian bread into thick slices. Brush with some of the garlic oil and grill in a hot pan until toasted, 1-2 minutes per side. Spread the **TOAST WITH BEAN PURÉE** and pile on the tomatoes.

MEDITERRANEAN BARLEY TIMBALES ◀◀ 278

This dish can also be used as a **VEGETARIAN APPETIZER** served in roasted Portobello mushroom caps. If dairy, add in crumbled feta cheese.

APPETIZERS

GAME PLAN

The word *appetizer* means to tease or stimulate the appetite. The appetizer course should set the stage and make your guests hungry, excited, and curious about what is to come. Select thoughtfully. Appetizers should complement the rest of the menu. Don't serve Nori-Wrapped Salmon and then follow it with salmon as the main course. Most importantly, watch the portion size. The equivalent of a whole meal should not be served before the dinner has arrived. If you are using a main dish or salad as the appetizer, remember that the recipe will yield a lot more portions. If your main dish is a heavier protein like meat, look for a vegetable-based appetizer. Downsize portions on very rich foods. Vary colors and textures throughout the meal.

PLATING AND GARNISHING TECHNIQUES

Appetizer courses tend to be plated. Plated courses give you a chance to show off some simple garnishing techniques. Although heavy garnishing techniques are out (radish swans anyone?), there are many easy techniques that will add the WOW factor to the presentation of your dishes.

Select larger, white or earth tone plates to allow the food to shine and to give the food plenty of white space. Interesting shaped plates like triangles or rectangles are nice as well.

Place sauces or flavored oils in squeeze bottles and use to make designs on a plated dish, or spoon them slightly off center on the plate.

Consider a vertical food arrangement. Stack items instead of placing them in a row.

Use an odd number of pieces of the food on the plate: one or three, not two or four. Odd numbers are often more pleasing to the eye.

Lay overlapping slices of chicken on a diagonal across the plate. Make vegetables visually interesting with the use of strategic placement to support an upward pile.

If the dish calls for a certain herb, use extra to decorate the plate. Choose a strategic sprig of basil for a pop of green on the plate.

Give height to piles of rice, potatoes, or grains by using molds or measuring cups that have been sprayed with nonstick cooking spray.

Before bringing your appetizer plates to the table, keep them restaurant-clean — wipe the rims of the plates with a towel dippped in white vinegar.

BEEF TOSTADAS

You can use ground turkey in place of the beef — just add the beans earlier so they have time to cook.

Corn tortillas are a must, as the flour ones won't become crispy. If making in advance, keep all the elements separate and assemble just before serving.

3 plum tomatoes, cut into ¼-inch dice

1 small red onion, peeled, cut into ¼-inch dice

¼ cup loosely packed cilantro leaves, chopped

2 scallions, root ends trimmed, very finely chopped

½ jalapeño pepper, seeded, very finely chopped
see p. 260

½ lime

fine sea salt

1 pound ground beef, can use ground turkey
see head note

½ teaspoon garlic powder

¼ teaspoon ground cumin

¼ teaspoon onion powder

10 small corn tortillas

1 tablespoon canola oil

¾ cup black beans (from a 15-ounce can), rinsed and drained

2 ripe avocados, peeled, pitted, mashed

¼ cup nondairy sour cream

hot sauce, such as Frank's Red Hot or sriracha

1. Prepare the salsa: In a medium bowl, combine the tomatoes, red onion, cilantro, scallions, jalapeño, and juice from lime half. Season with ⅛ teaspoon salt. Set aside.

2. In a medium bowl combine ground beef, garlic powder, ½ teaspoon salt, cumin, and onion powder. Mix well.

3. Heat an empty, large (12-14-inch) frying pan over medium heat. Add the tortillas and toast, flipping as each side becomes toasted. Remove from pan. Keep warm.

4. Add the oil to the pan and heat over medium-high. Add the ground beef mixture, using a wooden spoon to break up the chunks. Cook until the beef is browned and no longer pink. Add the black beans and cook for 5 minutes longer. Stir well.

5. Smear a little of the mashed avocado on 5 of the tostadas. Top with some of the meat mixture. Top each with second tortilla. Add a spoonful of the tomato salsa on top of each tostada. Add a small dollop of nondairy sour cream. Sprinkle each with a few shakes of hot sauce over the top.

2 tea bags Earl Gray or breakfast tea

2 cups water

1 cup golden raisins

1 large head green cabbage

1 tablespoon olive oil

1 small onion, peeled, thinly sliced

4 cloves fresh garlic, minced

½ cup white wine

1 zucchini, unpeeled, sliced in half lengthwise, seeds scooped out and discarded, cut into thirds, thinly sliced into matchsticks

1 teaspoon fine sea salt

½ teaspoon dried oregano

⅛ teaspoon ground cinnamon

½ cup pine nuts

1 (25-28 ounce jar) marinara sauce

1 (15-ounce) can tomato sauce

VEGETABLE STUFFED CABBAGE

As opposed to old-fashioned methods of boiling or freezing the heads of cabbage, this microwave method for removing whole, intact leaves is incredibly easy. It will change your view on the tedium of making stuffed cabbage forever! If only our Bubbies could see us now!

1. Bring a large pot of water to a boil. Preheat oven to 350°F.

2. Place the tea bags into a small pot with 2 cups water. Bring to a simmer. Turn off the heat and allow the tea bags to steep for 5 minutes. Remove the tea bags and add the raisins to the water to soften and infuse with the tea flavor.

3. Meanwhile, using a paring knife or steak knife, cut around the core of the cabbage. Cut out and discard the core. Place the whole head into the microwave and cook on high for 3 minutes. Remove from microwave and peel off the intact large dark green leaves. If necessary, microwave for another minute and repeat until you have 10 intact leaves. Once you get to the pale part, thinly slice the rest of the cabbage and set aside.

4. Submerge the big leaves in the pot of boiling water. Cook until just pliable, 1-2 minutes. Remove and allow to cool.

5. Prepare the filling: Heat the olive oil in a medium-large pot over medium-low heat. Sauté the onion for 4-5 minutes until soft; do not allow to brown. Add the garlic and cook until it is fragrant and shiny. Add 3 cups of the shredded cabbage and the wine. Raise heat to high. After the cabbage cooks down, add zucchini, salt, oregano, and cinnamon, allowing all the flavors to braise together. Reduce heat to medium-low. Cook, uncovered, for 15 minutes. Add the pine nuts and raisins, discarding the tea. Cook for 5 minutes longer, uncovered.

6. Working with 1 softened cabbage leaf at a time, cut a line on either side of the rib in a "v" shape to remove it. Place ½ cup

stuffing in the center of the leaf. Fold in the sides and roll from the bottom up. Place into a 9 x 13-inch casserole dish. Repeat with remaining leaves and stuffing.

7. Top with the marinara sauce and tomato sauce. Shake the pan so that sauce reaches the bottom. Bake, covered, for 2 hours, until cooked through.

CHICKEN CACCIATORE STICKS

My family jokes that we are going to open a restaurant called "Schtick" where everything is served on a stick. Think about it — EVERYTHING is better on a stick — pickles, steak, cheesecake, brownies, dipped bananas — well, this recipe is no different. This dish does it all — sticks and spaghetti for the kid in you, upscale chicken dish for the adult.

- 4 boneless, skinless chicken breasts halves, with tenders
- 1 cup all-purpose flour
- ½ teaspoon fine sea salt
- ½ teaspoon freshly ground black pepper
- 2 tablespoons olive oil
- 1 onion, peeled, cut into 1-inch dice
- 1 red bell pepper, seeded, cut into 1-inch dice
- 1 teaspoon dried oregano
- 1 (15-ounce) can diced tomatoes, with juices
- 3 cloves fresh garlic, minced
- 1 cup white wine
- 1½ cups chicken stock
- 1½ cups jarred marinara sauce
- ¼ cup water
- 2 tablespoons ketchup
- 8 ounces (½ box) angel hair pasta or 8 angel hair pasta nests
- fresh basil leaves, for garnish

1. Remove the tenders. Cut each chicken breast lengthwise into 4 long strips. Set aside.

2. Place the flour, salt, and pepper into a shallow dish. Stir to evenly distribute the spices. Coat 1 strip of chicken at a time in the flour, shaking off excess. Place onto a jellyroll pan. Repeat with remaining chicken, including the tenders.

3. Heat the olive oil over medium-high in a large (12-14-inch) skillet. When the oil is hot, add the floured chicken and brown on both sides, using tongs to flip each piece as it turns golden brown, about 3-4 minutes per side. Remove the chicken to a plate or tin.

4. To the same pan, add the onion, bell pepper, and oregano. Sauté for 5 minutes, until the onion is shiny and limp. Add the diced tomatoes and garlic and cook for 5-6 minutes. Add the wine, chicken stock, marinara sauce, and water. Mix well. Return the chicken to the pan, raise heat, and bring to a boil. Turn down to a simmer and cook for 10 minutes, stirring every few minutes.

5. Remove the chicken to a cutting board. Stir the ketchup into the sauce and mix well. Meanwhile, prepare the angel hair pasta according to package directions until al dente. Drain.

6. Stick skewers through the chicken strips. Dip skewered chicken into the sauce, coating both sides. Spoon some of the sauce into a bowl or plate. Place the pasta on the sauce, lay the cacciatore skewers on the pasta or standing up in it; spoon on more sauce. Garnish with fresh basil.

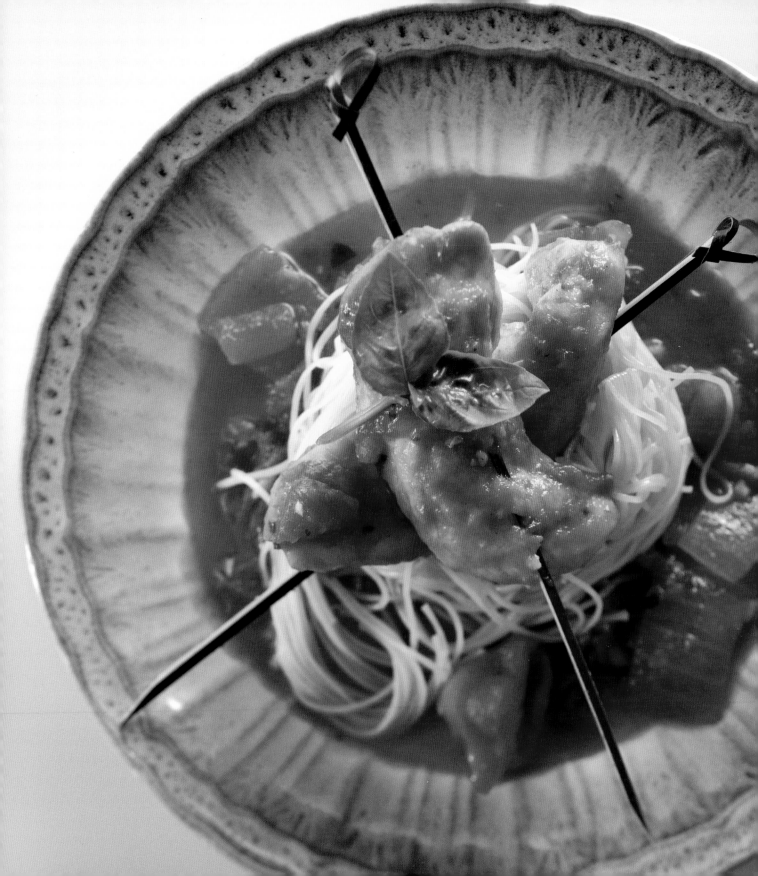

TOMATO TARTE TATIN

This is a twist on the famous French dessert, Tarte Tatin, in which apples are caramelized and baked in an upside-down tart. This dish is great as a vegetarian appetizer or lovely as a side for meat dishes. It also pairs wonderfully with a salad as a light meal. I learned this dish while leading a culinary adventure at Bayit Bagalil in Israel. Chef Dror Marco shared his kitchen and this recipe, which was the buzz of the dining room.

12 medium, ripe, firm plum tomatoes

extra-virgin olive oil

6 sprigs fresh thyme

6 cloves fresh garlic, thinly sliced

5 large shallots, unpeeled

4 ounces raw, shelled, pistachio meats

1 cup firmly packed fresh basil leaves

1/2 teaspoon coarse sea salt or kosher salt

1/4 cup balsamic vinegar

1/4 cup honey

nonstick cooking spray

2 sheets puff pastry, defrosted at room temperature for 20 minutes

8 (4-ounce) aluminum tins or ramekins

1. Preheat oven to 275°F.

2. Cut the tomatoes in half lengthwise. Place cut-side-up on a jellyroll pan. Brush the tops of each tomato half with olive oil. Arrange the thyme sprigs and slices of garlic over the tomatoes. Bake for 1 hour.

3. Raise the oven temperature to 350°F.

4. Place each shallot onto a square of aluminum foil. Drizzle with olive oil. Close up each packet and place in the oven alongside the tomatoes; the packets can be placed directly on the oven rack. Bake for 1 hour. Remove tomatoes and shallots from oven. Raise the oven temperature to 425°F.

5. When the shallots are cool enough to handle, open each foil packet and squeeze the roasted shallots out of their skins into a food processor fitted with a metal "S" blade. Discard the skins and stem ends. Add the pistachios, basil leaves, and salt. Pulse a few times to make a paste; make sure the nuts are finely chopped.

6. In a small pot over medium heat, cook the balsamic and honey until it is reduced slightly. Don't overcook, as it will thicken a lot as it cools.

7. Spray foil tins or ramekins with nonstick cooking spray. Brush the inside of the tins with the balsamic reduction. Arrange and overlap 3 tomato halves in each, pressing to make a cup to hold the pesto. Top with some of the pistachio pesto.

8. Using a cookie cutter or drinking glass, cut out circles of puff pastry slightly bigger than the opening of the foil tin; the pastry will shrink when it bakes and will become the bottom crust when unmolded. Top each tart with a puff pastry round, lightly pressing it to the tin. Place tins on a jellyroll pan.

9. Bake for 15 minutes, until the pastry is puffed and golden. Turn each tart out onto a plate or platter. Serve warm or at room temperature.

FAUX CRAB CAKES

PARVE

YIELD: 10-12 CRAB CAKES
OR 18-24 MINI CRAB CAKES

- 1 package (300 grams) surimi imitation crab seafood flakes or sticks, defrosted
- 3 large eggs
- 1 cup panko breadcrumbs
- 2½ teaspoons Old Bay Seasoning Spice blend
- ¾ cup mayonnaise, divided
- 1 lemon, divided
- ½ teaspoon sriracha chili sauce or other hot sauce
- ½ cup fresh parsley leaves, finely chopped
  canola oil
- ⅛ teaspoon cayenne
- ¼ teaspoon dried dill

Old Bay is a spice blend that is the quintessential seafood spice, although I have used it in hamburgers, on grilled corn, and in cole slaw as well. It originated in Maryland over 70 years ago and is the spice of choice for authentic-tasting "crab" cakes. The little yellow spice box is easy to spot in any supermarket. Feel free to experiment with other spice blends. You can try blackening spice for blackened faux crab cakes, which are yummy too.

1. Place the imitation crab into a food processor fitted with a metal "S" blade. Using a few on-off pulses, pulse until evenly chopped but not ground. If using the sticks, cut each in half before processing. You will need a few extra pulses to get these to the right consistency so that the fish is almost ground, not shredded in appearance. Transfer to medium bowl.

2. Mix in the eggs, breadcrumbs, Old Bay spice blend, ¼ cup mayonnaise, juice of ½ lemon, hot sauce, and parsley. With wet hands, form into 12 small cakes. If you prefer, you can use a ring mold or 2-3-inch biscuit cutter to shape them so they are all the same size.

3. Heat a thin layer of canola oil in a skillet over medium heat. Add the cakes, a few at a time; do not crowd the pan. Cook for 1-2 minutes per side until golden brown. Remove to a plate or platter. Repeat with remaining cakes.

4. In a small bowl, whisk the remaining ½ cup mayonnaise, cayenne, dill, and juice from remaining lemon half. Serve with the "crab" cakes.

PANCAKE DOUGH

$2^1/_2$ cups all-purpose flour

1 teaspoon fine sea salt

1 cup water

1 bunch (4-5) scallions, roots trimmed, very thinly sliced on the diagonal

$^1/_2$ cup all-purpose flour for kneading

canola oil

DIPPING SAUCE

$^1/_2$ cup low-sodium soy sauce

3 tablespoons honey

2 tablespoons water

$1^1/_2$ tablespoons rice vinegar

1 teaspoon cooking sherry

$^1/_4$ teaspoon dried ground ginger

$^1/_4$ teaspoon roasted or toasted sesame oil

2 cloves fresh garlic, minced

$^1/_8$ teaspoon red pepper flakes

》 *These are best served right out of the pan.*

SCALLION PANCAKES

This ancient Chinese secret won't stay secret for long. Your guests will be clamoring for the recipe once they taste this homemade version of the very popular take-out dish.

1. Place the $2^1/_2$ cups flour and salt into a food processor fitted with a metal "S" blade. While using on-off pulses, pour the water through the top of the machine $^1/_2$ cup at a time until the dough is just sticky. Transfer the dough to a bowl, knead into a ball, making sure all the flour is incorporated. Cover with a towel and allow the dough to rest for 45 minutes.

2. Meanwhile prepare the dipping sauce: In a small pot, combine the soy sauce, honey, water, vinegar, sherry, ginger, sesame oil, garlic, and red pepper flakes. Bring to a boil. Turn off the heat and allow the flavors to infuse. Set aside.

3. Using your fingertips, on a lightly floured surface, press the dough into a large (12-14-inch) circle. Sprinkle the scallions over the top of the dough. Fold the dough in half. Using $^1/_2$ cup flour in total, sprinkle a little flour over the top. Press down. Fold into quarters and press again. Twist the dough 3 times; replace on the work surface. If scallions are popping through, press them into the dough. Sprinkle with a little more flour. Fold in half again, pressing the dough flat with your fingertips. This helps to fold layers into the pancake. Cut into quarters. Shape each piece into a round. Using a rolling pin, roll each piece into a thin circle to form 4 pancakes, each with a diameter of 6-7 inches, about $^1/_8$-inch thick. Turn each pancake over, pat with flour.

4. Heat 1 tablespoon canola oil in a large (12- 14-inch) nonstick skillet over medium heat. If your pan is not nonstick, you may need another teaspoon or so of oil. Swirl to very lightly coat the bottom of the pan. Cook one pancake, for 2-4 minutes per side or until the pancake is golden brown in spots. Add 2 teaspoons or so more oil to coat the pan for the second side. Remove to a cutting board. Wipe out pan with a dry paper towel and re-oil. Repeat with the other three pancakes. Cut into wedges and serve immediately with the dipping sauce.

- 2 tablespoons canola oil
- 1 pound dark meat ground turkey
- 1 (1.25-ounce) packet Ortega taco seasoning mix
- 3/4 cup water
- 5 ounces (1/2 of a 10-ounce box) frozen spinach, completely defrosted
  see p. 254
- 1 (1-pound) package eggroll wrappers; I like Nasoya brand
- 1 large egg beaten with 1 tablespoon water, for egg wash

  canola oil, for frying

  bottled taco sauce or hot sauce for dipping

HELENE'S TURKEY TACO EGGROLLS

My friend Helene Wengrofsky is a fabulous cook. With 3 teenage sons, she is constantly cooking and coming up with new recipes. Her son Steven dropped off 6 of these eggrolls at my house one afternoon. When Helene texted to see how my whole family liked them I had to report that Kal and I loved them so much we had polished off all the eggrolls ... my kids didn't even get a whiff.

1. Heat 2 tablespoons canola oil in a large (12-14-inch) skillet over medium-high heat. Add the turkey, breaking up the chunks with a wooden spoon. Cook for 2-3 minutes until no longer pink and just starting to brown. Add the taco seasoning packet and the water. Bring to a simmer.

2. Squeeze all the liquid out of the 5 ounces of spinach. Add spinach to the pan and cook for 5 minutes longer. Stir to distribute the spinach. Cook until all liquid is cooked out. Remove from heat. Cool completely or the eggrolls will be soggy.

3. Arrange an eggroll wrapper on your cutting board facing you like a diamond. Brush the eggwash along the edges of the wrapper. Place 2 tablespoons of filling horizontally in the middle of the eggroll, form into a 4-inch log. Fold the bottom corner over the filling toward the top corner. Fold the two sides in toward the center. It should now look like an envelope. Roll firmly toward the top corner, making a roll 4 inches wide. Be careful not to tear wrapper, and seal the final edge with a brushing of the egg wash. Set aside, seam-side-down. Continue with remaining filling and wrappers.

4. In a deep fryer or in a medium pot, heat canola oil to 355°F. If using a pot, oil should to be deep enough to keep eggrolls from touching bottom of pan, at least 3 inches of oil. Fry eggrolls in batches, about 2-3 minutes until golden brown, turning occasionally; don't crowd the pot. Drain on paper towels. Serve with taco sauce.

PARVE
YIELD: 6 SERVINGS

NORI-WRAPPED SALMON WITH WASABI GINGER SAUCE

4 (3-ounce) portions salmon fillet, (6-inch strips) skin and pin bones removed

coarse sea salt or kosher salt

freshly ground black pepper

dried dill

1 cup lowfat mayonnaise

2 tablespoons minced fresh ginger

1 tablespoon wasabi powder

1 teaspoon roasted or toasted sesame oil

6 sheets toasted nori, each cut in half with scissors

1 lemon

2 tablespoons chopped fresh dill

2 tablespoons sriracha chili sauce

mixed sesame seeds and pinch cayenne, optional garnish

This is a fun and funky alternative to gefilte fish. Nori, the dried roasted seaweed that is used to wrap sushi, is a mineral-dense sea vegetable that adds flavor and texture to a dish.

1. Preheat oven to 400°F. Line a jellyroll pan with parchment paper. Set aside.

2. Place the salmon portions on your cutting board. Cut each in thirds to make 12 rectangles, approximately 2 x 1-inch each. Season each with salt, pepper, and a small pinch of dried dill.

3. In a medium bowl, whisk the mayonnaise, ginger, wasabi powder, and sesame oil. Remove ½ cup and reserve. Brush some of the remaining ½ cup over the salmon and onto all sides of each fillet.

4. Lay out a nori sheet with the short end toward you. Brush the nori with the wasabi mayonnaise to make it pliable. Place a fillet on the bottom of the sheet. Squeeze on a little lemon juice and sprinkle with fresh dill. Fold bottom up over the salmon to cover it; press. Fold in the sides and roll, pressing to seal. Place on prepared pan, seam-side-down. Repeat with remaining fillets and sheets.

5. Bake uncovered, for 10 minutes, until the packets pop slightly. The fish is steamed in the nori and should feel firm when you press the packet.

6. Meanwhile, stir the sriracha chili sauce into the reserved wasabi mayonnaise. Drizzle over the packets. Garnish with sesame seeds and a pinch of cayenne, if desired.

1-2 bunches large fresh spinach leaves, not baby leaves

1½ pounds ground beef

2 large eggs, lightly beaten

1½ teaspoons dried Italian seasoning

¾ teaspoon dried oregano

¾ teaspoon garlic powder

1 teaspoon onion powder, divided

¼ teaspoon fine sea salt

¼ teaspoon freshly ground black pepper

1 (15-ounce) can diced tomatoes, divided

nonstick cooking spray

1 teaspoon olive oil

2 cloves fresh garlic, minced

FLORENTINE MEATLOAVES

Select bunches of spinach that have large beautiful leaves.
This will make lining the muffin tin with them very easy.
If you have trouble arranging the leaves, microwave them for
10-15 seconds to soften slightly and make them more pliable.

1. Preheat oven to 350°F.

2. Set aside 32-40 of the largest spinach leaves. Chop the remaining leaves into small pieces. Set aside.

3. Place the ground beef and eggs into a medium bowl. Add the Italian seasoning, oregano, garlic powder, ¾ teaspoon onion powder, salt, and pepper. Sprinkle in 1 cup chopped spinach leaves and ¼ cup diced tomatoes. Mix well. Divide into 8 equal portions, each a little smaller than a baseball.

4. Spray a muffin tin with nonstick cooking spray. Set onto a cookie sheet to catch drips. Arrange 3-4 of the largest leaves in each cup, overlapping and extending from the cups. Keep 8 large leaves in reserve. Place a balled portion of the meat into each spinach-lined cup. Bring the excess spinach leaves over the top to wrap each meatloaf.

5. Bake for 15 minutes. Remove from oven; allow the meat to rest for 5 minutes. Wet the 8 reserved large spinach leaves and cover each meatloaf with one of the wet leaves. Use a spoon to help ease the leaf into the muffin cup to wrap the loaf. Return to the oven for 10 more minutes. Remove from oven, allow the meat to rest for 5 minutes. Remove the meatloaves from the muffin tin.

6. While the meatloaves are baking, in a small pot, heat the oil and garlic over medium heat. Add the remaining diced tomatoes, their juice, and remaining ¼ teaspoon onion powder. Stir. Spoon a bit of tomato sauce over each meatloaf.

BUILDING A CHEESE PLATE

SOFT CHEESES
- brie
- camembert
- goat

HARD CHEESES
- yellow and white Cheddar
- gouda
- Swiss
- muenster
- Monterey jack
- Manchego

BLUE CHEESES
- Blue
- Gorgonzola
- Roquefort

People usually think of serving cheese plates at open house-style parties or as hors d'oeuvres, but a cheese plate can be a stunning simple appetizer for a dairy lunch or dinner. Not only is it delicious, but it can be also be a conversation piece as people share and indulge.

When planning a cheese plate for an appetizer course, a simple guideline is to count on 3 ounces of cheese per person and a mix of 3-4 cheeses showcasing a variety of milks and textures. Include one soft-ripened cheese, one hard cheese, and one blue. You can decide on the intensity from mild to intense, based on your own taste as well as that of your guests. Label the cheeses by name, milk variety, and/or country of origin.

For maximum flavor, allow the cheeses to come to room temperature for an hour before serving. Keep the wrappers on so they don't dry out. Unwrap just before serving.

Display the cheeses on a wooden cutting board, a piece of slate, or a marble slab or tile.

Use a separate utensil for each cheese to prevent the mingling of flavors. A cheese plane works great for harder cheeses, a rounded knife for softer spreadable ones. Cheese knives that have tines at the end are nice for cutting and transferring the cheeses.

Finish the cheese board with an assortment of simple crackers, grissini, crusty bread, fruit and nut breads, fresh fruit, berries, olives, toasted nuts, honey, grapes, fresh figs, or some of the wonderful fig preserves that are now available kosher.

Remember that cheese platters can also be great as dessert courses paired with chocolate, or can stand alone at a party paired with wine or beer.

ASIAN CHICKEN WINGS

15-20 chicken wings, cleaned of feathers *see head note*

½ cup apricot jelly

5 tablespoons soy sauce

5 tablespoons red wine

1 tablespoon plus 1 teaspoon roasted or toasted sesame oil

3 cloves fresh garlic, minced

1½ teaspoons ground ginger

heaping ¼ teaspoon red pepper flakes

>> *This marinade is great on Cornish hens as well.*

It is difficult to remove stray feathers from chicken wings when they are raw. Rinse and pat the wings dry but disregard the feathers that are too hard to remove. Once the wings are cooked, the feathers are very easy to pull out using strawberry hullers, tweezers, or your fingers.

1. Preheat oven to 400°F.

2. Line a jellyroll pan with aluminum foil. Place the chicken wings in a single layer on the prepared sheet. Set aside.

3. Place the apricot jelly, soy sauce, red wine, sesame oil, minced garlic, ground ginger, and red pepper flakes into a quart-sized container. Using an immersion blender or whisk, blend the ingredients into a smooth marinade. Remove ¼ cup of the marinade into a bowl and set it aside to use for dipping.

4. Brush both sides of each wing with the remaining marinade. Place them on the prepared sheet, bone-side up. Bake for 35 minutes.

5. Remove the jellyroll pan from the oven. Set the oven to broil. While the oven is heating, use tongs to turn over each wing. This is the time to pull out any feathers. Brush the wings again with the original marinade. Return to the oven and broil, 6-8 inches from heat source for 2-4 minutes until chicken is done. Watch the whole time to make sure the marinade doesn't burn.

6. Serve the wings with the reserved marinade.

SUSIE'S BOSCH MIXER CHALLAH

PARVE

YIELD: 10 LBS. DOUGH,
5 MEDIUM CHALLAHS

3 tablespoons active dry or bread machine yeast

1/2 cup warm water

1 tablespoon sugar

4 1/2 cups water at room temperature

15 egg yolks (from size large eggs)

4 teaspoons salt

2 cups sugar

1 cup canola oil

1 (5-pound) bag bread flour plus 1 1/2 cups

   nonstick cooking spray

1 large egg, beaten with 1 teaspoon water, for egg wash

   poppy seeds

   sesame seeds

>> *Proof yeast, even if the label says it is not necessary. Yeast is alive. The warm water wakes it up and the sugar activates its growing power. If the water is too hot, it will kill the yeast; a bit above lukewarm (100°F- 110°F) is perfect. Touch it to your top lip or wrist if you don't have a thermometer. It should feel warm, not hot. Use a bowl with plenty of surface area. As the yeast works, it produces carbon dioxide foam: bubbles. Don't proof yeast longer than 5-10 minutes; it will lose much of the power needed to make the dough rise.*

1. **A** Place the yeast, 1/2 cup warm water, and tablespoon sugar into a large Pyrex measuring cup. Stir. Allow to proof as you proceed.

2. **B** Place the 4 1/2 cups water, yolks, salt, sugar, and oil into the Bosch mixing bowl with the dough hook attached. Start on low to prevent splashing, then mix at medium speed until slightly foamy and yolks are beaten. If your yolks aren't breaking, stop the machine and use a whisk to break them. **C** Add the yeast mixture. Mix for 1 minute at medium speed.

3. **D** With the machine running, slowly add the 1 1/2 cups bread flour plus 2/3 of the 5-pound bag. Mix 5-7 minutes. Add the remaining flour. Snap on the cover. Increase speed slightly. **E** Mix until dough looks smooth and shiny, about 4-5 minutes. **F** Remove the dough to a very large bowl. Cover the bowl with plastic wrap that has been sprayed with nonstick cooking spray. **G** Allow to rise until the dough has more than doubled, about 1 1/2 hours.

4. Place one oven rack on the lowest rack and one in the center of your oven. Preheat oven to 350°F. Cover 2 jellyroll pans with parchment paper. Set aside.

5. Turn the dough out onto your lightly floured work surface. **H** This is where you would take *challah* and make the *berachah*. Using a bench scraper, divide the dough into 5 parts, each weighing 2 pounds. Divide each part into 3 equal portions. Roll each into a 15-inch log. Braid and place on parchment lined jellyroll pans, 2 per pan. Brush the challahs with the egg wash. Sprinkle with poppy seeds and sesame seeds. Bake, uncovered, for 35 minutes. Switch pans halfway through baking time for even baking. If you don't have a double oven and you need to bake in batches, keep the braided dough out for the 35 minutes, but in a cool part of your kitchen if possible. When the tops appear done, turn the challah over. Tap it; it should sound hollow and the bottom should be golden brown.

A

B

C

D

E

F

G

H

MAKING CHALLAH BY HAND Use the same ingredients in the same amounts. You will do the work of the mixer manually. Whisk the 4½ cups water, egg yolks, salt, sugar, and canola oil in a large bowl until foamy. Add the proofed yeast, whisk again. While rotating the bowl, use a rubber spatula to start mixing in the flour. When it is stiff, switch to a wooden spoon. Mix for 4 minutes. By hand, knead in remaining flour for 4 more minutes. Turn out onto work surface; knead for 5 minutes. When smooth dough forms, return to the bowl. Cover with plastic wrap sprayed with nonstick cooking spray. Set aside in a warm place to rise for 1½ hours. Continue as per recipe.

MAKING CHALLAH WITH A STAND MIXER Use the same ingredients in the same amounts. With the paddle attachment, beat the 4½ cups water, egg yolks, salt, sugar, and canola oil on medium speed until foamy. Add the proofed yeast, beat again. Switch to the dough hook. Add half the flour. Mix at medium speed until a sticky dough forms. Keep adding flour, as much as you can fit into two-thirds of your work bowl. Turn out onto work surface; knead remaining flour into the dough. When a smooth dough forms, place it into a large bowl. Cover with plastic wrap sprayed with nonstick cooking spray. Set aside in a warm place to rise for 1½ hours. Continue as per recipe.

CHALLAH VARIATIONS

Rosemary Olive Challah

- 2 cups chopped kalamata olives
- 2 tablespoons dried rosemary
- ½ red onion, peeled, cut into ¼-inch dice

  dried rosemary, for sprinkling

  coarse sea salt, for sprinkling

1. Before all the flour is mixed into the dough, add the olives, 2 tablespoons dried rosemary, and red onion. Allow the machine to knead well into the dough. Allow to rise as usual.

2. Divide the dough into 2-pound balls. Shape the challahs and brush with a little olive oil. Sprinkle with dried rosemary and coarse sea salt. Bake for 35 minutes at 350°F.

Cinnamon Raisin Challah

- 2-3 cups raisins
- ¼ cup butter or margarine, melted

  cinnamon sugar

1. While making the dough, before all the flour is mixed in, add raisins. Allow the machine to knead well into the dough.

2. After dough has risen, divide it into 2-pound balls. Shape each ball into however many logs you are using (3 for a braid, or 1 for a round) and brush with melted margarine. Sprinkle surfaces with cinnamon sugar. Braid or form into rounds. Brush with egg wash. Sprinkle with cinnamon sugar and bake for 35 minutes at 350°F.

Babka Challah

12 oz (1 bag) good-quality
chocolate chips

$^3/_4$ cup sugar

3 tablespoons all-purpose
flour

4 tablespoons canola oil

$^3/_4$ teaspoon ground
cinnamon

nonstick cooking spray

1. While making the dough, before all the flour is mixed in, add chocolate chips. Allow the machine to mix well into the dough. Allow the dough to rise as usual.

2. With a spatula or using your fingers, in a small bowl combine the sugar, flour, oil, and cinnamon into coarse crumbs. Once the dough has risen, divide the dough into 2-pound balls. Braid the challah and put in parchment-lined loaf pan that has been sprayed with nonstick cooking spray. Brush with egg wash. Sprinkle babka crumbs over and bake for 50 minutes at 350°F. If braided and baked on a jellyroll pan, bake for 35 minutes.

Spiced Pull-Apart Challah

za'atar seasoning

chili power

ground turmeric

curry powder

raw, shelled sunflower
seeds

prepared pesto

1 tablespoon olive oil

1 clove fresh garlic, minced

2 teaspoons fresh
chopped parsley

dried minced onion

1. Spray a 9-inch round disposable aluminum tin with nonstick cooking spray. Line with parchment paper round. Divide 2$^1/_2$ pounds of dough into 6 balls. Place 1 ball in the center and surround with the 5 others. The dough will expand as it bakes, so leave even spaces between the balls. Brush egg wash over all the dough balls. Sprinkle one of the balls with za'atar seasoning.

2. Sprinkle the second with chili powder; the third with turmeric, a tiny pinch of curry powder and raw sunflower seeds. Brush the fourth with prepared pesto; the fifth with a mixture of olive oil mixed with minced garlic and chopped parsley; and the last ball with dried minced onion. Bake for 35 minutes at 350°F.

Onion Rolls

1 large onion

1 tablespoon canola oil

dried minced onion

1. Spray a 6-compartment large-capacity muffin tin with nonstick cooking spray.

2. Cut onion into $^1/_4$-inch pieces. Sauté in canola oil until caramelized and golden, about 15 minutes.

3. Divide 1 pound of risen dough into 6 balls. Flatten balls slightly. Place 1 tablespoon of sautéed onion onto center of each piece. Roll back into a ball, pinching to conceal onions. Place 1 ball, seam-side-down, into each compartment of the tin. Brush with egg wash; sprinkle with dried minced onion. Bake for 35 minutes at 350°F.

SOUP

GAME PLAN

Soups are a great, healthy way to start a meal. They can pack vegetables and vitamins into your family painlessly and deliciously. The techniques are simple so once you master them, you can be free to experiment with whatever ingredients you have on hand or what looks good at the market.

SOUP STARTERS

STOCK OR BROTH-BASED SOUPS

Many people ask me the difference between broth and stock. They are virtually the same finished product. Broth is created by cooking just the meat, while stock is made from meat with the bones that are then strained out. Think chicken soup. Although stock will have a bit more body and mouth-feel from the gelatin in the bones, I find that you can use either in any soup recipe where the stock is not the star of the show.

Chicken, beef, and vegetable broths/stocks are the most common, but broths can be made from veal or fish or other meats as well.

PURCHASING BOXED STOCKS

Although making your own vegetable stock is simple and a great way to use up the wilting veggies in your refrigerator bin, few people, including me, go to the trouble of making their own beef or chicken stock to use as the liquid in another soup recipe. If I am spending 2 hours making a big batch of chicken soup, it is to serve chicken soup, not to strain it all out and use it as the base for broccoli soup. So although in a perfect world, fresh (or frozen homemade stock) would be best, sometimes it is just not a real-world option. Boxed stocks are a nice option. The aseptic packaging is better for the environment than cans, and can allow for fewer preservatives and better flavor than the old methods. However, high sodium is still an issue for some brands, so make sure to read labels. Make sure those labels reflect real ingredients: vegetables, chicken, or meat should all be on the label. You will also find a variety of tastes, aromas, and thickness, so check out a few brands before selecting the one you use as your staple. Some are unnaturally orange or thick and have a bad flavor that will affect your end results.

DRIED CONSOMMÉ POWDER

Reconstituted dried consommé powder can be used in place of boxed stocks as the liquid in soups or stew. It also adds flavor to rice and other vegetable dishes. 1-2 teaspoons of powder should be whisked into 1 cup hot water until it is dissolved and then used as needed. Consommé powder is made with dehydrated vegetables and seasonings as well as starches, often MSG and most importantly, a lot of sodium. So, if you are watching your sodium (and we all should be), be careful about how much consommé powder you use in your dishes and cut out other salt from those recipes.

COOKING TECHNIQUES

SWEATING

The background note to many soups, and a technique used in many soup recipes, involves "sweating" vegetables. By gently coaxing flavor out of vegetables like onions, celery, garlic, leek, shallots, or carrots, you are creating a flavor base and a depth to support the main ingredients of the recipe.

The key is to allow these "aromatics" to slowly release their liquid, "sweat" out their natural water and enhance their flavor. It is easiest to see in the onions as they become translucent, but other vegetables will get shiny. Temperature is key here. Heat a little oil or butter in a big pot over medium heat. If the heat under the pan is too high, the vegetables will burn and lose their flavor. If it is too low, the vegetables will take longer to soften and may start to caramelize, accentuating too much of their natural sweetness and making the soup sweeter.

SPICING

Dried spices are sometimes added to the aromatics right after the "sweating' process and given a few minutes to toast. This develops their flavor before liquid is added.

SIMMERING

Once the liquid is added and brought up to temperature, fat and impurities may rise to the top. I have a tiny strainer that I can easily manipulate over the top of the soup to grab those impurities. After 45 minutes or so, the flavor is cooked out of most herbs and vegetables, so I find that soup bags are a great way to cook things like parsley, dill, peppercorns, and other things you would need to tie up in a "bouquet garni" and makes fishing them out once their flavor is gone, a snap. I do the same with bones I am adding to the pot. In the case of chicken soup, the bones are where you get a lot of flavor but I am always worried about a small loose bone ending up in a guest's bowl. Tying them up in a soup bag is a great way to ensure they all come out and are discarded together.

BLENDER VS. IMMERSION BLENDER

Vegetable-based soups have varied textures. Some soups are meant to be chunky, others to have the vegetables, beans, or other ingredients left whole and separate, and yet others, smooth and creamy. For years I touted my immersion blender as my best friend in the kitchen, and don't get me wrong, I am not a fair-weather friend and still love and use my immersion blender. The ease of sticking it right into the pot makes for a no fuss—no mess experience. For chunky soups this is still true. A couple of whirls with the immersion blender and I am done. However, I will admit, I have gone old-school in my thinking. For the creamiest, velvetiest textures on vegetable soups, nothing beats a good old-fashioned blender. Remember to never fill it more than halfway if your soup is hot, and to always hold a towel over the lid with pressure from your hand to keep the lid on and your soup from exploding all over your kitchen. With either appliance, don't buy by brand name; buy by horsepower or wattage. The stronger the motor, the better the result, in the shortest of time.

COOLING

It is not a good idea to put a big pot of hot soup into your refrigerator. It will warm up everything else in it and mess with the thermostat. In the winter, place the pot in the cold garage — this gets the soup to cool down faster.

I also use this technique when I am in a rush to cool my soups: I keep full water bottles, labels removed, in the freezer. I use these "ice wands" to quickly take the heat down.

Leftover chicken soup can be stored in ice cube trays. Each cube yields 2 tablespoons of soup. 8 ice cubes will give you a cup of stock to use in other future recipes.

» *Heat your soup bowls by pouring in a ladle of hot water. After a minute or so, pour out the water before adding your soup. This will warm them so that they are not cold when the soup is ladled into them.*

LENTIL AND SAUSAGE SOUP

Chopping the thyme releases its aroma. It will also allow you to pick out and discard the small stems.

1. Heat the oil in a large soup pot over medium heat. Add the sausage meat, searing it and breaking it up with a wooden spoon as it browns or turns a deeper red. Remove the meat to a bowl, reserving the fat in the pot.

2. Add the onion, celery, and carrot to the pot. "Sweat" the vegetables over medium-low heat until they are shiny and translucent, about 5-6 minutes.

3. Add the lentils, water, pepper, thyme leaves, and oregano. Bring to a boil, then turn down to a simmer and cook uncovered, for 30-35 minutes. Most of the liquid will be absorbed and the lentils will be soft to the bite.

4. Return the cooked sausage meat to the pot along with the stock. Warm through. Season with salt and pepper as needed.

1 tablespoon canola oil

2 links (1/2-pound) raw sausage links, spicy or hot Italian beef, casings removed and discarded

1 small onion, peeled, cut into tiny dice the size of the lentils

1 rib celery, cut into tiny dice the size of the lentils

1 carrot, peeled, cut into tiny dice the size of the lentils

1 1/2 cups green or Puy lentils, rinsed and picked over for pebbles or debris

4 cups water

1/4 teaspoon freshly ground black pepper, more as needed for seasoning

leaves from 4-5 sprigs fresh thyme, chopped

1/2 teaspoon dried oregano

5 cups chicken stock

pinch salt, as needed for seasoning

SPICY FISH HOT POT

PARVE
YIELD: 6 SERVINGS

8 cups water

2 teaspoons salt, divided

3 stems fresh basil

8-10 sprigs fresh cilantro, root ends trimmed

4 ounces shiitake mushrooms, stems discarded, sliced

1 pound cod or halibut fillet, skin removed, cut into equal 2 x 1-inch chunks

1/2 red bell pepper, seeded, cut into 1/2-inch dice

1 jalapeño pepper, pierced with a knife in 3-4 places
see p. 260

2 stalks celery, ends trimmed, very thinly sliced on the diagonal

1 large white onion, peeled, halved, cut into 1/2-inch dice

8 ounces Udon noodles or brown rice spaghetti

1/2-1 1/2 teaspoons chili garlic sauce

juice of 1 lime

chopped purple or Thai basil, for garnish

If you are making this soup in advance, cook the pasta separately. If allowed to sit in the soup, it will release its starch and turn the soup into a thick mess. Another option is to make the soup in advance and just add the noodles and fish when heating to serve.

1. In a medium pot, bring the water and 1 teaspoon salt just to a boil.

2. Place the basil and cilantro into a mesh bag, or tie with kitchen twine. Add this bundle to the water along with the mushrooms.

3. Place the cod into a medium bowl and toss well with the remaining 1 teaspoon salt. This will help firm the fish. Set aside.

4. Add the red pepper, jalapeño, celery, and onion to the pot. Turn heat down and simmer for 15 minutes, uncovered.

5. Add the Udon or brown rice spaghetti to the pot, breaking as necessary. Cook until just under al dente, 1-2 minutes less than the package directions suggest.

6. Add the cod to the pot. Cook for 2-3 minutes until the fish is white and just flakes when pierced by a fork.

7. Scoop out and discard the jalapeño and the herb bundle, squeezing any liquid back into the pot. Taste the soup. Add 1/2 teaspoon chili garlic sauce. Stir. Taste again. If not spicy enough, add another 1/2 teaspoon—1 teaspoon of the sauce. The amount needed will vary based on personal taste and the heat of the jalapeño, which you can't predict.

8. Add the lime juice to the pot.

9. Ladle into bowls and garnish with basil.

OSSO BUCCO SOUP

This soup is a take-off on Osso Bucco, a traditional Italian dish from Milan. The name means "bone with a hole" or "hollowed bone." This refers to the veal shank bone that has a large and rich marrow filling. The long slow cooking of the soup results in tender meat that falls off the bone. Traditionally, Osso Bucco is served over risotto, so taking on that theme, there is rice in this dish.

Leaving the papery brown skin on the onion helps the stock develop a richer brown flavor and deeper color. I also use this trick when I make chicken soup.

SOUP

- 2 veal osso bucco, with bone, tied (ask the butcher)
- 1 tablespoon all-purpose flour
- 1/2 teaspoon fine sea salt
- 1/4 teaspoon freshly ground black pepper
- 2 tablespoons canola oil
- 8 cups chicken stock
- 4 cups water
- 1 carrot, peeled, cut crosswise in half
- 1 rib celery, cut crosswise in half
- 1 onion, with skin, washed, cut in half
- 2 sprigs fresh thyme

RICE

- 1 tablespoon canola oil
- 1/2 onion, peeled and cut into 1/4-inch dice
- 1/2 rib celery, cut into 1/4-inch dice
- 1/2 teaspoon turmeric
- 1/4 teaspoon dried oregano
- 1 cup raw basmati rice
- 2 cups water

1. Place the osso bucco on a cutting board. Pat it dry. Lightly sprinkle both sides with the flour, salt, and pepper. Pat into both sides.

2. Heat the oil in a large pot over medium heat. Sear the osso bucco 5 minutes per side, until golden brown, using tongs to turn them. Lower the heat. Cover with the chicken stock and water. Add the carrot, celery, onion, and thyme. Raise heat, bring to a boil, turn down to a simmer, and cook, covered, for 1½ hours.

3. During the last half hour of cooking the meat, prepare the rice: In a medium pot, heat the tablespoon canola oil. Sauté the onion and celery, stirring, until they are translucent and shiny, 4-5 minutes. Stir in the turmeric and oregano. Add the rice and stir again. Cover with 2 cups water. Raise heat, bring to a boil, turn down to a simmer, and cook, uncovered, for 15 minutes. Set aside.

4. When the osso bucco is done, discard the carrot, celery, onion, and thyme sprigs. Shred the meat off the bones. Place a mound of rice into each bowl; top with a little of the shredded meat. Add soup. If preparing in advance, keep the rice separate until serving.

- 2 tablespoons olive oil
- 1 small onion, peeled, cut into 1-inch dice
- 2 cloves fresh garlic, sliced
- 2 ribs celery, cut into 1-inch dice
- 1 (10-ounce) package sliced button mushrooms
- ¼ teaspoon dried thyme
- 1 (3.5-ounce) bag roasted, peeled chestnuts, sliced
- 1 medium celery root, root ends trimmed, peeled, cut into 1-inch pieces
- 6 cups chicken stock or water flavored with consommé powder; more if needed to thin soup

CHESTNUT MUSHROOM SOUP

This soup follows the rule of starting with simple, good ingredients to yield good food that is big on flavor. The chestnuts and celery root are so savory and yield a wonderful creamy result.

1. Heat the olive oil in a large soup pot over medium heat. Add the onion. Allow the onion to "sweat," release its liquid, and become translucent — but don't let it brown, 4-5 minutes. Add the garlic and celery. Continue to cook slowly, stirring occasionally, for 3 minutes. Add the mushrooms. Cook for 3-4 minutes to release their liquid. Add the thyme and stir.

2. Measure 1½ tablespoons of the sliced chestnuts and reserve for garnish. Place the remaining chestnuts and celery root into the pot along with the stock. Cook until celery root is fork-tender, about 30-35 minutes. Transfer in batches to a blender or, using an immersion blender, purée right in the pot until smooth. Thin with additional stock until desired consistency is reached.

3. Ladle into bowls and garnish with reserved chestnuts.

JERUSALEM ARTICHOKE SOUP

4 cups vegetable or chicken stock

2 pounds sunchokes, aka Jerusalem artichokes, the largest you can find, peeled, rinsed and chopped into chunks

1 large Yukon Gold potato, peeled, cut into chunks

2 ($1/4$-inch) slices fresh, peeled ginger

1 bay leaf

3 whole black peppercorns

extra-virgin olive oil or white truffle oil

I once led a culinary adventure at Bayit Bagalil for R&R Tours in Israel. Chef Dror Marco welcomed me into his kitchen, where he was assisted by a lovely sous chef, Amit Barshap. They opened up a new world to me when they served and taught me how to make this soup, which I think is my all-time favorite of any soup I have ever cooked or eaten. It is an elegant adventure in easy home cooking. It is the recipe that will demonstrate why it is sometimes worthwhile to go out of your way to seek out a special ingredient like sunchokes, also called Jerusalem artichokes. If you can only find small ones, buy an additional pound, since much can be lost to peeling between the small knobs. The season for sunchokes is fall and into winter but some stores, including Pomegranate in Brooklyn, source them all year.

1. Pour the stock into a large soup pot. Add the Jerusalem artichokes, potato, ginger, bay leaf, and peppercorns. Bring to a boil over high heat. Cover the pot, reduce to a simmer on medium-low for 30 minutes or until the artichokes and potato are fork-tender.

2. Remove and discard bay leaf. Transfer the soup in batches to a blender or use an immersion blender right in the pot and purée until very smooth.

3. Ladle the soup into individual bowls. Finish each bowl with a drizzle of extra-virgin olive oil or truffle oil.

CHICKEN POT PIE SOUP

- 1 sheet puff pastry, at room temperature for 20 minutes
- 4 chicken thighs, bone-in, skin on
- 1 onion, peeled, cut into ¼-inch dice
- 1 russet potato, peeled, cut into ½-inch dice
- 2 carrots, peeled, cut into ¼-inch dice
- 2 ribs celery, cut into ¼-inch dice
- 2 parsnips, peeled, cut into ¼-inch dice
- 6 cups chicken stock
- 1 turnip, unpeeled, cut in half
  handful parsley sprigs
- 2 sprigs fresh dill
- 1 bay leaf
- 1 large egg, well beaten
- ½ teaspoon dried dill
- ¼ teaspoon cayenne
- ⅛ teaspoon fine sea salt
- 1 teaspoon cornstarch
- ¼ cup unsweetened, plain soymilk

Growing up, my sister Karen loved chicken pot pies from the freezer section of the supermarket. This healthier homemade version is what you will want for supper when it is cold and rainy; a modern twist on comfort food. This recipe is a cross between two classics — hearty chicken pot pie, and heavenly cream of chicken soup.

1. Preheat oven to 400°F. Cover a cookie sheet with parchment paper. Set aside.

2. Once the puff pastry is pliable enough, open it and set it aside on your counter to continue to defrost while you start the soup.

3. Heat an empty soup pot over medium heat. Add the chicken, skin-side-down and cook for 4-5 minutes, to render out some of the fat. Once the skin is brown, use tongs to flip the chicken skin-side-up. Add the onion, potato, carrots, celery, parsnips, and stock. Bring to a boil. Turn down heat to simmer for 8 minutes.

4. Place the turnip, parsley, dill, and bay leaf into a mesh soup bag. Tie the bag and add it to the pot. Continue to simmer for 30 minutes. Remove from heat; allow to cool slightly.

5. Meanwhile, brush the puff pastry with the beaten egg. Sprinkle evenly with the dried dill, cayenne, and salt. Cut the pastry horizontally into 1 x 9-inch strips. Tightly twist each strip to hide the spices. Place on prepared cookie sheet. Lightly brush the outside with egg. Bake for 8 minutes, rotate pan, bake for an additional 8 minutes until crisp and golden.

6. Remove and discard the mesh bag of herbs and turnip. Remove the chicken. When cool enough to handle, discard the bones and skin. Chop the chicken meat and reserve.

7. Dissolve the cornstarch in the soymilk. Whisk it into the pot. Return the heat to medium and allow the soup to simmer. The cornstarch will thicken the soup. Add the chicken back to the pot. Heat through. Ladle into crocks or bowls and serve with puff pastry twist.

YEMENITE BEEF SOUP

- 3 tablespoons canola oil
- 2 pounds beef marrow bones
- 1½ pounds cubed shell roast or beef stew meat
- 1 onion, peeled, cut into ½-inch dice
- 6 cloves fresh garlic, sliced
- 2 teaspoons hawaij Yemenite spice mixture
- ¼ cup tomato paste (from a small can)
- 3 carrots, peeled, cut into thick rounds
- 6 cups chicken stock
- 2 large or 3 small russet potatoes, peeled, cut into large chunks
  chopped fresh cilantro for garnish

>> *Serve this soup with fresh thick pita bread to complete your meal in a bowl.*

Hawaij is a flavorful Middle Eastern spice mixture. It is delicious but not fiery; a basic version contains cumin, cardamom, turmeric, coriander, and black pepper. You can buy it at any well-stocked kosher supermarket or on the internet.

If you have the time, refrigerate the soup overnight. Before you reheat the soup, remove the solidified layer of fat from the top.

1. Heat the oil in a large soup pot, over medium heat. Add the beef marrow bones. Stir, cover, and cook for 5 minutes. Add the beef cubes, cover, cook for 10 minutes longer, until there is some brown coloring on both the bones and the meat.

2. Uncover the pot and add the onion and garlic; cook for 5 minutes. Sprinkle in the hawaij. Stir and cook for 3 minutes. Stir in the tomato paste, coating the meat and bones. Cook for 3-4 minutes to deepen the tomato flavor. Add the carrots and stock. Cover the pot. Turn the heat to low and cook, simmering for 1 hour. Skim off any foam or fat.

3. Add the potatoes. Cover and cook for an additional hour.

4. Discard the bones. Ladle soup into bowls. Garnish with chopped cilantro.

PARVE OR MEAT
YIELD: 6 SERVINGS

1   tablespoon olive oil

3   shallots, peeled, thinly sliced

2   large yellow squash, with skin, cut into ½-inch dice

    kernels cut from 2 ears of corn on the cob

¼   teaspoon turmeric

¼   teaspoon ground white pepper

4   cups vegetable or chicken stock

YELLOW SQUASH AND CORN SOUP

Here's a great tip that I once read in Cook's Illustrated Magazine for cutting raw corn off the cob. Hold the corn in the tube opening of a bundt pan. Run your knife down the corn, scraping off all the kernels. This way, as you cut, the kernels fall right into the pan and don't fly all over your counter.

1. Heat the olive oil in a large soup pot over medium-low heat. Sauté the shallots for 3-4 minutes until shiny and translucent. Add the squash and sauté for 5-6 minutes.

2. Add the corn kernels to the pot. Sprinkle in the turmeric and white pepper. Pour in the stock and simmer for 25 minutes.

3. Transfer the soup in batches to a blender or use an immersion blender right in the pot and pureé until very smooth. The blender will give a more velvety texture. Reserve a few corn kernels and shallots for garnish, if desired, before blending. Ladle into bowls.

nonstick cooking spray

5 large beefsteak tomatoes, each cut in half

2 large Italian eggplants, each cut in half lengthwise

olive oil

1 whole head garlic, top ½ inch cut off and discarded

fine sea salt

freshly ground black pepper

3 tablespoons tomato paste

3 shallots, peeled, thinly sliced

1 teaspoon paprika

1 teaspoon fine sea salt

½ teaspoon dried oregano

½ teaspoon freshly ground black pepper

¼ teaspoon cayenne

3½ cups vegetable or chicken stock

½ cup white wine

1 tablespoon balsamic vinegar, plus additional for garnish

ROASTED EGGPLANT AND TOMATO BISQUE

Chef Lito Tan shared this soup recipe with me during the summer when the tomatoes are bursting with flavor. But it is an all-season soup, since it is warm and filling in the winter and the roasting brings out great flavor from the out-of-season tomatoes. You can serve it hot or cold. If you decide to make it dairy, garnish with a flick of sour cream.

1. Preheat oven to 450°F.

2. Cover 2 jellyroll pans with foil and spray with nonstick cooking spray. Place tomatoes and eggplant, cut-side-up, on the prepared pans. Brush all the exposed surfaces with olive oil. Turn the eggplant cut-side-down. Brush the cut head of garlic with olive oil as well, sprinkle with a little salt and pepper, and wrap in a square of aluminum foil. Place on one of the pans. Roast for 35 minutes.

3. Remove pans from the oven and brush the tomatoes and cut side of the eggplant with tomato paste. Leave the eggplant cut-side-up. Return the pans to the oven for a final 10 minutes. Remove pans from oven and allow to cool. If desired, reserve a little eggplant and some tomato to chop up for garnish.

4. Meanwhile, heat 1 tablespoon olive oil in a large soup pot over medium heat. Add the shallots and cook until translucent, 4-5 minutes. Stir in the paprika, salt, oregano, pepper, and cayenne. Hold the head of garlic over the pot (use a paper towel to protect your hand if it is still hot), and squeeze the cloves of roasted garlic out of the skin and into the pot. Add the tomatoes and the pan juices into the pot.

5. Using a large spoon, scoop the flesh from the eggplants and add to the pot, discarding skins.

6. Pour in the stock and wine. Stir well. Raise heat, bring to a boil, then turn down to a simmer and cook for 5 minutes. Stir in the

balsamic. Transfer the soup in batches to a blender or use an immersion blender right in the pot and purée until smooth. Ladle into bowls. Garnish with additional balsamic drizzled from a narrow squeeze bottle and with the reserved roasted eggplant and tomato if you had set it aside earlier.

GREEK WHITE BEAN FETA SOUP

1 cup dried navy beans or other small white beans, placed in a bowl and covered with water to soak for at least 2 hours or overnight

2 teaspoons olive oil

2 ribs celery, cut into ¼-inch dice

1 medium onion, halved, peeled, and thinly sliced

½ teaspoon dried oregano

1 cup grape tomatoes, halved lengthwise

6 cups water flavored with 4 teaspoons vegetable consommé powder

2 cups fresh baby spinach leaves

4 ounces feta cheese, broken into small chunks

If you want to substitute boxed vegetable broth, be aware that some of the brands that I have used become very thick when cooked, so don't substitute it for more than half the amount of liquid, using water for the other half. You may also need to add an additional cup or two of consommé-flavored water at the end of the cooking time if your soup is very thick.

1. Heat the oil in a large soup pot over medium heat. Add the celery and onion, cook for 4-5 minutes. Allow the vegetables to "sweat," release their liquid, and become translucent, 5-6 minutes, but don't let them brown. Add the oregano and tomatoes. Stir and cook for 1 minute.

2. Drain the beans and add them to the pot. Pour in the consommé-flavored water. Bring to a boil, then bring down to a simmer. Continue to cook, uncovered, for 50-60 minutes, or until the beans are tender. Add the spinach and allow it to wilt, about 1 minute. Add the cheese. Remove from heat.

3. Ladle into bowls.

PARVE
YIELD: 12 SERVINGS

1 small onion, peeled

2 ribs celery

2 carrots, peeled

2 zucchini, with skin

5 cloves fresh garlic

1 tablespoon olive oil

1½ tablespoons dried oregano

1 teaspoon dried basil

½ teaspoon dried parsley

½ teaspoon dried rosemary

¼ teaspoon dried thyme

⅓ cup tomato paste

8 cups vegetable stock

1 (28-ounce) can diced tomatoes, with liquid

2 bay leaves

2 tablespoons fresh chopped parsley

1 cup packed fresh baby spinach leaves

1 (15-ounce) can red kidney beans

1 (15-ounce) can small white beans

1 cup fresh green beans, ends trimmed, cut into thirds

½ cup red wine

2 cups water

1 cup ditalini or other small pasta, uncooked

VEGETABLE MINESTRONE SOUP

This recipe is a dieter's dream: days' worth of veggies packed into a delicious soup. If you are making it in advance, cook the pasta separately; if it is allowed to sit in the soup it will absorb too much broth. Keep additional broth or stock on hand in case you need more liquid, or you can use a cup or two of water.

1. Cut the onion, celery, carrots, and zucchini into ¼-inch dice. Chop the garlic.

2. Heat the oil in a large pot over medium-high heat. Add the onion, celery, carrots, zucchini, garlic, oregano, basil, parsley, rosemary, and thyme. Stirring every few minutes with a wooden spoon, cook until the vegetables are shiny and the onion translucent, 5-7 minutes.

3. Add the tomato paste and stir into the vegetables. Cook for 2 minutes. Pour in the stock and tomatoes. Add the bay leaves, fresh parsley, and spinach. Rinse and drain kidney beans and white beans, and add them to the pot along with the green beans. Stir in the wine and allow to simmer for 25 minutes.

4. Add the water. Bring to a boil; turn down to a simmer. Add the pasta and cook for 10 minutes, or until the pasta is tender. You may need to add more vegetable broth or water if the pasta absorbs too much liquid. Remove and discard bay leaves.

5. Ladle into bowls and serve hot.

3-BEAN CHILI SOUP

DAIRY, PARVE, OR MEAT
YIELD: 6-8 SERVINGS

1 tablespoon canola oil

1½ medium onions, peeled, thinly sliced

2 teaspoons chili powder

2 teaspoons ground cumin

¾ teaspoon salt

6 cloves fresh garlic, minced

1 (15-ounce) can chick peas, with its liquid

1 (15-ounce) can black beans, with its liquid

1 (15-ounce) can red kidney beans, with its liquid

1 (16-ounce) can or bottle lager beer; I like Budweiser brand

2 cups vegetable or chicken stock

sour cream or nondairy sour cream, optional, for garnish

grated cheddar cheese, optional, for dairy garnish

Different brands of chili powder vary in heat.
I like the Morton & Bassett brand, it has great kick.

1. Heat the oil in a large soup pot over medium heat. Add the onions and cook until shiny and translucent, 5-6 minutes; do not allow them to brown. Add the chili powder, cumin, and salt. Stir well to distribute the spices. Add the garlic and cook for 4-5 minutes to toast the spices and develop their flavor. Use a wooden spoon to scrape the bottom of the pot.

2. Empty the cans of chick peas, black beans, and kidney beans, with their liquid, into the pot. Add the beer and stock. Bring to a boil, turn down to a simmer and cook, covered for 30 minutes.

3. Garnish with a dollop of dairy or parve sour cream and a sprinkle of cheddar cheese if using for dairy.

SALAD

GAME PLAN

Salad is very versatile. Salad can be used as a light and lovely starter. Add a protein and it can be a main. A pasta, rice, or vegetable salad can make a great side dish, and fruit salad can be served as a refreshing dessert.

Green salads have 3 components: lettuce, dressing, and add-ins.

LETTUCE

The lettuce you choose determines the taste, texture, and color of the salad. Greens can be mild, spicy, or bitter and are the foundation of the salad. Make sure they are the freshest you can find. Look for crisp tender leaves. Avoid heads that are brown at the tips or bags with leaves that look wet or mushy.

CLEANING AND STORING

Bagged and fresh lettuce need to be cleaned and checked for bugs. Many kashrut agencies offer booklets and online instruction with detailed directions for checking greens. Once cleaned, greens must be dried completely or you will end up with soggy salad, and if you are prepping the greens in advance, they will not survive in the refrigerator if stored too wet. Even if serving immediately, if the leaves are wet, the dressing won't stick. Salad spinners work really well to dry lettuce quickly. I like the kind with the pump top, not the string mechanism, which can easily tangle.

DRESSINGS

Dressings tie salads together. They should not overwhelm the other ingredients.

CREAMY DRESSINGS

Creamy dressings have their base in mayonnaise, sour cream, yogurt, and often, buttermilk. These should be paired with crisp sturdy lettuces such as romaine, endive, and iceberg, which tend to be heavy in consistency.

>> *To easily remove the core from a head of lettuce, smack it firmly, core-side-down against your countertop. This will break the core and make it easy to twist out and discard.*

Salad Spinner

>> *Creamy dressings stand in nicely as dips for vegetables.*

VINAIGRETTES

Vinaigrettes are emulsions of 2 liquids that don't easily mix. The standard ratio is 1 part acid to 3 parts oil. This is a starting point. If lemon is your acid, it may need less oil than if you use a strong vinegar. Make sure to taste and adjust accordingly.

My favorite go-to dressing is a simple balsamic/olive oil combination with some coarse sea salt and freshly ground black pepper.

ADD-INS

Used as accents, add-ins make your salads creative, unique, and seasonal. Some examples: **CRUNCHY VEGETABLES** — cucumber, peppers, onions, celery, carrots, mushrooms, radish, broccoli, cauliflower, cabbage, scallion, red onion, corn **NUTS** — pine nuts, walnuts, almonds, macadamia, pecans **SEEDS** — pumpkin, sunflower **DRIED FRUIT** — cranberries, blueberries, crystalized ginger, fresh citrus zest **FRESH FRUIT** — diced or sliced apples or pears, orange or tangerine segments, avocado, watermelon **BERRIES** — blueberries, strawberries, raspberries, blackberries **CHEESES** — Parmesan, goat cheese, feta, blue cheese **ROASTED VEGETABLES** — squash, portobellos, bell peppers, beets, sweet potatoes, garlic **FRESH HERBS** — basil, mint, thyme, rosemary **PROTEINS** — sliced deli meat, tuna, chicken, steak, salmon, beans, chick peas, tofu, eggs **TOMATOES** — cherry, grape, heirloom, sundried **CAPERS**

TOSSING AND SERVING

Although many people use wooden salad bowls, I am not a fan. They retain odor and can warp over time. Often the shape is wrong for dressing salads as well. If the sides are too deep, the smaller ingredients, like nuts and seeds, fall to the bottom. I prefer a lightweight stainless steel shallow bowl. I toss with gloved hands to get a feel for dressing the leaves and making sure all are coated but not soaked. Overdressing will ruin a salad, so add a little at a time. When having a large group, I will use a plastic shopping bag to dress the salad. Transfer dressed greens to a shallow serving bowl. Dress salads right before serving or they will wilt.

» *A quarter-cup of vinaigrette dressing coats 8-10 cups of lightly packed greens.*

» ACIDS: *balsamic vinegar, rice vinegar, red wine vinegar, white wine vinegar, white vinegar, buttermilk, citrus juice, lemon juice.*
Mustard and mayonnaise bind and emulsify vinaigrettes, but are not necessary.

» TYPES OF OILS: **extra-virgin olive oil, canola, sunflower, grapeseed, nut oils** — *like walnut or hazelnut oil; buy these in small quantities — they turn rancid quickly* **sesame oil** *— I like the dark toasted or roasted kind but use in small quantities, as it has a very strong flavor*

CUTTING BELL PEPPERS

Slice off the whole stem end. Grasping with your fingers, remove and discard the seeds and innards. Make a cut so the whole pepper opens flat. Trim any ribs. Slice or dice as desired.

CITRUS

My favorite way to zest citrus is using a rasp-style grater, like a Microplane. It removes only the bright colored zest, leaving the bitter white pith behind. Zest can be frozen for up to 3 months.

To get the most juice out of your citrus, make sure it is at room temperature. You can microwave it for 10 seconds if it is cold. If you roll it between your palm and your countertop, applying pressure, you will break the membranes and more juice will be released. I like using a press like the one pictured above. It gets all the juice from the citrus half and holds on to the pits. If you buy one, make sure it is all metal, not plastic, incuding the hinges.

TRIMMING GREEN BEANS

Grab a big handful of beans and quickly trim the ends using scissors. Flip them and then do the other side. Scissors are also a great tool for cutting dill.

SEEDING A CUCUMBER

In salads, I like using English hothouse cucumbers. These usually come shrink-wrapped. They are called seedless, but there are seeds and I remove them using a melon baller. You can keep the skin on or peel it off with a vegetable peeler. Kirby cucumbers are best for pickling.

FENNEL

Fennel is a great crunchy vegetable that tastes a bit like licorice or anise. Don't slice too thickly or it will be fibrous. It can be shaved with a mandolin or sliced into salads or braised until tender. Make sure you buy firm bulbs with no sign of browning. Slice off the whole tops, including the fronds, and discard. Cut the bulb in half lengthwise like an onion. Trim bottom and discard. Remove the core. Slice thinly against the grain.

AVOCADO

Look for Haas avocadoes, the ones with very rough skin. They are creamier and richer than the smooth-skinned variety. Purchase ones that give just a bit when pressed. If too hard, allow to ripen at room temperature. Cut in half around the whole length of the avocado. Twist the two ends in opposite directions to divide. Whack your knife into the pit and twist to dislodge it. Avocados turn brown when cut open and exposed to light, air, and heat. Some people say to keep the pit in place to avoid discoloration. An avocado is often green underneath the pit but brown on the exposed surfaces surrounding it because the surface underneath the pit is protected from light and air. So it's not about the pit itself, only the way the pit acts as a barrier. Try to limit the exposure of the cut surface by tightly pressing a piece of plastic wrap over the cut surface and stick it in the refrigerator. It's not ideal but will buy you a little time.

HAND-HELD MANDOLIN

Slicing perfect and paper-thin vegetables could not be easier. I love my hand-held mandolin and use it for vegetables, slicing potatoes for homemade fries and for gratins, for apples, for getting paper-thin fennel or onion shavings in a salad, and so much more. Get one that is adjustable so you have the versatility to make slices that are thicker and thinner based on your need. I like the ceramic blade kind because they never rust. It is vital that at the same time, you also purchase a steel-core glove to protect your fingertips; these blades are very sharp and dangerous pieces of equipment if you are not careful and they should not be used by children.

seeding a tomato

halved

seeded

sliced

diced

SEEDING AND DICING TOMATOES

Buy local tomatoes whenever possible, as they don't ship well. Look for firm tomatoes that are heavy for their size. For sandwiches, I like beefsteak tomatoes; for salads I like grape or cherry tomatoes, or Roma, also called plum tomatoes (which are also good in sauces). They are less watery. Remove seeds with a melon baller. Never refrigerate a tomato; it will become mealy and lose its flavor.

HERBS

Fresh herbs are a great way to boost flavor in a salad or other dish.

Choose herbs that have a vibrant color. Black or yellowing spots show signs of aging or spoilage.

parsley

sage

dill

basil

cilantro

thyme

rosemary

oregano

STRIPPING THYME

To remove thyme leaves by hand, pluck off the leaves you need, or if your thyme has firm stalks, not flimsy ones, grasp the tip of a stalk with one hand, pinch it with the other hand, and run your pinched fingers down the stem. This will remove most of the leaves at once. This works for rosemary as well.

SCRAPING PARSLEY

Grab the parsley bunch by the stem end. Pointing the leaves down toward your cutting board, run the knife down the outside of the bunch to shave off the leaves.

STORING HERBS

When you get home from the market, cut off any rubber bands or fasteners from the herbs. Wet a paper towel. Squeeze out all the water. Tightly wrap the herbs in the damp towel and place into the refrigerator. Your herbs will keep for days like this. If the towel gets dry, wet your hand and squeeze the towel to remoisten.

PARSLEY AND CILANTRO

Although they look similar, parsley and cilantro taste very different and are not interchangeable. Cilantro is the leaf of the young coriander plant. It is used often in Asian and Mexican dishes. Parsley is milder in flavor and is often used as a garnish.

Some people have a hard time distinguishing one from the other, but learning the difference ensures that you pair the herbs with the right foods and achieve the best flavor.

Cilantro has rounded leaves with serrated edges. Parsley leaves have a more oval/pointed appearance with serrated edges.

cilantro

parsley

SHAVED ASPARAGUS SALAD

PARVE
YIELD: 6-8 SERVINGS

The key to this salad is using good sweet asparagus. Look for firm, bright green stalks with tight, compact tips. Avoid spears that are dry, limp, or wrinkled, or have dried-out, separated tips.

1. Lay one asparagus spear flat on your cutting board. Holding the spear on one end for support, pull a vegetable peeler down the length of the spear to shave the asparagus stalk into thin strips. Continue until the entire spear is shaved. Repeat with remaining asparagus. Place the asparagus strips into a medium bowl until ready to serve.

2. In a small bowl, whisk the honey, balsamic, olive oil, and pepper.

3. When ready to serve, toss the arugula with the asparagus. Mound a handful of the salad on each plate or on the platter. Gently drizzle with the dressing. Arrange the tomatoes and pine nuts in and around the mound. Sprinkle with a pinch of the sea salt.

1½ pounds thick asparagus, bottom 2 inches cut off and discarded

2 tablespoons honey

2 tablespoons balsamic vinegar

2 tablespoons extra-virgin olive oil

¼ teaspoon freshly ground black pepper

2 ounces baby arugula leaves

12 cherry tomatoes, halved

⅓ cup pine nuts

coarse sea salt or other finishing salt

ORANGE-TERIYAKI STEAK SALAD

Tender grilled steak, crispy lettuce, and a smooth Asian-inspired dressing make this dish a winner for lunch or dinner.

1½ pounds shoulder London broil or minute steak fillet

fine sea salt

freshly ground black pepper

nonstick cooking spray

2 large or 3 small heads Romaine lettuce

½ cup shredded carrot

2 scallions, roots trimmed, thinly sliced on diagonal

leaves from 5 sprigs fresh cilantro, chopped

leaves from 2 sprigs fresh mint (8-10 leaves), chopped

2 (11-ounce) cans mandarin oranges, drained

½ navel orange

6 tablespoons light mayonnaise

2 tablespoons teriyaki sauce; I like Kikkoman brand

½ teaspoon ground ginger

½ teaspoon lime juice

¼ teaspoon roasted or toasted sesame oil

1-2 cups thin Chinese chow mein or rice noodles; I like La Choy brand

1. Season the steak with salt and pepper on both sides. Spray a large skillet or grill pan with nonstick cooking spray. Heat over medium until hot but not smoking. Sear the steak, cooking 6-10 minutes per side, depending on thickness; the shoulder London broil will be thicker than the minute steak fillet. Allow to rest for 10 minutes and then slice thinly on the diagonal.

2. Separate the Romaine lettuce leaves. Stack the leaves and chop into bite-sized pieces, to make about 12 cups chopped. Place into large bowl. Add the carrot, scallion, cilantro, mint, and mandarin oranges. Toss the steak slices into the salad. Squeeze the orange half over the salad.

3. In a small bowl, whisk the mayonnaise, teriyaki, ginger, lime juice, and sesame oil. Drizzle over the salad and toss to coat the steak and vegetables well.

4. Garnish with the noodles.

2 boneless, skinless chicken breast halves

2 large flour tortillas

2 cups panko breadcrumbs

1 cup lowfat mayonnaise

1 tablespoon favorite barbecue sauce

1 tablespoon water

$\frac{1}{2}$ teaspoon dried dill

$\frac{1}{2}$ teaspoon onion powder

$\frac{1}{4}$ teaspoon garlic powder

$\frac{1}{8}$ teaspoon freshly ground black pepper

$\frac{1}{8}$ teaspoon dry mustard powder

canola oil for frying

$\frac{1}{4}$ teaspoon dried dill

$\frac{1}{8}$ teaspoon fine sea salt

$\frac{1}{8}$ teaspoon chili powder

4 ounces salad greens

12 small cherry tomatoes

1 small (8.5-ounce) can corn kernels, drained

3 tablespoons canned black beans, rinsed

juice of half a lime

1 avocado, peeled, pitted, diced

$\frac{1}{4}$ cup canola oil

2 tablespoons apple cider vinegar

$\frac{1}{4}$ teaspoon ground cumin

$\frac{1}{4}$ teaspoon chili powder

COWBOY CHICKEN SALAD

Dinner in a bowl with some Southwestern flair! If you are counting calories, don't let the pan-frying of the chicken scare you off. Instead, put the coated chicken pieces onto a cookie cooling rack set in a jellyroll pan and bake them for 10-15 minutes at 350°F. Serve with just a few tortilla strips.

1. Slice the chicken breasts lengthwise into thin strips, 6-7 strips per breast. Set aside.

2. Fold the tortillas in half and slice into thin strips. Set aside.

3. Meanwhile, place the panko into one part of a 2-part breading station. In the second part, whisk the mayonnaise, barbecue sauce, water, $\frac{1}{2}$ teaspoon dill, onion powder, garlic powder, black pepper, and mustard powder.

4. Dip the chicken strips into the mayonnaise mixture and then into the panko. Place onto a cookie sheet until all are breaded. Allow to air-dry for 10 minutes so that the panko will adhere better during cooking.

5. Heat 1-inch canola oil in a medium pot. When the oil is hot, add the chicken, in a single layer, in batches. The oil should bubble vigorously; don't over-crowd the pot. Fry until medium golden, about 2 minutes. Remove with tongs or a slotted spoon to paper towels. Discard any burnt coating pieces from the pot.

6. When all the chicken is done, add the tortilla strips to the oil and fry until golden. Remove to paper towels and sprinkle with $\frac{1}{4}$ teaspoon dill, salt, and chili powder.

7. Place salad greens into a large bowl. Halve the cherry tomatoes; add to bowl. Add the corn, black beans, lime juice, and avocado.

8. In a small bowl, whisk the $\frac{1}{4}$ cup oil, vinegar, cumin, and chili powder. Dress the salad, tossing to coat. Top with chicken and tortilla strips.

CHICK PEA AND FENNEL SALAD

1 small bulb fennel, stalks and feathery fronds discarded

1 (15-ounce) can chick peas or garbanzo beans, rinsed and drained

1/2 cup gaeta or kalamata olives, pitted, coarsely chopped

1/4 red onion, peeled, very thinly sliced

3 tablespoons fresh lemon juice

3 tablespoons extra-virgin olive oil

1/4 teaspoon fine sea salt

1/8 teaspoon freshly ground black pepper

   leaves from 5 stems fresh parsley, roughly 1/2 cup, loosely packed

4 leaves fresh mint, chopped

You can let this salad sit overnight in the refrigerator. Add the parsley and mint just before serving.

When buying fennel, look for rounded, moist-looking bulbs; they are sweeter. The leafy dill-like fronds should not be limp.

1. Using a vegetable peeler, shave off the outer layer of the fennel bulb. Discard the shavings. Cut the bulb into quarters, and then use a mandolin to cut into paper-thin slices against the grain. Place into large bowl. Add the chick peas, olives, and onion.

2. Toss with the lemon juice, olive oil, salt, and pepper. Sprinkle in the parsley and mint. Transfer to serving bowl.

STRAWBERRY-GOAT CHEESE SALAD

- 4 ounces goat cheese
- 2 ripe strawberries, stems removed, halved
- 2 teaspoons white wine vinegar or apple cider vinegar
- 2 tablespoons extra-virgin olive oil
- 2 tablespoons honey
- 1 tablespoon water
- ¼ teaspoon fine sea salt
- ¼ teaspoon freshly ground black pepper
- 3 ounces spring mix or mesclun lettuce leaves

  handful glazed walnuts; I like the Emerald brand
- 6 strawberries, stems removed, quartered

My daughter Katie has great instincts in the kitchen. She developed this recipe knowing that I love every ingredient in this salad. The dressing has just the right blend of tart and sweet.

1. In the container of a food processor fitted with the metal "S" blade or in a quart-sized container with an immersion blender, process the goat cheese, 2 strawberries, vinegar, olive oil, honey, water, salt, and pepper. Pulse until creamy. Set aside.

2. Place the salad greens into a large bowl. Drizzle with dressing to taste. Toss. Arrange the walnuts and strawberries over the salad.

GRILLED SALAMI AND FIG SALAD

- 2 ounces pine nuts
- 2 tablespoons red wine vinegar
- 6 tablespoons extra-virgin olive oil
- 1 (11-ounce) jar fig preserves
- 1 tablespoon nondairy cream cheese, such as Tofutti brand
- 1 pound sliced beef salami (4-inch diameter slices)
- 4 ounces baby arugula leaves

  additional pine nuts, for garnish

I'll always remember the day my doorbell rang and I looked down to see the cutest little boy standing there, out of breath, Nate Savitz was holding a bouquet of these salami fans that his mom, Naomi, had skewered and wanted me to try so she sent him racing through the connecting yards with her fabulous creation. They were fabulous indeed; I ate them all before even crossing back over the threshold. The addition of the salad piece makes it the perfect starter course that will appeal to young and old alike. The bite of the arugula plays off the sweetness of the figs perfectly.

1. Place the 2-ounces of pine nuts into a large empty skillet or grill pan over medium heat. Toast until fragrant, shaking the pan, for about 2 minutes. Transfer the pine nuts to a quart-size container. Add the vinegar and olive oil. Using an immersion blender purée the mixture into a dressing. This can also be done in a food processor fitted with metal "S" blade.

2.. Place the fig preserves into a second quart-sized container. Add the nondairy cream cheese. Using an immersion blender, process until the figs are evenly chopped. If you don't have an immersion blender, finely chop the fig preserves and whisk them into the cream cheese.

3. Preheat the skillet or grill pan over medium heat. Place the salami slices on your work surface. Spread the fig mixture evenly on one side of each salami slice, about ½ teaspoon per slice. Fold each slice of salami in half twice to form a fan. Place the salami fans into the hot pan. Cook, using tongs to turn each fan once, 1-2 minutes per side or until the salami is grilled. Set aside. Do in batches and rinse out pan between batches if necessary.

4. Place the arugula into a large bowl or platter. Toss with the dressing. Set the salami fans into the lettuce. Garnish with pine nuts.

BUFFALO CHICKEN SALAD

DRESSINGS

- ¹/₂ cup mayonnaise
- 1 teaspoon dried tarragon, crumbled
- juice of 1 lemon
- ¹/₂ cup hot sauce; I like Frank's Red Hot brand
- ¹/₄ cup extra-virgin olive oil
- 1 teaspoon garlic powder
- ¹/₂ teaspoon onion powder

BUFFALO CHICKEN

- 3 boneless, skinless chicken breast halves
- 2 teaspoons fine sea salt, divided
- 1¹/₂ cups all-purpose flour
- ¹/₈ teaspoon freshly ground black pepper
- 4 large eggs
- 3 tablespoons hot sauce; I like Frank's Red Hot brand
- 2¹/₂ cups panko breadcrumbs
- nonstick cooking spray
- 3 carrots, peeled
- 2 ribs celery, ends trimmed
- 1 head Romaine lettuce, root end trimmed, cut into bite-sized pieces

Last year, my son Eli and his third-grade buddies had culinary worlds open to them. Their friend AJ Keiser, a ketchup fanatic, made the big move to hot sauce and it started a rage! Eli went from eating nothing to everything, as long as it had a sprinkling of hot sauce. This salad falls into that category, so I know that the hot-sauce lovers in your life will love it, just like mine does.

1. Preheat oven to 375°F. Place a cookie cooling rack on a cookie sheet or jellyroll pan. Set aside.

2. Prepare the creamy dressing: In a small bowl whisk the mayonnaise, tarragon, and lemon juice. Set aside. Prepare the Buffalo sauce dressing: In a second small bowl, whisk the ¹/₂ cup hot sauce, olive oil, garlic powder, and onion powder. Set aside.

3. Remove the tenders and cut each tender in half. Place into a medium bowl. Cut each breast in half lengthwise and then into 2-inch cubes. Place into bowl. Season with 1 teaspoon salt, kneading it into the chicken until evenly seasoned.

4. Prepare a 3-part breading station. Place the flour with the pepper and remaining 1 teaspoon fine sea salt into the first section. Place the eggs whisked with the 3 tablespoons hot sauce into the second part. Place the panko into the third part.

5. Working with a few pieces of chicken at a time, and keeping one hand for wet ingredients and one hand for dry, coat the chicken in the flour, the egg mixture, and then into the panko, pressing it to coat. Place on prepared rack on cookie sheet in a single layer. Repeat until all the chicken is used.

6. Using a sweeping motion, lightly spray the tray of chicken with the nonstick cooking spray. Bake, uncovered, for 15 minutes.

7. Halve carrots lengthwise. Thinly slice on diagonal; place into large bowl. Repeat with the celery. Add the Romaine. Set aside.

8. Toss the salad with the creamy dressing until evenly coated. Serve in a large salad bowl or portion onto plates. Top with the baked chicken.

9. Drizzle the Buffalo sauce dressing over the salad.

PARVE
YIELD: 8 SERVINGS

FRUIT AND NUT SALAD

- 1/2 pound sugar snap peas, strings discarded, reserve a few for optional garnish
- 8 ounces (or 8-10 large handfuls) mesclun lettuce or spring mix
- 2 ounces baby arugula
- 1 cup fresh firm raspberries
- 1 cup fresh firm blueberries
- 1/4 cup raw unsalted sunflower seeds
- 1/4 cup raw shelled pistachios, finely chopped
- 2 tablespoons chopped pecans
- 2 tablespoons pine nuts
- 2 tablespoons raw shelled pumpkin seeds
- 6 tablespoons extra-virgin olive oil
- 3 tablespoons raspberry vinegar
- 1/2 teaspoon fine sea salt
- 1/2 teaspoon freshly ground black pepper
- 1/2 lemon

For a pretty presentation, mold the salad into a mound using a ring mold. If you don't have one, use a can opener and remove both sides of a tuna can; wash well to eliminate the odor. Place the can or ring mold into the center of your serving dish. Pack the salad firmly into the mold. Lift the can or ring. Garnish the plate with a few whole sugar snap peas, arranged in a fan.

International Spice makes a nice raspberry vinegar but if you can't find kosher raspberry vinegar, steep 2 red raspberry tea bags in 1/4 cup white vinegar. Squeeze out tea bags and discard. Mix in 2 tablespoons light corn syrup, 1 teaspoon sugar, and 1/2 teaspoon balsamic vinegar. Use as directed in recipes.

1. On a cutting board, stack the snap peas, 3-4 at a time; trim and discard ends. Slice thinly on the diagonal. Repeat with remaining snap peas.

2. Place the lettuce leaves and arugula into a large mixing bowl. Add the sliced snap peas. Add the raspberries, blueberries, sunflower seeds, pistachios, pecans, pine nuts, and pumpkin seeds.

3. In a quart-sized container or cruet, combine the olive oil, vinegar, salt, and pepper. Whisk or cover and shake the container until the ingredients are emulsified. Pour over the salad. Squeeze the lemon half over the salad, making sure to catch and discard the seeds. Using gloved hands, toss the salad to coat all the lettuce; be gentle so you don't squish the berries.

4. Transfer to a bowl, or serve individually plated as described in the note, and garnish with whole sugar snap peas, if desired.

25 shiitake mushrooms, stemmed and sliced

1 bunch thick asparagus, ends trimmed, cut into thirds

1 bunch scallions, ends trimmed, cut into thirds

olive oil

coarse sea salt or kosher salt

½ small sweet onion, such as Vidalia or Maui, peeled

2 cloves fresh garlic

¼ cup (small handful) fresh basil leaves, stemmed

1 teaspoon fine sea salt

¾ teaspoon freshly ground black pepper

¼ teaspoon dry mustard powder

juice of ½ lemon

2 teaspoons Worcestershire sauce
see note on p. 166

¼ cup balsamic vinegar

2 tablespoons water

½ cup extra-virgin olive oil

5 ounces baby Romaine lettuce leaves or spring mix

SLOW-ROASTED SHIITAKE ASPARAGUS SALAD

Slow roasting the mushrooms develops their "umami" and results in a deep meaty flavor.

1. Preheat oven to 275°F.

2. Cover 2 cookie sheets with parchment paper. Spread the sliced shiitake mushroom caps on one of the sheets. Arrange the asparagus and scallions in a single layer on the other sheet. Drizzle all the vegetables with olive oil, rubbing it in to coat. Sprinkle lightly with a few grains of coarse sea salt. Slow-roast the vegetables for 1 hour.

3. Meanwhile, prepare the dressing: Place the onion half, garlic, basil, salt, pepper, dry mustard, lemon juice, Worcestershire sauce, balsamic, and water into the bowl of a food processor fitted with a metal "S" blade. Process until smooth. With the motor running, drizzle in ½ cup olive oil and blend until smooth.

4. Place the lettuce into a large bowl. Add the roasted mushrooms, asparagus, and scallions. Drizzle with dressing. Toss to coat the leaves well.

ISRAELI EGGPLANT PEPPER SALAD

3 medium Italian dark purple eggplants, unpeeled, ends trimmed, cut into ¾-inch dice

fine sea salt

½ cup ketchup

2 tablespoons white vinegar

1 tablespoon lemon juice, from about ½ lemon

3 cloves fresh garlic, minced

⅛ teaspoon ground cumin

canola oil for deep frying

2 red bell peppers, seeded and cut into ½-inch dice

1 large onion, peeled, very thinly sliced

fresh parsley, chopped, for garnish

I did a show a few years back for a Chabad in John's Creek, Georgia. The group had hired a fabulous team of caterers, Donna Meyer and Jodie Sturgeon, to set up a table of appetizers for the guests as they were arriving for the show. This salad was so gorgeous and delicious, I had a hard time tearing away from the table when my show began. Jodie was kind enough to share the recipe.

1. Put cut eggplant pieces in single layers on two cookie sheets. Sprinkle with salt. Let them sit for 30 minutes. Drain and pat dry with paper towels. Line a large colander with more paper towels. Set aside.

2. In a large bowl, mix the ketchup, vinegar, lemon juice, garlic, and cumin.

3. In a deep pot, heat enough oil to come a little less than halfway up the side of the pot. Allow the oil to get very hot, 350°F. Carefully add the eggplant and fry until golden. You will need to do this in 2-3 batches, depending on the size of your pot. Remove with a slotted spoon or a spider. Cool the eggplant in the paper towel-lined colander to remove excess oil. Transfer to the bowl of sauce. Replace the paper towels in the colander for subsequent batches.

3. Add the red pepper and onion to the hot oil in the pot and fry until limp and shiny, about 3-4 minutes. Add to the colander if it is big enough; if not, drain on paper towels.

4. Transfer peppers and onion to the large bowl. Gently stir the ketchup mixture into the vegetables.

5. Cover and refrigerate the salad. This salad is best when it sits for a few hours or overnight. Garnish with fresh parsley before serving.

ISRAELI EGGPLANT PEPPER SALAD

3 medium Italian dark purple eggplants, unpeeled, ends trimmed, cut into ¾-inch dice

fine sea salt

½ cup ketchup

2 tablespoons white vinegar

1 tablespoon lemon juice, from about ½ lemon

3 cloves fresh garlic, minced

⅛ teaspoon ground cumin

canola oil for deep frying

2 red bell peppers, seeded and cut into ½-inch dice

1 large onion, peeled, very thinly sliced

fresh parsley, chopped, for garnish

I did a show a few years back for a Chabad in John's Creek, Georgia. The group had hired a fabulous team of caterers, Donna Meyer and Jodie Sturgeon, to set up a table of appetizers for the guests as they were arriving for the show. This salad was so gorgeous and delicious, I had a hard time tearing away from the table when my show began. Jodie was kind enough to share the recipe.

1. Put cut eggplant pieces in single layers on two cookie sheets. Sprinkle with salt. Let them sit for 30 minutes. Drain and pat dry with paper towels. Line a large colander with more paper towels. Set aside.

2. In a large bowl, mix the ketchup, vinegar, lemon juice, garlic, and cumin.

3. In a deep pot, heat enough oil to come a little less than halfway up the side of the pot. Allow the oil to get very hot, 350°F. Carefully add the eggplant and fry until golden. You will need to do this in 2-3 batches, depending on the size of your pot. Remove with a slotted spoon or a spider. Cool the eggplant in the paper towel-lined colander to remove excess oil. Transfer to the bowl of sauce. Replace the paper towels in the colander for subsequent batches.

3. Add the red pepper and onion to the hot oil in the pot and fry until limp and shiny, about 3-4 minutes. Add to the colander if it is big enough; if not, drain on paper towels.

4. Transfer peppers and onion to the large bowl. Gently stir the ketchup mixture into the vegetables.

5. Cover and refrigerate the salad. This salad is best when it sits for a few hours or overnight. Garnish with fresh parsley before serving.

CHICKEN SOUVLAKI SALAD

2 boneless, skinless chicken breast halves

1½ teaspoons dried oregano, divided

1 teaspoon ground cumin, divided

¼ teaspoon garlic powder
fine sea salt
freshly ground black pepper

1 medium lemon, very thinly sliced

4½ tablespoons extra-virgin olive oil, divided

3 tablespoons fresh lemon juice, from 2-3 lemons

3 ounces mesclun lettuce or spring mix

½ small red onion, peeled, thinly sliced

½ cup grape tomatoes, halved, lengthwise

1 clementine, peeled, segments separated

⅓ cup pitted kalamata olives, sliced

2 pita breads, or more if serving whole pitas

Traditional Greek souvlaki is fast food and is served on skewers. It can be made with any kind of meat, not just poultry.

1. Preheat oven to 400°F.

2. Place the chicken on a large rectangle of aluminum foil. Season with ½ teaspoon oregano, ½ teaspoon cumin, garlic powder, salt, and pepper. Cover each chicken breast with overlapping slices of lemon. Fold up the packet and place on a jellyroll pan. Bake for 20-25 minutes until no longer pink inside.

3. Meanwhile, whisk 4 tablespoons extra-virgin olive oil with 3 tablespoons fresh lemon juice, remaining 1 teaspoon oregano, remaining ½ teaspoon cumin, and ⅛ teaspoon salt. Set aside.

4. Place the mesclun into a large mixing bowl. Add the onion, tomatoes, clementine segments, and olives. Set aside.

5. During the final 5 minutes of the cooking time for the chicken, brush the pita breads with remaining ½ tablespoon olive oil and place into the oven, uncovered, on the jellyroll pan.

6. When the chicken is done, open the packet; discard the lemons. Add the juices to the dressing. Slice each breast on the diagonal into ½-inch-thick slices and then lengthwise down the center, to create chunks of chicken. Add the chicken to the salad. Cut the pita bread into 8 triangles, like a pizza. Arrange in a bowl or platter, with the pita as garnish. Drizzle with the dressing. Or just serve a portion for each person in or on pita.

LENTIL AND BEET SALAD

Lentils are a healthy legume that are low in fat, high in protein and fiber, and cook quickly. Get Puy lentils if possible; they may take a little longer to cook but they will hold their shape best, although I have had good results from Arrowhead Mills green lentils.

Lentils have a mild, often earthy flavor, and are best if cooked with strong flavorings. Before cooking, rinse lentils and pick out stones and debris. Lentils cook more slowly if they're combined with salt or acidic ingredients, so add these last. Bigger or older lentils need more cooking time. Dried lentils can be stored for up to a year in a cool, dry place.

water

2½ teaspoons fine sea salt, divided

4 red beets, washed, roots trimmed and discarded

1 cup Puy or green lentils, rinsed

2 sprigs fresh thyme

2 cloves fresh garlic

1 rib celery, root end trimmed

1 carrot, peeled, ends trimmed and discarded

2 tablespoons extra-virgin olive oil, plus extra for drizzling on arugula

½ teaspoon freshly ground black pepper, divided

1 small red onion, peeled, halved, very thinly sliced

¼ cup red wine vinegar

leaves from 2 sprigs fresh tarragon, finely chopped, to make 1 teaspoon

4 cups baby arugula, divided

leaves from 2 sprigs fresh parsley, finely chopped, to make 1 tablespoon

1. Fill a large pot halfway with water. Add 1 teaspoon salt. Add the beets. Bring to a boil, cover, turn down to medium heat and cook for 45 minutes, until the tip of a knife can easily pierce a beet.

2. Place the lentils into a medium pot with 2 cups water. Add the thyme, garlic, celery, and carrot. Bring to a simmer and cook for 20 minutes. Check the water level toward the end of the 20 minutes and add more water ¼ cup at a time, if lentils are not soft to the bite (they should still hold their shape). When the lentils are done, turn off the heat. Discard the thyme, garlic, celery, and carrot. Drain off any excess water. Add the olive oil, ½ teaspoon salt, and ¼ teaspoon black pepper to the lentils. Stir and set aside.

3. Place the onion slices into a large bowl.

4. Drain the beets. Let them cool until you can handle them. Grasping the beet with paper towels, to color-protect your hands, peel off and discard the skin from each beet. Trim off the ends and any remaining skin from each beet. Cut each beet in half and then into ½-inch cubes. Add to the onion.

5. Drizzle with the vinegar, ¾ teaspoon salt, and remaining ¼ teaspoon black pepper. Sprinkle on the tarragon. Mix well. Allow to stand so the flavors can meld. You can even do this a night before serving.

6. Place the arugula into a mixing bowl. Drizzle with olive oil and remaining ¼ teaspoon salt. Arrange a 3-cup layer of baby arugula in the bottom of a large serving bowl or platter. Top with the beets, creating a well in the center. Fill with the lentils. Garnish with chopped parsley. Top with the remaining arugula in a mound.

Dressing both brings out the flavors of the ingredients in the bowl and adds new flavors. There are plenty of kosher dressings on the market, but they are loaded with stale herbs, inferior ingredients, gums, and starches. For a fraction of the cost, you can whip up your own dressings. They will be bright and fresh, and you can control the quality of the ingredients. You need nothing more than a small jar to shake them up or a bowl and whisk. You can even recycle glass jars from jelly or condiments, they are a perfect size.

As far as meal planning goes, always think, what can I do today so that I don't have to do something tomorrow? Tonight's vinaigrette may be tomorrow night's fish, chicken or grilled vegetable marinade. It can be brushed onto green beans or asparagus before roasting for a great side dish. Basic vinaigrettes and dressings can keep for days in the refrigerator, so make a big batch if you like. Just remember to shake or whisk before serving.

Garlic Vinaigrette
PARVE

- ¼ cup white-wine vinegar
- 1 tablespoon Dijon mustard
- 2 cloves fresh garlic, minced
- ¼ teaspoon sugar
- ½ teaspoon coarse sea salt
- ½ teaspoon freshly ground black pepper
- ¾ cup extra-virgin olive oil

In a blender, food processor, or in a quart-sized container with an immersion blender, pulse the vinegar, Dijon, garlic, sugar, salt, pepper, and olive oil. Store in an airtight container.

Kate's Blue Cheese Dressing
DAIRY

- 4 ounces blue cheese
- 3 tablespoons whipped cream cheese
- 2 tablespoons milk; plus more if needed for thinning
- 1 tablespoon white vinegar
- 1 tablespoon water
- ¼ small onion, peeled, roughly chopped
- 1 clove fresh garlic
- ¼ teaspoon fine sea salt
- ¼ teaspoon freshly ground black pepper
- 2 tablespoons extra-virgin olive oil

In a blender, food processor or in a quart-sized container with an immersion blender, pulse the blue cheese, cream cheese, milk, vinegar, water, onion, garlic, salt, pepper, and olive oil. Store in an airtight container. Thin with milk as needed if it becomes too thick.

Alix's Honey Shallot Dressing
PARVE

- 1 tablespoon olive oil
- ½ cup (about 3 shallots) shallots, chopped
- ¼ cup apple cider vinegar
- ¾ cup canola oil
- ¼ cup honey
- 1 tablespoon Dijon mustard
- ¼ teaspoon fine sea salt
- ¼ teaspoon ground white pepper

Heat the oil in a pan over medium heat. Add the shallots. Cook for 5-6 minutes until golden and caramelized, stirring occasionally. Add the vinegar to deglaze the pan. Pour into a blender or food processor. Add the canola oil, honey, Dijon, salt, and pepper. Pulse until emulsified. Store in an airtight container.

Simple Vinaigrette
PARVE

- 1 tablespoon minced shallot
- 1 teaspoon Dijon mustard
- 3-4 tablespoons best-quality balsamic or red wine vinegar
- ¾ cup best-quality extra virgin olive oil
  coarse sea salt
  freshly ground black pepper

Place the shallot, Dijon, vinegar, and olive oil into a small jar. Season with salt and pepper. Seal the jar and shake. This can also be whisked in a bowl. Store in an airtight container.

Sesame Vinaigrette
PARVE

- 3 tablespoons roasted or toasted sesame oil
- 3 tablespoons canola or peanut oil
- 3 tablespoons soy sauce
- ¼ cup rice vinegar
- 2 tablespoons brown sugar
- 1 clove fresh garlic, minced
- 1 teaspoon red pepper flakes
- ¼ teaspoon ground dried ginger
- 2 scallions, roots trimmed, finely chopped

Place the sesame oil, canola oil, soy sauce, vinegar, brown sugar, garlic, red pepper flakes, ginger, and scallions into a small jar. Seal the jar and shake. This can also be done in a bowl with a whisk. Store in an airtight container.

Lemon-Truffle Oil Dressing
PARVE

- zest of 1 lemon
- 3½ tablespoons fresh lemon juice (from 1-2 lemons)
- ½ cup good-quality extra virgin olive oil
- 1 tablespoon white truffle oil
- 3 chives, finely chopped
- ½ teaspoon sugar
  coarse sea salt
  freshly ground black pepper

Place the lemon zest, lemon juice, olive oil, truffle oil, chives, and sugar into a small jar. Season with salt and pepper. Seal the jar and shake. This can also be done in a bowl with a whisk. Store in an airtight container.

EDAMAME SLAW

From the picnic table to the dining room table, this one fits in anywhere.

¼ cup rice vinegar or apple cider vinegar

¼ cup water

¼ cup soy sauce

3 tablespoons sugar

1 (0.7-ounce) packet dry Italian Seasoning mix, such as Good Seasons

6 tablespoons canola oil

8 ounces shelled edamame

1 small head Napa cabbage, thinly sliced into shreds

2 stalks bok choy, ends trimmed, thinly sliced

3 scallions, roots trimmed, thinly sliced on diagonal

¼ cup pine nuts

¼ cup raw shelled sunflower seeds

1. In a large bowl, place the vinegar, water, soy sauce, sugar, seasoning mix, and oil. Whisk thoroughly until combined. Add the edamame, cabbage, bok choy, scallions, pine nuts, and sunflower seeds. Toss to coat well. Gloved hands work well here.

2. Cover the bowl with plastic wrap or transfer to a large ziplock bag. Allow to stand for 2-3 hours before serving.

POULTRY

GAME PLAN

turkey   duck   chicken   hen

Chicken and turkey are two of the most popular meats in the world. Relatively inexpensive, healthful, and easy to work with, they can be prepared in endless ways. The four most popular members of the poultry family are turkey, duck, chicken, and hen. A broiler is a small chicken; a roaster is one that is over 2½ pounds.

HOW TO BUTTERFLY A CHICKEN BREAST

Butterfly means to split a chicken breast half down the center without cutting through. The breast can then be flattened to resemble a butterfly shape. This allows for greater surface area and more even cooking.

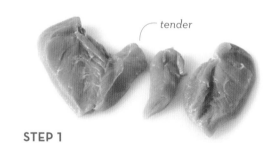

tender

STEP 1

STEP 1 Remove the tender. It is a perfectly good piece of white meat but makes for uneven cooking, so cook it separately. Lay the breast on your cutting board. **STEP 2** Rest one hand on top of the chicken and, using a sharp knife, slice the chicken in half, holding your knife parallel to your work surface — but don't cut all the way through. **STEP 3** Open like a book or butterfly.

STEP 2   **STEP 3**

A turkey breast, or turkey London broil, can also be butterflied so it can grill quicker or be used to stuff and roll for a fancier meal like a roulade. It works the same way as the chicken. Place the turkey breast on your cutting board smooth-side-down. Holding your blade parallel to your board, cut into the thickest part, through the thickness of the meat, stopping

½-inch from the edge. Press it open like a book. Cover with a sheet of parchment or plastic wrap. Pound slightly with a meat mallet until the turkey is a thin, even thickness throughout.

HOW TO SPATCHCOCK A CHICKEN

Spatchcocking a whole chicken, Cornish hen, or turkey is the same thing as butterflying it. By cutting out the backbone and pressing it flat, the fowl cooks evenly and quickly, and results in fabulous crispy skin. It is a great technique for grilling a whole chicken on the barbecue or roasting in the oven. **STEP 1** Place the poultry on your cutting board breast-side-down. Using sharp scissors or poultry shears, starting at the bottom, cut just to the side of the backbone all along the length of the bird right through the ribs. Do the same on the other side of the backbone. **STEP 2** Remove the backbone (save it for when you are making chicken soup). **STEP 3** Turn the bird over and press to flatten and open.

HOW TO POUND A CUTLET TO AN EVEN THICKNESS

» *Place the cutlet between 2 sheets of plastic wrap and lightly pound with a mallet or the side of your chef's knife to an even thickness.*

STEP 1

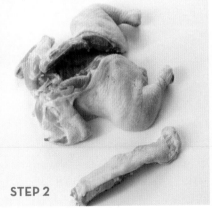

STEP 2

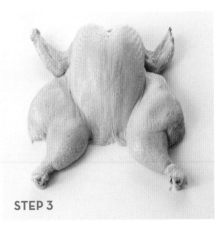

STEP 3

WORKING WITH DUCK BREAST

Duck skin has a thick creamy layer of fat that you must render, or melt out. This is easy to do. Place the duck skin-side-up on your cutting board. With a sharp knife, gently score the skin in a crisscross pattern. This will create channels through the fat to help it flow away as it melts off into your hot skillet. Don't pierce the tender flesh beneath. In restaurants, the rendered duck fat is a delicacy that the chefs fight over. It makes the best homefries, latkes, or other potato dishes. You can keep yours stored in the refrigerator.

TEST FOR DONENESS — TEMPERATURE

Chicken cutlets are done at 170°F; they will be opaque and firm. Whole chicken and parts are cooked to doneness at 180°F. For whole birds, stick a meat thermometer into the thickest part of the thigh, underneath the drumstick joint. Make sure it is not touching bone. The juices will run clear when pierced, the legs will move easily in their sockets and the meat will release easily from the bone. You can also check for doneness by cutting into the chicken to make sure it is no longer pink. Bone marrow pigment, especially in frozen chicken, sometimes leaches out as the chicken cooks. This creates red areas near the bone; this is not the same thing as flesh being pink. This is safe to eat as long as you have cooked the bird to the required temperature. Large whole birds and turkey will continue to cook after being removed from the oven. To avoid dryness, you should remove them a few degrees below the ideal temperature. Always let turkey and chicken stand for 10 minutes to give the juices time to settle and redistribute. If you cut into them too early, the juices will spill out onto your cutting board.

TYING

Tying a chicken or turkey gives it a smooth compact shape. It also keeps the legs from flopping open and tearing the skin. You can tie with kitchen twine but I love the silicone bands pictured here. They are heat-safe and available on the internet.

kitchen twine

silicone band

DEFROSTING/ FREEZING

Thaw frozen poultry slowly and safely in the refrigerator, not on the counter, and wear disposable gloves when handling it to avoid the spread of bacteria. Always cook poultry to doneness.

COOKING TECHNIQUES

GRILLING

Grilling cooks food quickly with dry, direct heat. Whether you are using a grill pan or cooking directly on a grill, make sure to coat the surface with oil to prevent food from sticking. Try not to move the food around once it hits the pan so it can sear properly. Create nice grill marks by placing food skin-side-down on the hot grill pan or grates. If you imagine you're looking at a clock, you would put the chicken breast on the grates or in the grill pan facing toward ten o'clock, and then once you get the marks, about 3-4 minutes, turn it toward two o'clock. Make sure to pick it up with tongs and place the chicken down correctly the first time, so you get good, even crosshatch marks.

SAUTÉING OR PAN-FRYING

To sauté is to cook in a large, hot, shallow pan, using a small amount of fat, like canola oil. When you sauté chicken parts, you get great flavor by browning and caramelizing the skin. This also leaves behind bits to flavor a sauce. To ensure this, don't overcrowd the pan or you will steam the chicken.

DEEP FRYING

Deep frying calls for large amounts of oil brought to a specific temperature (355°F-375°F) that creates crisp crust and locks in moisture. A thermometer is a must. If you don't have one, heat the oil till almost smoking. Drop in a cube of bread. It should brown in 30 seconds.

Make sure your food is at room temperature, as cold food lowers the temperature of the oil. Canola oil and peanut oil are ideal for frying, as they have a neutral taste and a high smoking point. You need oil that can come up to a high temperature without smoking, burning, or breaking down. Also, whichever way you are doing it, don't fry too much at a time. Leave some space so all surfaces will cook evenly.

» *Never discard a large amount of oil down your drain or directly into the garbage. Let it cool; then funnel it into a container and throw it out with the trash.*

» *Oil can be safely reused as long as it is light colored and doesn't smell. Strain it through a strainer or coffee filter to remove any particles and place it into a dry, clean container. Cover and store in a cool dark place. Use within one month.*

» *I use either a deep fryer or a large cast iron pot. The deep fryer has a built-in thermometer and levels marked off to show how high the oil should come. In a pot, be sure there is at least 3 inches above the level of the oil to allow for the oil to rise as food is added.*

large cast iron pot

deep fryer

ROASTING AND BAKING

The standard difference between roasting and baking is that baking happens at 350°F or lower and roasting at 400°F or more. I use the term roasting when I describe cooking something uncovered in the oven. Whole chickens roast especially well, and putting them on a v-shaped rack, to elevate them out of their juices, will result in dry, crisp skin all around. The heat of an oven can dry out foods that need longer cooking times, such as a turkey, so make sure to baste to return moisture and flavor to the dish.

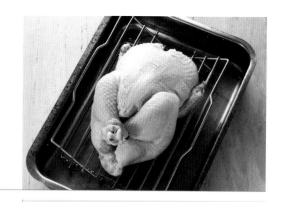

STANDARD BREADING PROCEDURE

This procedure is the same for breading vegetables, fish, chicken cutlets, chicken parts, veal chops, or anything else. If you follow the steps, you will have a nice even coating that will not fall off during cooking.

Select 3 shallow containers, small aluminum tins, pie plates, or plastic containers. Make sure they are not too large or your breading will be too spread out. Pictured is my set of 3 interlocking trays that I love because they are perfectly sized.

THE FIRST compartment is for the flour, which is usually seasoned with salt and pepper, although any spices can be added at this point. The seasoned flour sticks to the food being breaded.

THE SECOND is for the "wet" ingredient, beaten eggs, salsa, soymilk, etc. This prepares the item for the breading, almost like a glue.

THE THIRD is for the breading, which can be anything including panko, ground nuts, cornmeal, potato flakes, and cornflake crumbs.

Both hands must be used in this procedure. Use one hand to handle the wet and one to handle the dry ingredients. This will keep the breading from clumping on your fingers and from getting the dry ingredients wet.

> Once food is breaded, allow it to set for 10 minutes before frying or pan-searing.

> Always discard any leftover egg or coatings that have touched raw proteins.

BAKED "FRIED" CHICKEN CUTLETS

If you are watching your fat intake, this is a good technique to try. Place a cookie cooling rack in a jellyroll pan. After breading your chicken, place it on the rack. This will elevate it out of its juices and allow air to circulate above and below the breaded cutlet as it cooks. Spray with nonstick cooking spray for a little crispness. Bake in a preheated oven, usually 375°F for 20 minutes.

HOW TO CARVE A TURKEY OR CHICKEN

STEP 1 After allowing the bird to rest to redistribute the juices, place it on a cutting board that is set in a jellyroll pan to catch the juices. Cut away the trussing string. **STEP 2** Pull the thigh away from the bird and when you can see the joint, wiggle the thigh and cut through the joint. **STEP 3** Separate the drumstick from the thigh in the same way. **STEP 4** Remove the wings. **STEP 5** Remove second thigh and drumstick. **STEP 6** Carve a long deep cut, as close to the breast bone as possible. **STEP 7** Removing the breast in 1 piece. **STEP 8** Repeat on other side. **STEP 9** Slice the breast meat.

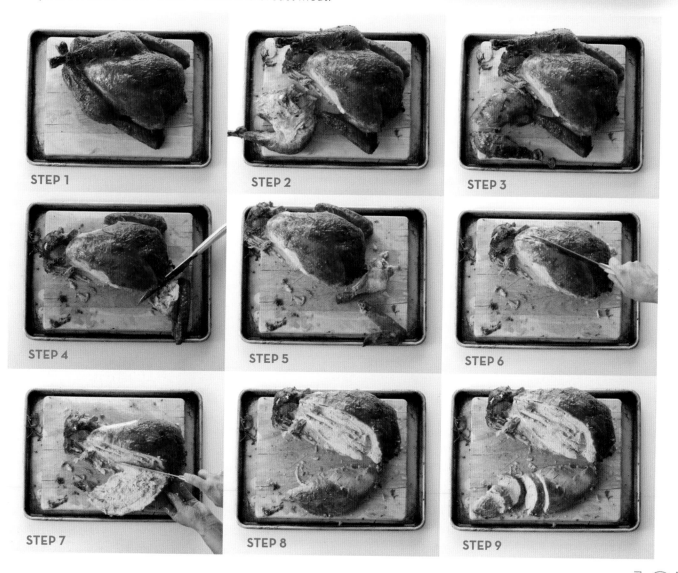

STEP 1

STEP 2

STEP 3

STEP 4

STEP 5

STEP 6

STEP 7

STEP 8

STEP 9

- 6 boneless, skinless chicken breast halves, with tenders
- 6 ounces fresh raspberries
- 3 tablespoons seedless red raspberry preserves
- 1/4 cup grainy Country Dijon mustard
- 1 tablespoon whole mustard seeds
- 2 tablespoons honey
- 1/2 teaspoon fine sea salt
- 1 1/2 cups cornflake crumbs
- 1 1/2 cups finely chopped pecans

  honey for drizzling

  fresh raspberries, for garnish

RASPBERRY MUSTARD-CRUSTED CHICKEN

Here's one simple chicken dish that has WOW factor. The raspberries are stunning and work so nicely with the mustard.

Cook what's in season; corn and tomatoes in summer, pumpkins in fall, and a raspberry dish like this one in early summer. The ingredients will really shine.

1. Cut each chicken breast through the thickness to create 12 thin cutlets. Set aside.

2. Place the raspberries, raspberry preserves, mustard, mustard seeds, honey, and salt into a quart container. Using an immersion blender, blend until smooth. This can also be done in a food processor fitted with a metal "S" blade. Pour the raspberry marinade into a heavy-duty ziplock bag. Add the chicken to the bag and massage in the marinade. Allow to marinate in the refrigerator for at least 1 hour.

3. Preheat oven to 400°F. Cover a cookie sheet with parchment paper. Place a cookie cooling rack on the cookie sheet. Set aside.

4. In a shallow dish, combine the cornflake crumbs and the pecans. Remove the chicken from the marinade one piece at a time, breading the chicken on each side with the cornflake mixture. Use your palm to press the coating into the chicken. Place onto prepared rack. Drizzle some raspberry marinade over the chicken. Lightly drizzle additional honey over the chicken.

5. Bake for 20 minutes or until cooked through and no longer pink inside. Slice and transfer to plate or platter. Garnish with fresh raspberries.

CHICKEN SCARPIELLO WITH RED SAUCE

- 4 teaspoons canola oil, divided
- 6 boneless, skinless chicken breast halves, tenders separated, pounded to an even thickness
- 6 large button mushrooms, sliced
- 2 spicy raw beef sausages, casings removed, roughly chopped
- 1 red bell pepper, seeded, cut into $\frac{1}{2}$-inch dice
- 1 yellow bell pepper, seeded, cut into $\frac{1}{2}$-inch dice
- 1 red onion, peeled, cut into $\frac{1}{2}$-inch dice
- 3 hot cherry peppers, from a jar, thinly sliced, stems discarded
- 1 teaspoon dried basil
- 1 teaspoon garlic powder
- $\frac{1}{2}$ cup white wine
- 1 (28-ounce) can tomato sauce
- 1 pound box orzo, cooked according to package directions until al dente

  fresh basil, for garnish

Ask true Italians how to make chicken scarpiello and you will get a different answer from each one. My true Italian friend Damian Sansonetti includes sausages, hot cherry peppers, and a tomato sauce. The orzo is the perfect complement to absorb all the flavors.

Hot cherry peppers are sold with the pickles and olives. You can do this dish with chicken parts as well, but increase the baking time to 1 hour, 15 minutes.

1. Preheat oven to 350°F.

2. Heat 2 teaspoons canola oil in a large (12-14-inch) skillet over medium-high heat. If you only have smaller skillets, divide into two pans or make in batches. Sear the chicken and tenders, about 2-3 minutes per side, getting some color on each side. Remove the chicken breasts to a 9 x 13-inch baking pan. You may need to overlap them.

3. Add remaining 2 teaspoons oil to skillet. Heat. Add mushrooms and cook until they have released their liquid and all the liquid has cooked out. Add the sausage to the pan; sauté for 2 minutes, until it starts to brown, using a wooden spoon to break up chunks. Add the red pepper, yellow pepper, onion, and cherry peppers. Sauté for 3-4 minutes, until the vegetables start to wilt and become shiny. Season with basil and garlic. Add the wine. Stir and simmer on medium for 3 minutes. Stir in the tomato sauce. Pour over chicken.

4. Bake, uncovered, for 25 minutes.

5. Serve over orzo. Garnish with fresh basil.

- 1 (2½-3-pound) turkey London broil, butterflied
- 1½ cups unflavored croutons
- 1 (5.2-ounce) bag roasted and peeled chestnuts, roughly chopped
- ½ teaspoon garlic powder
- ¼ teaspoon dried ground sage
- ⅛ teaspoon ground nutmeg
- ½ red onion, peeled, minced
- ½ cup golden raisins
- 3-4 cups chicken stock or broth, divided
- 3½ tablespoons olive oil, divided
- ½ teaspoon paprika
- ½ teaspoon fine sea salt
- ¼ teaspoon turmeric
- ¼ teaspoon freshly ground black pepper
- 7-8 sprigs fresh thyme, divided
- 3 leaves fresh sage
- 1 cup carrot coins
- 2 ribs fresh celery, cut into ½-inch dice
- ¼ teaspoon cracked black pepper

CHESTNUT-STUFFED TURKEY LONDON BROIL

Boneless white meat turkey is one of the healthiest lowfat proteins around. Fill it with a gorgeous pinwheel of roasted chestnut stuffing and you have a centerpiece that your guests will go crazy for.

1. Preheat oven to 375°F.

2. Place the turkey on a large cutting board, smooth-side-down. Cover with parchment paper. Using a meat pounder or bottom of a heavy skillet, pound the turkey into a large rectangle of even thickness, ¾-1 inch thick. Remove parchment.

3. Place the croutons and chestnuts into a large bowl. Sprinkle on the garlic powder, sage, and nutmeg. Add the red onion and raisins. Moisten with ½ cup chicken stock. Toss the mixture to combine. It should stick together when compressed; if not, add stock, 1 tablespoon at a time, so that the croutons absorb the liquid.

4. Spread the stuffing in an even layer over the turkey, leaving a ½-inch border. Press it down, using both palms. Starting with a shorter side, roll tightly, tucking the stuffing in as you roll. Secure with kitchen twine or silicone bands every 3 inches (about 3-4 ties). Tucking the ends in, place one tie around the length of the roll.

5. Rub 2 tablespoons olive oil all over the roll. Season with paprika, salt, turmeric, and pepper, rubbing it over the turkey.

6. Pour 2 cups of chicken stock into an oven-to-table casserole or baking pan that holds the turkey snugly. Add the leaves from 4 sprigs thyme, sage, carrots, and celery. Place the tied turkey on the carrots and celery. Cover the pan with tented foil so foil doesn't touch the roast. Roast for 1 hour, brushing with pan juices halfway through. Uncover, baste, and roast for another 30 minutes, basting again during the last 5 minutes. Roast until a thermometer inserted into the center reaches 160°F and the turkey is no longer pink. Remove from oven.

7. In a small bowl, mix remaining 1½ tablespoons olive oil with the leaves from remaining 3-4 sprigs fresh thyme and ¼ teaspoon cracked black pepper. Brush all over the roast. Allow the roast to rest for 10 minutes before slicing. Serve with pan juices and vegetables.

HOT AND CRISPY CHICKEN WITH MANGO SLAW

MANGO SLAW

- 1 bag (16-ounces) coleslaw mix (cabbage and carrots)
- ½ small red onion, thinly sliced
- 1 ripe mango, peeled, pitted, cut into small dice
- ½ cup sliced almonds
- 1 cup mayonnaise
- 5 tablespoon sweet chili garlic sauce; I like Oxygen brand *see note on p. 260*
- 3 cloves fresh garlic
- ½ jalapeño pepper, with seeds *see p. 260*
- ½ teaspoon fine sea salt
- ¼ teaspoon freshly ground black pepper

HOT AND CRISPY CHICKEN

- all-purpose flour
- 3 large eggs, lightly beaten
- 2 cups cornflakes
- ½ cup sliced blanched almonds
- ⅓ cup sesame seeds
- 2 tablespoons sugar
- 1½ tablespoons red pepper flakes
- 2 teaspoons coarse sea salt or kosher salt
- 6 boneless, skinless chicken breast halves
- canola oil

Although we shot this bright and early, my team at the photographer's studio could not help but devour these fantastic chicken fingers. The chicken is spicy hot, yet sweet at the same time. The slaw puts it over the top.

1. Place the coleslaw mix, onion, mango, and almonds into a large bowl. In a quart container using an immersion blender or in a food processor, combine the mayonnaise, chili garlic sauce, garlic cloves, jalapeño, salt, and pepper. Pour over the slaw and mix well. Allow to stand while you prepare the chicken.

2. Place the flour into the first part of a 3-part breading station. Place the beaten eggs into the second part.

3. Place the cornflakes, almonds, sesame seeds, sugar, red pepper flakes, and salt into the bowl of a food processor fitted with the metal "S" blade. Pulse a few times, leaving coarse crumbs. Place into the third part of the breading station.

4. Separate the tenders from the chicken breasts. Pound the cutlets to make them a little flatter. Pass each breast and tender through the 3-part breading station, starting with the flour, shaking off excess; then into the eggs, wetting the chicken evenly; then into the crispy coating. Press down to get a nice even coating.

5. Heat canola oil in a large heavy skillet over medium heat to come up ¼-inch on the skillet.

6. Test the oil to see if it is hot enough by dropping a bit of the coating into the oil. If oil bubbles around it and it turns golden, the oil is ready. Place the chicken into the hot oil and cook for 3-4 minutes per side until golden brown. You may need to do this in batches. Use tongs to carefully flip each piece. Remove to platter. Top each piece of chicken with some of the slaw.

BLUEBERRY AND FIG-GLAZED DUCK BREASTS

- 3 whole boneless duck breasts, with skin, or 6 duck breast cutlets
- 1 teaspoon dried rosemary, crumbled
- 1 teaspoon freshly ground black pepper
- ½ teaspoon fine sea salt
- ½ cup Cabernet Sauvignon
- 1 (12-ounce) jar good-quality blueberry preserves; I like Hero brand
- 5 fresh figs, stems removed, quartered; can use dried black Mission figs
- 1 tablespoon balsamic vinegar

  fresh blueberries, for garnish

Ah, romance on a plate. Duck is an elegant meal usually reserved for events like weddings or special parties. However, don't be fooled. This impressive dish could not be easier to prepare. Once you've mastered the rendering of the duck fat from the breast, it handles as easily as a chicken cutlet. It is easier to score the duck skin for rendering if it is well chilled.

The sweetness of the blueberries and figs complements the smoky flavor of the duck breast and adds fruity notes to the wine sauce.

1. Score the duck breast skin in a criss-cross fashion, cutting through the skin but not into the duck meat.

2. In a small bowl, mix the rosemary, pepper, and salt. Sprinkle evenly over each duck breast and rub into the scored fat.

3. Heat a large skillet over medium heat. Place the duck breasts into the hot skillet, fat-side-down. Slowly cook the breasts for 10 minutes, until the fat renders out, and the skin begins to brown. Carefully pour the fat out of the pan — it will be hot — and discard or save for another use. Turn the duck breasts over and cook on the other side for 5 minutes; duck should be slightly pink in the center.

4. Remove the duck from the pan. Pour out any rendered fat but leave the browned bits in the pan. Allow the duck to rest for 5 minutes.

5. Meanwhile, add the wine, blueberry preserves, figs, and balsamic to the browned bits in the pan. Whisk, cooking for 3-4 minutes, until the sauce is bubbly and the figs are slightly cooked.

6. On a cutting board, slice the duck on the diagonal into ½-inch strips. Transfer to serving plate. Spoon sauce over the duck. Garnish with fresh blueberries.

SICILIAN CHICKEN

The capers and artichokes have a pungent smell due to the brine they are canned and jarred in. Remember to rinse them well before chopping them and using in this or any other recipe. If you can't find canned artichoke bottoms, you can use a jar of marinated hearts; just rinse off the oil and spices.

- ³/₄ cup all-purpose flour, plus 1½ tablespoons
- 1 teaspoon fine sea salt, divided
- ³/₄ teaspoon freshly ground black pepper, divided
- 6 boneless, skinless, chicken breast halves, tender removed, pounded thin

  olive oil
- 1 medium onion, halved, peeled, very thinly sliced
- 10 ounces baby bella or cremini mushrooms, sliced
- 1 cup white wine
- ³/₄ cup chicken stock
- 1 (14-ounce) can artichoke bottoms, rinsed well and finely chopped
- 3 tablespoons capers, drained, rinsed, and finely chopped
- 10 grape tomatoes, chopped
- 1 teaspoon dried oregano

  chopped fresh parsley for garnish

1. Place ³/₄ cup flour into a shallow plate or pan. Season with ½ teaspoon salt and ½ teaspoon pepper. Dredge the chicken in flour. Shake off the excess flour.

2. Heat 2 tablespoons olive oil in a large pan. Sauté the cutlets, in batches if necessary, for 4-5 minutes per side, until golden brown and the chicken is cooked through. Add more oil, 1 tablespoon at a time, between batches as needed. Remove the chicken to a platter. Add the onion to the pan and scrape up the browned bits from the bottom. Cook the onion for 3-4 minutes until wilted. Add the mushrooms. Sauté for 3-4 minutes until shiny. Sprinkle with remaining 1½ tablespoons flour. Mix well.

3. Add the white wine and sauté for 3 minutes until the alcohol has evaporated. Add the stock. Sprinkle in the artichokes, capers, tomatoes, and oregano. Add ½ teaspoon salt and ¼ teaspoon freshly ground black pepper to season. Bring to a simmer and heat until the artichokes are warmed through. Pour the sauce over the chicken and garnish with fresh parsley.

CORNISH HEN IN PORT & CHOCOLATE SAUCE

CORNISH HENS

- 6 (1-pound) Cornish hens
- leaves from 2 sprigs fresh rosemary
- leaves from 2 sprigs fresh sage
- leaves from 3 sprigs fresh thyme
- 1/2 cup olive oil
- fine sea salt

PORT & CHOCOLATE SAUCE

- 2 tablespoons extra-virgin olive oil
- 1 small onion, cut into 1/4-inch dice
- leaves from 2 sprigs fresh thyme
- 1 (750 ml) bottle Port wine
- 2 1/2 ounces good-quality, semisweet chocolate, chopped

My family visited Spain and Portugal for a Jewish heritage tour in honor of my daughter Jodi's bas mitzvah. For our Shabbos in Portugal we were at a loss as to where we would be able to have a kosher and meaningful Shabbos. Luckily, my husband stumbled on an ad for an Emunah Woman's tour of Portugal running at the same time. They were lovely and gracious and allowed us to join them for a wonderful davening, illuminating walking tour, and unbelievable Shabbos meals. Knowing how hard it is to find kosher food in Portugal, we were fully expecting to be served airplane food. We were blown away by Naomi Caterers and their local chef Isaac Massias, who served a 4-course, 5-star meal that rivaled any we had ever eaten. The food was authentically Portuguese, which was fascinating to us and added a real level of excitement. Eric Goldberg, manager of Naomi Tours, graciously shared the recipe for this, my favorite dish of the night.

1. Preheat oven to 400°F.

2. Finely chop all the fresh herbs. Place into a small bowl. Mix with olive oil.

3. Place the 6 hens on a foil-lined jellyroll pan. Tie together the legs of each hen with a silicone band or kitchen twine so they roast in a nice shape. Pour on the oil mixture and rub all over the hens, both inside and out.

4. Sprinkle on sea salt and roast, uncovered, for about 40-45 minutes; check for golden, crisp-looking skin. The leg and wing should move very easily and the flesh should no longer be pink. Remove from oven; brush with pan juices.

5. Meanwhile prepare the Port sauce: Heat the 2 tablespoons olive oil in a medium pot over medium heat. Add the onion and sauté

until translucent and starting to turn slightly golden, about 6-8 minutes. Add the thyme and the bottle of Port. Bring to a boil until the Port has reduced to half of its volume (to about $1^2/_3$ cups). Reduce heat, add the chocolate, mix and melt, stirring to hasten the melting. Simmer together for about 2 minutes. When the sauce has a nice silky thickish texture, pass it through a sieve or fine mesh strainer. You will end up with a silky shiny sauce. Allow the sauce to rest for 10 minutes. It will get very shiny and thicker.

6. Place the hens on a large platter. Brush with pan juices.
   Drizzle with the Port sauce.

BALSAMIC ONION CHICKEN

- 1 tablespoon canola oil
- 5 cloves fresh garlic, chopped
- 4 medium red onions, peeled, thinly sliced into rings
- ¼ cup dark brown sugar
- 1 cup Cabernet Sauvignon or other good red wine
- 1 cup balsamic vinegar
  fine sea salt
  freshly ground black pepper
- 1 chicken cut into eighths or chicken parts, skin-on, bone-in
  fresh curly parsley, chopped, for garnish

This incredibly easy dish is crowned by the sweet, sticky onions that nestle the chicken as it bakes, sharing their juicy deliciousness.

1. Preheat oven to 400°F.

2. Heat the oil in a large pot. Add the garlic and onions. Sauté until shiny, about 4-5 minutes. Stir in the brown sugar, wine, and balsamic. Mix well. Cook, uncovered, for 20 minutes. Season with salt and pepper. Remove from heat.

3. Meanwhile, arrange the chicken parts in a baking dish that holds them in a single layer. Season the chicken with salt and pepper. When the onions are soft, pour them over the chicken. Bake, uncovered, for 45 minutes or until chicken is no longer pink at the bone. Transfer to serving platter and smother with the onions. Garnish with chopped parsley.

1 whole (3-4 pound) chicken, spatchcocked

3 cloves fresh garlic

1 teaspoon onion powder

1 teaspoon paprika

½ teaspoon coarse sea salt or kosher salt

½ teaspoon garlic powder

½ teaspoon crushed dried rosemary

½ teaspoon dried thyme

½ teaspoon freshly ground black pepper

1 lemon

2 teaspoons olive oil

LEMON-GARLIC SPATCHCOCKED CHICKEN

See the photos on p. 121 that show you how to "spatchcock," or butterfly, a whole chicken. The advantage of this technique is that by removing the backbone, and pressing the bird flat, the chicken cooks quickly and evenly, and all the skin cooks to a crisp golden brown. This works perfectly on a rack in the oven, in a skillet on the stove, or when grilling a whole chicken on the barbecue.

1. Preheat oven to 375°F. Place a rack into a jellyroll pan. Place the chicken on the prepared pan. Set aside.

3. Mince the garlic on your cutting board. Sprinkle with onion powder, paprika, salt, garlic powder, rosemary, thyme, pepper, and the zest from the lemon. Using the side of your knife, drag and press the garlic and spices to make a dry paste. Place into a bowl and combine with the olive oil and juice from the lemon.

4. Rub the spice mix all over the chicken, including under the skin.

5. Roast, skin-side-up, uncovered, for 55-60 minutes, until no longer pink and a thermometer inserted in the thigh reads 160°F.

6. Transfer to platter. Pour any pan juices over the chicken. Use a pastry brush to spread the pan juices over the chicken.

CURRIED SUNFLOWER CHICKEN

If you like schnitzel but are getting a little bored by its simplicity, shake things up with this great rendition of a breaded chicken cutlet. It is bursting with flavors and textures and can be served with any kind of dipping sauce, from tartar sauce to barbecue sauce to spicy mayonnaise.

4   plump boneless, skinless chicken breast halves, with tenders

2   cups panko breadcrumbs

2   teaspoons curry powder

2   teaspoons chicken-flavored consommé powder

1   teaspoon turmeric

1   teaspoon onion powder

1   teaspoon garlic powder

1   teaspoon celery salt

1   teaspoon dry mustard powder

1   cup raw, shelled, sunflower seeds, not roasted or salted

1   large egg

2   egg yolks

½   cup plain unsweetened soy milk, not vanilla flavored

1   cup all-purpose flour

¼   teaspoon fine sea salt

¼   teaspoon freshly ground black pepper

    canola oil

1. Preheat oven to 400°F. Line 2 jellyroll pans with parchment paper. Set aside.

2. Remove the chicken tenders and reserve. Cut through the thickness of each cutlet to make each into 2 thin cutlets.

3. Place the panko into a shallow pan or one part of a 2-part breading station. Add the curry powder, consommé powder, turmeric, onion powder, garlic powder, celery salt, and mustard powder. Mix well.

4. Place the sunflower seeds into the bowl of a food processor fitted with a metal "S" blade. Process for a count of 10 until coarsely chopped; result will be uneven. Add the panko mixture and pulse 3-4 times. Pour back into shallow pan.

5. In the bowl of the food processor or in a quart container with an immersion blender, pulse the egg, yolks, and soy milk. Add the flour and pulse until it is the consistency of a thick pancake batter. Season with salt and pepper. Pour into a second shallow pan or second part of breading station.

6. Dunk the chicken cutlets and tenders, one at a time, into the batter, shaking off excess, and then into the breading. Place on one prepared pan until all the chicken is breaded.

7. Heat 3 tablespoons oil in a large skillet over medium heat. Sear chicken in a single layer in batches, leaving room between cutlets, until golden, about 2 minutes per side. Add 1-2 tablespoons oil before each batch. Transfer to the clean pan and bake in the oven until cooked through, 5-7 minutes, depending on thickness. Serve 2 cutlets per plate.

16 bone-in, skin-on chicken parts, legs, thighs, breasts

4 cups plain, unsweetened soy milk, divided

1 lemon

canola oil

3¼ cups all-purpose flour, divided

4 teaspoons baking powder

4 teaspoons garlic powder

4 teaspoons onion powder

4 teaspoons dried oregano

4 teaspoons seasoning salt; I like Mrs. Dash original flavor, no MSG

2 teaspoons freshly ground black pepper

2 teaspoons fine sea salt

2 tablespoons hot sauce; I like Frank's Red Hot brand

SOUTHERN FRIED CHICKEN

You don't need Southern hospitality to get people to the table if this chicken is on it. My family devours this authentic treat hot out of the pot or, just as happily, cold the next day. The results are all about following the technique, so make sure you set up your breading station and rack. Allowing the breading to set for 10 minutes really keeps the crust sticking to the chicken, so don't skip this step.

1. Place the chicken into a pan that can hold it in a single layer or into a large heavy-duty ziplock bag. Combine 2 cups of soymilk and juice from the lemon. Stir. Pour over the chicken. Allow to marinate in the refrigerator for at least 2 hours.

2. Set a cookie cooling rack into a jellyroll pan. Set aside.

3. Fill a large, very heavy pot, cast iron if possible, halfway with canola oil. Heat until a thermometer reads 350°F. You can also use a deep fryer.

4. In a medium bowl, whisk 3 cups flour, baking powder, garlic powder, onion powder, oregano, seasoning salt, pepper, and salt. Transfer to a shallow pan or first part of a breading station.

5. In a second shallow pan or in the second part of a breading station, whisk the remaining 2 cups soy milk, remaining ¼ cup flour, and hot sauce to make a slightly thickened batter.

6. Remove the chicken from the marinade. Discard the marinade. Dip each piece into the dry flour mix, into the batter, and then back into the dry flour, coating well, shaking off excess. Place on prepared rack to set for 10 minutes.

7. Using a thermometer, check the temperature of the oil to ensure it is at 340-350°F. This is a crucial step. If the oil is too hot, the coating will burn; if too low, the chicken will be greasy. Add the

chicken to the pot in 2-3 batches; do not crowd the pot. Cover the pot or fryer and fry until chicken is brown and crisp. Remove the lid after 5 minutes, and use tongs to turn each piece. It should take 12-14 minutes for dark meat and 10 minutes for white meat. Keep checking the oil temperature to make sure it doesn't get above 350-355°F. Drain the chicken on a wire rack set over paper towels to catch any drips. Recheck the temperature of the oil between batches. Serve hot or at room temperature.

LATIN CHICKEN

6-8 boneless, skinless chicken breast halves, tenders separated

1 medium onion, peeled, quartered

5 cloves fresh garlic, peeled

½ jalapeño pepper, with seeds
see p. 260

2 tablespoons dried oregano

1 tablespoon paprika

1 teaspoon dried cilantro leaves

½ teaspoon chili powder

½ teaspoon fine sea salt

½ teaspoon freshly ground black pepper

⅓ cup lime juice, fresh or bottled

¾ cup olive oil

canola oil

Latin foods such as Mexican tacos and chimichurri sauce have made it to popular culture, but Latin cuisine reflects a diverse array of influences from all over the globe. Much of Latin cuisine is characterized by rice- and maize-based favorites, including tortillas and tamales, along with guacamole, salsa, and pico de gallo. Spices and marinades also play a big part in this cuisine. This recipe is colorful and flavorful, with a bit of a kick. Even if you need only 6 servings, throw the extra cutlets into the marinade bag. There is enough marinade and you can use the leftover grilled chicken, sliced or shredded over some greens or in a wrap, to make a Latin lunch.

This recipe can also be prepared by pouring the marinade over chicken parts (bone-in, with skin) and baking immediately — no marinating time necessary — on a jellyroll pan, uncovered, at 350°F for an hour. This preparation is my husband's current favorite dish.

1. Place the chicken breasts and tenders into a large ziplock bag or container.

2. In the bowl of a food processor fitted with a metal "S" blade, pulse the onion, garlic, jalapeño, oregano, paprika, cilantro, chili powder, salt, pepper, and lime juice. With the motor running, pour the olive oil through the chute. Pour the marinade over the chicken and marinate for a few hours or overnight.

3. Preheat oven to 350°F. Preheat a grill or grill pan. Brush the grates or pan with canola oil. Remove the chicken from the marinade, discarding marinade. Grill each breast for 5 minutes per side, until you get nice grill marks and a deeper color. Transfer to a cookie sheet and finish in the oven until no longer pink inside, about 8-10 minutes. The tenders will cook faster than the breasts and won't need the time in the oven. Slice each breast on the diagonal into thick slices and place on plate or platter.

water

6 large sweet potatoes, peeled, cut into $\frac{1}{2}$-inch chunks

$\frac{1}{3}$ cup real maple syrup, NOT pancake syrup

$\frac{1}{2}$ teaspoon fine sea salt

$\frac{1}{8}$ teaspoon cayenne

1 tablespoon plus 2 teaspoons canola oil, divided

2 pounds ground turkey

1 medium onion, peeled, cut into $\frac{1}{4}$-inch dice

3 cloves fresh garlic, minced

$1\frac{1}{2}$ teaspoons dried oregano

$\frac{1}{2}$ teaspoon ground sage

$\frac{1}{4}$ teaspoon freshly ground black pepper

$1\frac{1}{2}$ cups chicken stock

$1\frac{1}{2}$ teaspoons cornstarch dissolved in 2 teaspoons water

1 cup (6-ounces) frozen green peas

$1\frac{1}{2}$ tablespoons dark brown sugar

TURKEY SHEPHERD'S PIE WITH SWEET POTATO TOPPING

An old childhood favorite of mine gets a makeover for the year 2012! The gorgeous sweet potato crust hides a healthy and delicious turkey filling, a nice change from the less-healthy ground beef of its ancestors.

1. Bring a large pot of water to a boil. Add the sweet potatoes. Boil until fork-tender, about 15-20 minutes. Drain very well. Mash with the maple syrup, salt, and cayenne. Set aside.

2. Heat 1 tablespoon canola oil in a medium skillet over medium heat. Add the turkey in one piece, as it comes from the package. This allows for good caramelization and flavor. Once caramelized and brown, flip the turkey to sear the second side. Use a wooden spoon to break up the chunk and cook until just no longer pink in the center, about 3 minutes — not longer, since turkey dries out easily. Transfer to a bowl, chopping more with the spoon. Set aside.

3. Add remaining 2 teaspoons canola oil to the pan. Heat. Add the onion and garlic. Use a wooden spoon to stir up the fond from the drippings. Cook until the onion caramelizes, about 6-7 minutes. Add the oregano, sage, and black pepper. Cook for 3 minutes longer, until the spices are fragrant. Add the turkey to the pan. Add the stock and dissolved cornstarch. Stir well to distribute the onions. Bring to a simmer. Cook until slightly thickened. Add the peas and cook until they are shiny, 3 minutes. Transfer to a 9 x 13-inch oven-to-table casserole dish. Spread the sweet potato in an even layer over the turkey.

4. Preheat oven to broil. Sprinkle the top of the sweet potatoes with the brown sugar. Place the dish 3-4 inches from the heating element and broil for 5-6 minutes until the brown sugar starts to caramelize. Serve hot.

1 whole 13-15 pound turkey, fresh or defrosted if necessary

fine sea salt

freshly ground black pepper

1-2 navel oranges, halved

4 large sprigs fresh rosemary

½ cup Dijon mustard

½ cup real maple syrup, NOT pancake syrup

fresh rosemary, for garnish

ROAST TURKEY WITH MAPLE-MUSTARD GLAZE

When you are hosting for the holiday the last thing you want to be is tied to your turkey. This gorgeous bird is a snap to make. Just a few ingredients and you have a dish worthy of a magazine cover.

Just a few tips: Plan on 1 pound of turkey per person or 1 ½ if you want leftovers. Remember, a larger bird is an older bird so it may be a bit drier. Don't forget that by elevating the turkey on a rack out of its juices, you will get gorgeous roasted skin. Tie the legs to keep the skin from tearing and to keep the shape of the bird nice and rounded. A meat thermometer inserted into the thigh is a must; it's the only way to tell when you hit 165°F. Allow the cooked turkey to rest on a cutting board set into a jellyroll pan so when you slice it you will capture all the precious juices that you can then pour back over the turkey.

1. Preheat oven to 350°F. Set a rack inside a large, heavy metal roasting pan. Set aside.

2. Trim excess neck fat from the turkey and discard. Remove the neck and any giblets from the cavity, and discard.

3. Hold the turkey neck-side-down on the cutting board and season the interior cavity with 1 teaspoon salt and ¼ teaspoon black pepper. It penetrates through while cooking the turkey. Stuff the orange halves and rosemary into the cavity. Lay turkey flat on the cutting board, and using kitchen twine or a silicone rubber band, tie the legs together tightly. Rub and pat in ¼ teaspoon salt and ⅛ teaspoon black pepper all over the outside of the turkey.

4. In a small bowl, mix the Dijon and maple syrup together. Brush some glaze all over the turkey.

5. Place turkey breast-side-down on the roasting rack. Tent with foil, making sure it doesn't touch the turkey. Roast, tented, for 1 hour.

6. Flip the turkey, baste with the maple-mustard mixture, and cook breast-side-up for 1 hour, uncovered.

7. Remove from oven and generously brush with the glaze. Return it to the oven and roast, uncovered, for a final 1 hour. Baste with the maple-mustard sauce once or twice more during this final hour of roasting.

8. Insert a meat thermometer into the thickest part of the thigh. It should register 165°F. Measure this temperature in the thickest part of the breast and the thigh, just above the drumstick. Allow the turkey to rest for 10-15 minutes. Brush with pan juices. Place on platter. Garnish with fresh rosemary. Before serving, transfer to cutting board and carve. *See p. 125 for carving instructions.*

POMEGRANATE-HONEY CHICKEN

12 chicken parts, bone-in, with skin, legs, thighs, breasts

½ cup silan (date syrup) or honey

¼ cup dark brown sugar

¼ cup pomegranate juice

¼ cup teriyaki sauce; I like Kikkoman brand

2 tablespoons cornstarch

1 teaspoon tomato paste

½ teaspoon dried thyme

2 cloves fresh garlic, minced

1 tablespoon margarine

fresh pomegranate seeds, for garnish

This dish shouts Rosh Hashanah on a plate! Honey and other sticky ingredients are a cinch to measure. Just coat the measuring cup or spoon with nonstick cooking spray and the honey will slide right out.

Make sure to line your pan so cleanup will be a snap.

1. Use foil to line a baking dish that holds the chicken pieces snugly. Arrange the chicken in a single layer. Set aside.

2. Preheat oven to 400°F.

3. In a small pot over medium heat, whisk the silan or honey, brown sugar, pomegranate juice, teriyaki sauce, cornstarch, tomato paste, thyme, and garlic. Bring to a simmer over medium heat for a minute or two until thickened. Whisk in the margarine. Reduce heat slightly. Cook for 1 minute. Generously brush the pomegranate mixture on each piece of chicken. Drizzle additional sauce over the top of each piece.

4. Bake, uncovered, 45 minutes, until chicken is no longer pink at the bone. The dark meat may take a little longer; if so, remove the white meat to a platter and cook the dark until done. Brush with the sauce in the pan every 15 minutes during cooking. After 45 minutes, turn on the broiler and broil the chicken until the skin is brown and crispy; keep a close eye on it. Transfer to a platter and baste again with pan sauce. Garnish with fresh pomegranate seeds and some of the pan sauce.

MOROCCAN CHICKEN

12 dried apricots

10 dried pitted dates

1 red onion, peeled, cut into ½-inch pieces

½ cup pitted, sliced Spanish olives, without pimento

1 tablespoon olive oil

½ teaspoon coriander

½ teaspoon turmeric

½ teaspoon fine sea salt

¼ teaspoon ground cumin

¼ teaspoon ground ginger

¼ teaspoon white pepper

⅛ teaspoon ground cinnamon

1 whole (3-4 pound) chicken, legs tied

¾ cup white wine

½ cup chicken broth

This recipe is a perfect example of how your spice cabinet can be your ticket around the culinary world. Enjoy this tender, exotic, delicious dish with a side of couscous.

1. Preheat oven to 425°F.

2. Toss the apricots, dates, onion, olives, and oil into a 9 x 13-inch pan or casserole dish, mounding in the center of the pan.

3. In a small bowl mix the coriander, turmeric, salt, cumin, ginger, pepper, and cinnamon. Rub all over the chicken.

4. Place the chicken in the pan, breast-side-up, on the fruit mound. Tuck as much of the fruit under the chicken as possible. Pour the white wine and broth around the chicken in the pan. Bake, uncovered, for 45 minutes. Baste with pan juices and bake for an additional 10 minutes until chicken is cooked through.

》25

MEAT

GAME PLAN

This chapter is near and dear to me, as my grandfather, Morris Sokol, was a butcher. His customers on Division Avenue in Williamsburg, Brooklyn gathered in his shop to chat about current events, politics, and family. Home refrigeration was rare back then, so the butcher shop was an almost daily stop on women's errand runs. There was a butcher shop every few blocks, since people walked to do their errands, and almost everyone who came in was a regular customer. My grandpa made sure to remember their taste. If a woman ordered flanken, he would remind her that her husband really liked pot roast. Most importantly, people relied on him to share his knowledge of meat so they could cook wisely and economically.

Packaged meat is a fabulous modern-day convenience and, in some less kosher-populated areas, a necessity. Most days, the kosher meat aisle at my local supermarket suffices, although I do often adjust my menu based on what is in the case. I don't like to rely on it for the special meals of Shabbos or holidays. For those, I am lucky that the highest caliber butcher I know, Park East Kosher, delivers! So with advanced thought and a spare freezer, I'm always covered. You may be fortunate to live in a neighborhood with a great butcher or shop at a supermarket that has one.

SELECTING A CUT OF MEAT

Different stores and butchers use different names for the same cuts of meat. This can make it very confusing for the consumer. When an animal is butchered, it is broken down into primal cuts, or sections, five of which — **CHUCK**, **RIB**, **BRISKET**, **PLATE**, and **FORESHANK** — are kosher. If you learn their characteristics and recognize the part of the animal the meat is from, you will be able to understand how certain cuts react to heat and what the best cooking method is. It's also a good way to know how to work with an unfamiliar cut, which sometimes might be just a name change.

DO YOURSELF A BIG FAVOR — BEFRIEND YOUR BUTCHER.

» *He can tell you what is freshest. You won't have to wonder if the meat beneath the plastic wrap is as bright red and fresh as the top layer.*

» *You're not limited to what is in the showcase, and if you're on a budget, the butcher can tell you what less expensive cut will stand in perfectly in a recipe calling for a pricier one.*

» *He can introduce you to new cuts of meat. Just last year, to my delight, I discovered surprise steak, a gorgeously marbled cut of meat that wraps a standing rib roast. I had never tasted it and it's now one of my favorites.*

» *A butcher can help you figure out the quantity you will need based on how many servings, what else is being served, and if leftovers are desired.*

» *If your carving skills are lacking, your butcher can make up for what you lack. Ask him to slice the meat paper-thin for your bulgogi recipe or to trim the sweetbreads to save you the effort.*

If you know how cuts respond to various cooking methods, you can sub in meat you have on hand or purchase cuts that are on sale, knowing you will understand how to work with them.

The following pages contain information that will help you to become familiar with the different cuts. Each type of meat is discussed separately, so find the cut you want to use and learn the best way to prepare it so that its flavor really comes through. Remember, knowldege is power and knowing your meats will allow you to power through a recipe and even develop your own style.

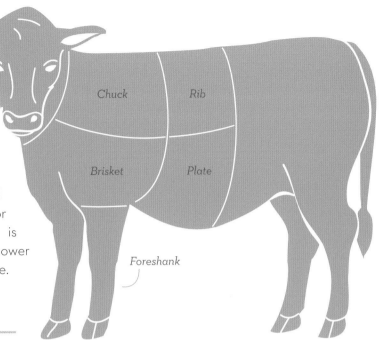

Chuck

Rib

Brisket

Plate

Foreshank

─BEEF─

CHUCK

Chuck, also known as shoulder cut or arm, includes the neck. The chuck area is used for movement and power and is a very exercised part of the cow; therefore it has the toughest muscles and lots of tendons or connective tissue. The amount of connective tissue determines the meat's tenderness; the greater the connective tissue, the less tender the meat. Most of these cuts need long, slow cooking to bring out the flavors and tenderize the meat. Slow braising, stewing, or roasting in liquids works well here. For the most part think pot roast, but there are also cuts from this primal cut that are lean, flavorful, and tender.

Many nice roasts come from the chuck and can be used interchangeably in recipes like pot roast, or in those that sear and then braise the roasts in liquids and then cook them slowly and covered. I receive the most questions on this part of the chuck primal, since butchers call the popular roasts by different names.

This roast is a **WHOLE CHUCK ROAST**, which can be sold whole and tied. If you untie it, you will see two distinct parts. The **SQUARE ROAST**, which sits on top, and the bottom part, which is called by

Whole Chuck Roast

various names, including: **CALIFORNIA ROAST, FRENCH ROAST,** and **BRICK ROAST.** You should know that they all slice very nicely, are a bit chewier than brisket, and are all cooked in the same fashion: low, slow heat with plenty of liquid. Some butchers will cut off a part of this larger roast and sell it as **SHELL ROAST.** I use this for pot roast as well as for beef cubes in stews.

BEEF CUBES

SQUARE ROAST

FRENCH ROAST

BRICK ROAST

SHOULDER LONDON BROIL is a nice stand-in for recipes calling for **LONDON BROIL, FLANK STEAK,** or any recipe using sliced beef, as in salads. Shoulder London broil is thick, so I usually sear it in a skillet or grill pan to get nice deep caramelization on both sides, and then finish it in a 350°F oven until medium rare, usually another 10-15 minutes. This cut can be cooked on the outdoor grill as well.

SILVER TIP ROAST

SHOULDER LONDON BROIL

SILVER TIP ROAST is cut from the shoulder part of chuck and is good for roast beef. Dry heat on a rack in the oven works well; for best results, don't cook it past medium-rare.

The top blade comes from the shoulder. **BEEF CHUCK BLADE STEAKS** are tough and have lots of connective tissue and gristle, but when sliced in a different way it can be trimmed of the connective tissue and is sold as a **FLAT IRON STEAK** or **MUSH STEAK.** This is an incredibly tender piece of meat. It is perfect for grilling outdoors or in a grill pan. It is also great for fajitas or stir fry.

FLAT IRON STEAK

OYSTER STEAK, sometimes called **MINI LONDON BROIL,** benefits from a quick, dry heat cook, such as grilling or searing.

OYSTER STEAK

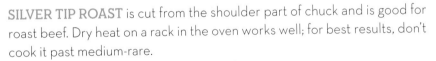
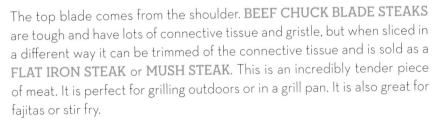

A very popular cut on the East Coast is **MINUTE STEAK ROAST**, a shoulder cut with a thick piece of gristle in the center. Sliced vertically, the meat is sold as minute steak, but it is difficult to eat around the gristle. If the meat is cut horizontally above and below the gristle, the two resulting pieces are called **FILET SPLIT** or **MINUTE STEAK FILLET**. They are fabulous for quick grilling and in recipes calling for London Broil or flat iron. I use them often in steak salads and at barbecues.

KOLICHOL

FILET SPLIT

KOLICHOL is also from the shoulder but, unlike silver tip, it is very tough. This makes it an economical choice. It is perfect for cholent or pot roast, as it benefits from the long, slow cooking time.

RIB

THE RIB contains tender roasts and steaks. The muscles in this primal are used for support and are not worked as much as the chuck. This results in naturally tender, well-marbled meat. The meat is exceptionally flavorful and commands a premium. This is the place to splurge. This quality of meat should always be dry cooked, never braised or stewed. Grilling, pan searing, and broiling are the way to go here.

STANDING RIB ROAST

A **STANDING RIB ROAST**, or **PRIME RIB** contains up to 7 bones. It is cooked whole as an extravagant centerpiece. For easy carving, you can have the butcher cut the rib bones and tie them on the roast, although I prefer to roast it whole.

WHOLE BEEF RIBS can be cut into **RIB STEAKS** and **RIBEYE STEAKS**. **RIB COWBOY STEAKS** are steaks that have had the bone frenched so the rib is exposed. Entrecôte is the French name for rib steak. When sold boneless, some butchers call these steaks **CLUB STEAKS**; others call them **DELMONICO**. If the whole center eye of a **PRIME RIB** is filleted out, it can be cut into **TOURNEDOS**, also known as **MOCK FILET MIGNON**, since real filet mignon is a nonkosher cut. There is a lot of waste in this process, making this a very expensive cut.

RIB STEAK

SURPRISE STEAK is the top flap of the prime rib. It is an incredibly tender, well-marbled large slab of meat that benefits from just a simple seasoning of salt and pepper and a quick grill.

SURPRISE STEAK

The only exception to the dry heat method used for all the tender cuts from this primal is **TOP OF THE RIB**. This piece lays above the Surprise Steak. It is a great choice to cook as you would a brisket or pot roast: slow, moist heat.

RIBS can come from two places. There is the 5-bone section of rib from the chuck/neck primal which are tougher but less fatty, and a 3- bone rib section in the plate primal. This is known as **PLATE FLANKEN** and is very rich but fattier; it is what I prefer to use, as the marbling yields wonderful taste.

TOP OF THE RIB

Ribs are rectangular sandwiches of fat, meat, and bone that are often cut into sections. They're very flavorful, but tough and fatty, so they're best if slowly braised. You can also grill them over low heat, but the dripping fat tends to cause flare-ups. To prevent this, I always braise or steam the ribs first and just finish them with their sauce on the grill. Short ribs, chuck short ribs, barbecue ribs, spare ribs, English short ribs, and flanken are all from the same two cuts. The differences come from the way they are cut.

SHORT RIBS are sold either boneless or bone-in and are the big chunks of meat found between the bones.

SPARE RIBS or **BARBECUE RIBS** are short ribs cut in half lengthwise; you can even see this from the side of the bone where the marrow is visible. **ENGLISH RIBS** are a 4 x 4-inch rectangle that includes 2 ribs and makes for a lovely, generous presentation.

FLANKEN

SPARE RIBS

If the cut is made across the first five ribs instead of between the ribs, the result is a slab of ribs, which include bone, called **FLANKEN**. They are best cooked in a braised method.

Toward the end of the chuck, right before the seven ribs that make up the rib primal, is the **DELMONICO ROAST**, sometimes called **CLUB ROAST**, which can also be sliced into **CLUB STEAKS**. This tender piece of meat benefits from dry heat methods, like grilling, pan searing, or broiling.

PLATE

The plate is the underside of the animal and sits below the ribs. **SKIRT STEAK** is from the plate. It is marbled with fat, making it very juicy. It is perfect for fajitas and needs just a quick grilling over high heat. **HANGER STEAKS** or **HANGING TENDERLOIN**, known as the "butcher's cut" since butchers used to take these home to their families, is great for grilling or broiling and has an almost aged taste. It hangs off the diaphragm so there is only one per carcass, making it a bit hard to find, but so worth trying for.

SKIRT STEAK

It is sold as one steak but is usually cut into two pieces. The French term for it is "onglet." Skirt and hanger are very salty, so watch the sodium that you add within the recipes; I would season these only with pepper. Both are best served rare or medium-rare. Some butchers use the navel bones in the plate for a fatty **FLANKEN** and some use the plate for **PASTRAMI**.

HANGER STEAK

BRISKET

Brisket muscles support about 60% of the body weight of a cow. This requires a significant amount of connective tissue, so the resulting meat must be cooked slowly and with moisture to break down the collagen and tenderize the connective tissue. When broken down properly, it becomes a soft, silky gelatin, which gives a wonderful rich mouth-feel, astonishingly tender meat, and a deep meaty flavor. A **WHOLE BRISKET** is quite large, 10-15 pounds. Most often you will see it sold in parts: the "flat cut" or **FIRST CUT** and the "point cut" or **SECOND CUT**. First-cut brisket is leaner and will slice nicely. Second cut is smaller and less expensive. The extra fat yields results that melt in your mouth, but it tends to shred, not slice. Both need slow, moist-heat cooking. I use both depending on the desired result. Some butchers call second-cut brisket **DECKLE**. Deckle means "covering" and can really be a number of different pieces; one place is the covering from the side of the rib, another and most popular is the breast covering or the "brust deckle," but all can be treated like brisket or pot roast. Acidity also helps to break down the connective tissue and tenderize the meat. That's why wine or tomatoes are so commonly used in making brisket, although naturally tenderizing enzymes found in fresh ginger, pineapple, and figs work well too. Some restaurants add ground brisket to chuck for incredible burgers. **CORNED BEEF** and **PASTRAMI** are briskets that have been brined and pickled, then steamed and smoked, respectively.

FIRST AND SECOND CUT

FORESHANK

FORESHANK primal does not yield much in the way of meat. It houses the **SHIN**, which is good for soup, beef for osso bucco, and rich **MARROW BONES**.

GROUND BEEF is generally made from lean meat and trimmings. I like an 80% lean/20% fat mix. The leaner the

MARROW BONES

SHIN

meat, the drier it is, so if you go leaner, you will need to compensate for the lack of flavor with spicing and be careful not to overcook it. Ground beef is best prepared by broiling, pan-broiling, pan-frying, roasting, or baking.

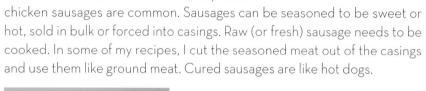
GROUND BEEF

SAUSAGE

SAUSAGE can be made from any kind of ground meat that is seasoned and has added fat. Beef, lamb, veal, turkey, and chicken sausages are common. Sausages can be seasoned to be sweet or hot, sold in bulk or forced into casings. Raw (or fresh) sausage needs to be cooked. In some of my recipes, I cut the seasoned meat out of the casings and use them like ground meat. Cured sausages are like hot dogs.

ORGAN MEAT — SWEETBREADS, LIVER, TONGUE

SWEETBREADS are the thymus gland. To prepare them, sweetbreads should be soaked in cold water overnight and then blanched for a few minutes in boiling water with some lemon juice in it. Drain, cool, remove any skin, membrane, and fat, and then pan-sear them or cut into chunks and sauté in a recipe.

SAUSAGE, OUT OF CASING

CALVES' LIVER is delicious for chopped liver or sautéed liver and onions but it must be treated to sufficiently remove the blood that is so concentrated in it. Please consult a Rabbinic authority for the specifics on how to broil liver in order to kasher it properly if your butcher has not done it for you.

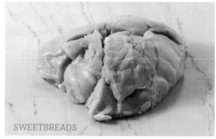
SWEETBREADS

BEEF TONGUE is a wonderful delicacy in many cultures. Some butchers sell it already "corned" and ready to boil, so you can prepare it like corned beef by simmering in water and then baking it smothered in a sweet-and-sour sauce. If the tongue is untrimmed and the skin is still on, you will have to peel it after its initial boiling or using your favorite technique.

LIVER

—— VEAL ——

VEAL is from a calf, most often male. The meat is very tender and lighter in color. It tastes different because the muscles are not formed the way they are in a mature cow.

VEAL SCALOPPINI

VEAL OSSO BUCCO

VEAL SHOULDER

VEAL CHOP

SCALLOPINE, SCALLOPINI are sautéed cutlets (usually veal or poultry) that have been pounded thin and coated with flour.

OSSO BUCCO and **VEAL SHOULDER** need slow cooking over low heat, while braising in some liquid.

VEAL CHOPS benefit from a quick sear, as in grilling on an outdoor grill or grill pan.

LAMB

BABY LAMB CHOPS don't come from baby lambs! They're called baby because they're smaller than the shoulder or round bone lamb chops. The meat on the baby lamb chops is the best, most tender meat on the lamb, in the same way first-cut veal chops are the most tender cut of veal. Both baby lamb chops and **SHOULDER LAMB CHOPS** benefit from a quick sear, as in grilling on an outdoor grill or grill pan.

LAMB SHANKS and **LAMB CUBES** need slow cooking over low heat, while braising in some liquid.

BABY LAMB CHOPS

LAMB CUBES

SHOULDER LAMB CHOPS

LAMB SHANK

GETTING STARTED

Make sure to bring your meats to room temperature for about 20-40 minutes before starting to cook. This will ensure the correct cooking time and evenly cooked results. Set up your cutting board and knife. Keep bacteria at bay and glove up! Buy boxes of latex powder-free gloves and keep them handy. Train yourself to remove your gloves every time you take your hands away from your cutting board, and re-glove after finding that spice jar or closing that cabinet. Make sure your cutting board can be sanitized easily, such as a polythene one that can go through the dishwasher. Always pat your meat dry with paper towels. This will allow the seasoning to stick better.

SEASONING

Seasoning meat both adds flavor and brings out the natural flavors within the meat itself. By varying dry spice rubs for seasoning, you can go from an Italian to a Latin to a Mediterranean dish just by changing which spice blend you use. A truly great steak needs nothing more than salt and pepper. Salt also helps break down the meat and improve the texture. If seasoning with just salt and pepper, do so right before searing or the salt will draw out some moisture. When seasoning, do so from a height. As you can see from the picture, it is the most efficient way to get a good even seasoning. Season too closely to the meat and the spices will be concentrated in one small area.

MARINADES

Marinades are wet seasonings and can be used alone or in conjunction with a dry rub. The length of time you marinate a piece of meat depends on the size and type of the meat and the desired end result. Often, it is useful to make score marks or small cuts in the meat so that the marinade can seep in for deeper flavor.

too low   *correct height*

》 *True Worcestershire sauce contains anchovies. If the kosher certification mark stands alone, then the percentage of anchovies is less than 1.6% of the whole product. Many rabbinical authorites say that this is okay to use with meat.*

If the kosher certification on the label has a fish notation next to it, the level exceeds 1.6%; do not use it in meat dishes.

SELECTING A PAN

18-gauge stainless steel is the material I like best for skillets and pans. It transfers heat to the food evenly and quickly. Stainless steel pans can reach the high temperatures ideal for searing meat. Also, stainless steel helps develop fond, or flavor on the bottom of the pan, which allows for gravies and sauces. I am a big fan of 14-inch skillets that leave plenty of room for big batches of food without overcrowding.

Nonstick pans are great for delicate foods like eggs and stir fries. Never heat an empty nonstick skillet; the coating will break down.

Ovenproof handles and tight-fitting lids are necessary when starting a dish on the range and then transferring from direct heat to the oven. Cast iron and stainless work great here.

When roasting or baking, sturdy pans or oven-to-table casseroles are crucial. Disposable tins can buckle from the weight of the food. Choose a pan that the meat fits snugly, with just a few inches to spare on each side. If your roasting pan is too big, juices will evaporate, leaving nothing for sauce. If the pan is too small, the meat won't cook evenly.

ROASTING AND BAKING

Both roasting and baking take place in the oven; the terms are often used interchangeably. Baking takes place at a lower temperature, often 350°F, and roasting at a higher temperature. Roasting can be used to achieve a brown crust, as for a standing rib roast. The high heat can dry out certain foods, so basting is often used in roasting. You can baste with the fat and juices released by the meat or with other marinades or oil. Baking gives the fibers a little more time to break down. A rack can be a useful tool to elevate the meat out of the juices or marinade, as when making roast beef.

BRAISING

Braised meats are seared and then cooked for a long period of time in a covered, heavy pot such as a cast iron pot, using a small amount of liquid. This technique is used for tougher cuts of meat that need longer cooking times. It results in tender, flavorful, moist dishes like pot roast or osso bucco. An advantage to braising is that the fat slowly renders out during the cooking; if the dish is chilled overnight, the fat is easily removed and discarded. It is also economical, as braising works well on inexpensive cuts. Once everything is in the pot, your work is done. Often vegetables or legumes are cooked with the meat, and so your sides are also taken care of. Stewing is similar to braising, but uses smaller, uniform pieces of meat completely covered in liquid, as for a beef stew.

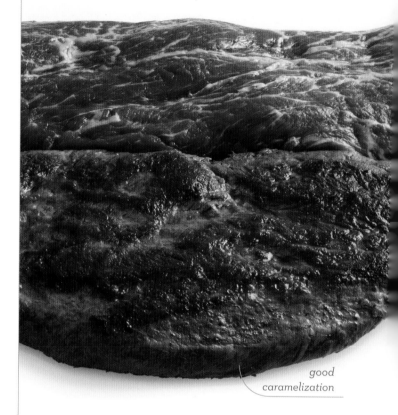

good caramelization

SEARING

Searing meat in a bit of fat over high heat is an important step in cooking lean high-end cuts such as rib steaks, as well as in preparation for braising. A good sear can make or break a steak. The thick, flavorful brownish "crust" created during the sear is the caramelization of the amino acid proteins in the meat. This caramelization is called the Maillard reaction (named for French chemist Louis Camille Maillard, pronounced may-yar). Preheating is a must; you can't just turn on the burner, grill, or broiler and toss on the steak. There is debate about whether searing actually "seals in juices." Regardless, the browning, or caramelization of the sugars and proteins on the surface of meat, adds deep flavor and should never be skipped.

SAUTÉING

Sautéing or pan-frying is a cooking method that uses quick dry heat. In French, sauté means "to jump." Bite-sized pieces of meat and/ or vegetables are tossed or stirred, usually in a flat-bottomed pan over high heat, until cooked through. To get the sizzle going, heat the pan very well before food is added. Once the pan is hot, add enough oil to keep the food from sticking. Your ears are key here. If you don't hear a sizzle when the food hits the pan, the oil is not hot enough. Remove the food and heat the pan longer. If it splatters and pops, the pan is too hot. Leave space between the pieces of meat: if you overcrowd the pan, your meat will steam.

DEGLAZING A PAN TO MAKE A PAN SAUCE

After sautéing, searing, or roasting the meat, remove it from the pan. Little bits of caramelized browned bits will be stuck to the bottom. These bits are called fond, "foundation" in French, and form the foundation for sauces and for flavor. Fond needs liquid, such as wine, beer, stock, or vinegar, to release its incredible flavors and help start a sauce or pan gravy.

STEP 1 To deglaze the pan, pour in twice as much of your selected liquid as the amount of sauce you want. **STEP 2** With the heat on medium and using a wooden spoon to really scrape the bits, stir and scrape the particles into the liquid. **STEP 3** Bring to a boil, turn to a simmer, and **STEP 4** cook down to half the volume of the liquid. For extra body, you can whisk in a pat of margarine. Season the sauce. Garnish with fresh parsley.

STEP 1

STEP 2

STEP 3

STEP 4

MAKING GRILL MARKS

Grill marks are not necessary but add an upscale touch to steaks and burgers, and the blackened marks add a deeper charred flavor. Only one side is necessary to mark since the side on the plate won't be seen. If you don't get it right the first time, you have another chance on the second side.

Place steak or burger on a hot oiled grill or grill pan, pointing to 2 o'clock on an imaginary clock. Once the meat hits the grill, don't move it or press down on it. After searing for $1/4$ of the total cooking time, use tongs to rotate the steak, or a thin metal spatula to rotate the burger, to point to 11 o'clock. Cook for an additional $1/4$ of the total cook time. Flip the steak or burger, and cook on the second side until cooked to desired temperature.

HOW TO TELL WHEN MEAT IS DONE

Cutting into meat to check if it is done should be avoided, as you will lose precious juices and mar the appearance of the meat. Every recipe gives a cooking time but to be a precise cook, you should really rely on those times only as guidelines. Not everyone's oven is exactly the same. Maybe the roast you bought was $1/2$ pound in weight more than the recipe called for. Perhaps your oven's thermostat is off by a few degrees. I may have developed and tested the recipe in a heavy-bottomed pan but yours is thinner. Or maybe my standard range throws off less heat than your higher BTU output range. These factors will all affect the cooking time and final results. There is only one real solution. Buy a good instant-read thermometer. Your results will be so much more accurate and tasty if you depend more on actual internal temperatures than on cooking times and oven temperature. Remember to take into account the resting period. Look for visual cues as well. The center of your roast should be pink, which will ensure the juiciness of a perfect medium-rare result.

INTERNAL TEMPERATURE BEFORE RESTING

Medium rare ››› 140°F.

Medium ››› 160°F.

Well-done ››› 170°F.

Ground beef ››› 160°F.

MEDIUM-RARE

MEDIUM

WELL-DONE

RESTING

Allow meat to rest for 10 to 20 minutes before cutting. Smaller cuts (like steak) should rest for the shorter time, while larger cuts (like roasts) should stand longer. During this time, the internal temperature rises, finishing the cooking. That's why you should keep your eye on the internal temperature and take the meat off the heat at least 5-10 degrees before the desired temperature. So when trying to reach an ideal internal temperature of 145°F for perfectly grilled rib steak, you want to cook it to 140°F and let it rest for 5-10 minutes until it reaches 145°F. The resting period also allows meat juices to redistribute. Rest the meat on a cutting board placed in a larger jellyroll pan before slicing. You will catch the precious juices that leak out; they can then be poured back over the meat. It also keeps cleanup of countertops and sometimes floors to a minimum.

CUTTING ACROSS THE GRAIN

Notice the grain, the strings, running along the top of the meat

We have all read in cookbooks, "cut your meat against the grain," but what does that mean and why does it matter? All pieces of meat have grain, the muscle fibers. In tender cuts like rib steaks they are harder to spot and will yield tender results no matter how you slice. But in cuts from harder-working muscles like shoulder London broil, skirt steak, hanger steak, and briskets, the muscle fiber bundles are thick. The grain looks like strings or lines running in the same direction. Cutting against the grain refers to cutting perpendicular to those fibers, rather than cutting parallel to them. If you cut with the grain, you get long and stringy, chewy, fibrous meat. Cutting against the grain yields shorter segments of muscle fibers that seem more tender to the bite.

Meat slices cut across the grain

POTATOES

- 3 pounds mix of very small red and white potatoes, each cut in half
- 16 cloves fresh garlic, minced
- 2 tablespoons olive oil
- ¼ teaspoon ground cumin
- ¼ teaspoon freshly ground black pepper

MEAT

- 1 teaspoon garlic powder
- ½ teaspoon fine sea salt
- ¼ teaspoon smoked paprika
- ⅛ teaspoon ground cumin
  olive oil
- 3 pounds shoulder London broil
- 1 lime, divided
- 1 orange, divided

MOJO BEEF AND POTATOES

Pronounced MO-ho, this garlicky flavoring is a staple in Cuban cuisine. It is nice on fish or grilled vegetables as well. The use of orange juice and lime juice approximates the sour orange juice in authentic mojo.

1. Preheat oven to 425°F.

2. Place the potatoes into a large bowl. Add the minced garlic, olive oil, ¼ teaspoon cumin, and pepper. Toss. Place into a 9 x 13-inch baking pan and roast in the oven, uncovered, for 15 minutes while you prepare the meat.

3. In a small bowl mix the garlic powder, salt, smoked paprika, and ⅛ teaspoon cumin. Rub 1 teaspoon olive oil into the London broil. Season both sides with the spice mixture. Squirt juice of ½ lime and ½ orange over the meat.

4. Heat 1 tablespoon olive oil in a grill pan over medium heat until very hot but not smoking. Sear the London broil for 3 minutes per side, until there is some nice caramelization on the meat.

5. Remove the pan of potatoes after the 15 minutes and lay the meat over them. Return the pan to the oven and cook for 25 minutes longer, until the meat is medium rare. Slice the meat on the diagonal. Squeeze the remaining ½ lime and ½ orange over the meat. Serve with the potatoes.

9 cups mini salted pretzel twists, divided

1 cup all-purpose flour

3 large eggs

1 tablespoon Worcestershire sauce
see note on p. 166

2 cloves fresh garlic, minced

3/4 teaspoon dried rosemary, crumbled, divided

12 baby lamb chops
canola oil, as needed

1/4 cup white wine

1/4 cup plain, unsweetened soymilk

1/4 cup spicy brown mustard

1/4 teaspoon fine sea salt

1/8 teaspoon dried dill

PRETZEL-CRUSTED LAMB CHOPS

Once you've read the title, does anything else need to be said?! A year after I served these lamb chops at a dinner party, my guests were still talking about them.

1. Set a cookie cooling rack into a jellyroll pan. Preheat oven to 375°F.

2. Place 1 cup of the pretzel twists into the bowl of a food processor fitted with the metal "S" blade. Process for a full 2 minutes, until the pretzels are flour-like. Combine the processed pretzels with the flour in the first part of a 3-part breading station or in a large shallow bowl.

3. In the second part of the breading station, whisk the eggs, Worcestershire sauce, garlic, and 1/2 teaspoon dried rosemary.

4. Break remaining pretzels as you place them into the food processor. Process, using on-off pulses, until they are coarse crumbs, larger than breadcrumbs; you should be able to see the texture of pretzels. Place into the third part of the breading station; do not use any powdered pretzels. Line up the flour, eggs, and pretzel crumbs, in that order.

5. Dredge both sides of each lamb chop in the flour, shaking off any excess, then in the egg, and then in the pretzel crumbs, pressing them in to adhere. Place onto the prepared rack.

6. Heat a thin layer of canola oil in large (12-14-inch) skillet over medium heat. Add the lamb chops, a few at a time, trying not to crowd the pan, and sear. Don't move the chops around once they hit the pan. When the crumbs are golden brown (about 1-2 minutes), use tongs to turn each lamb chop and cook for an additional 1-2 minutes, until the crumbs are golden. Return the lamb to the cooling rack and continue until all are done, wiping out the pan between batches and adding more oil as needed. Place the pan with rack of lamb chops into the oven and cook the lamb for 10 minutes. The middle of the lamb chops should still be pink.

7. Meanwhile, in a small pot over medium heat, whisk the wine, soymilk, mustard, remaining ¼ teaspoon rosemary, salt, and dill. Bring to a simmer. Cook for 1 minute until heated through.

8. Serve the lamb chops with the mustard sauce.

nonstick cooking spray

2 pounds ground beef

¼ cup panko breadcrumbs

1 teaspoon chili powder

1 teaspoon dried thyme

½ teaspoon ground black pepper, divided

1 teaspoon coarse sea salt or kosher salt, divided

3 large eggs, divided

½ cup ketchup

1 tablespoon honey

½ teaspoon Worcestershire sauce
see note on p. 166

¼ teaspoon hot pepper sauce; I like Frank's Red Hot brand

1 Vidalia or other sweet onion, peeled, halved, thinly sliced

2 tablespoons canola oil

2 tablespoons water

⅓ cup all-purpose flour

½ teaspoon baking powder

1 teaspoon onion soup mix

CRUSTLESS MEAT AND ONION PIE

This fancier version of meat loaf goes over the top with an onion-ring kind of topping that will have your family begging for more.

1. Preheat oven to 350°F. Spray the sides and bottom of a 9½-inch springform pan with nonstick cooking spray. Wrap the outside of the pan in foil to catch drips. Set aside.

2. Place the ground beef into a large bowl. Sprinkle in the panko, chili powder, thyme, ¼ teaspoon black pepper, and ½ teaspoon salt. Add 1 egg. Knead to thoroughly combine and distribute the spices. Pat the meat into the springform pan, use a small offset spatula to even the top. In a small bowl mix the ketchup, honey, Worcestershire sauce, and hot pepper sauce. Stir well. Pour over the meat and spread with a spatula. Set aside.

3. In a large bowl, whisk the remaining 2 eggs. Add the onions, oil, water, remaining ½ teaspoon salt, flour, baking powder, remaining ¼ teaspoon black pepper, and onion soup mix. Combine well. Pour on top of the glazed meat.

4. Bake uncovered, for 1 hour. Release sides of springform pan. Transfer the pie to a plate or platter.

VIETNAMESE BURGERS WITH PEANUT SAUCE

BURGERS

2 pounds ground beef

½ teaspoon fresh ground black pepper

½ teaspoon fine sea salt

½ teaspoon onion powder

¼ teaspoon cayenne

1 teaspoon soy sauce

1 teaspoon roasted or toasted sesame oil

3 scallions, roots trimmed, very thinly sliced on the diagonal

nonstick cooking spray

PEANUT SAUCE

⅓ cup reduced-fat creamy peanut butter

2 tablespoons soy sauce

1 tablespoon rice vinegar

1 tablespoon water

½ teaspoon sriracha chili sauce or hot sauce, such as Frank's Red Hot or Tabasco

8 hamburger buns

8 large or 16 small fresh basil leaves

Sriracha (pronounced SIR-rotch-ah) chili sauce has taken the cooking world by storm. It is the magic ingredient in spicy mayonnaise, which my kids use on everything from broccoli to turkey sandwiches. You can find it online or in a well-stocked kosher supermarket.

1. Place the ground beef into a medium bowl. Add the pepper, salt, onion powder, cayenne, 1 teaspoon soy sauce, sesame oil, and scallions. Using both hands, knead to combine. Form into 8 burger patties.

2. Heat a lightly greased barbecue or if indoors, a grill pan, sprayed with nonstick cooking spray, over medium heat. When the grill or pan is hot, add the burgers. Cook for 4 minutes per side; do not move the burgers around once they hit the pan.

3. Meanwhile, prepare the peanut sauce: In a small bowl, whisk the peanut butter, 2 tablespoons soy sauce, rice vinegar, water, and chili sauce or hot sauce. Keep whisking until very smooth and creamy.

4. Open the buns. Spread some of the peanut sauce on one or both sides of each bun. Add a burger and top with a basil leaf or two.

ZITI WITH SAUSAGE

- 1 (1-pound) box ziti, cooked in boiling salted water according to package directions until al dente, drained, set aside
- 1 (28-ounce) can whole, peeled Italian plum tomatoes
- 1 small head (1-pound) broccoli rabe
- 1 tablespoon olive oil, divided
- 4 links (1-pound) raw hot Italian beef or veal sausage
- 10 cloves fresh garlic, minced
- 1/8 teaspoon red pepper flakes
- 3/4 teaspoon fine sea salt
- 1 (15-ounce) can tomato sauce

I love this dish. I think of it as a grown-up version of ziti and meat sauce. Raw sausage is ground beef, veal, or lamb that is wonderfully seasoned and available from many butchers. All the kosher ones I have seen have been sold in casings so they look like hot dogs. Just cut them out of the casings and use like ground beef. If you can get bulk sausage, that is fine, just get 1 pound of it. You can break up the raw sausage chunks with a potato masher.

The broccoli rabe will cook down significantly but you will need a 14-inch frying pan or skillet to fit it all. It you don't have one, you may make it in two batches. My 14-inch frying pan has no lid, so when it comes to time to cover and steam the greens, I invert a second 14-inch pan over the first; you can also use an inverted jellyroll pan as a lid.

1. Remove the tomatoes from the can; reserve the juice. Cut each tomato into quarters, lengthwise. Place into a bowl. Set aside.

2. Cut the stems from the head of broccoli rabe and discard. Place the leaves into a bowl. Pull out the stalks with the florets and thinly slice those stalks and florets on the bias. Add to the bowl of leaves.

3. Heat 2 teaspoons olive oil in a large skillet over medium-high heat. Slit the casings to remove the sausages; discard the casings. Add the sausage meat to the hot oil, and use a wooden spoon to break up the meat. Cook until brown or deep red, about 4-5 minutes. Add remaining teaspoon olive oil. Sprinkle in the minced garlic and red pepper flakes.

4. Sauté until the garlic is fragrant, stirring to keep the garlic from browning and to pick up the fond from the bottom of the skillet. Remove the meat from the pan and set it aside.

5. Add the broccoli rabe, the drained tomatoes, and their juice to the same pan. Add salt. Cover the skillet; cook for 3 minutes. Add the sausage meat to the pan. Add tomato sauce. Cook for 2 minutes until heated through. Toss with the drained pasta.

LAMB COUSCOUS

This Moroccan-inspired dish comes together quickly but has complex flavors due to the assortment of spices.

- 2 mint tea bags
- 2 cups water
- 1 cup golden raisins
- 3 pounds boneless lamb cubes
- 1½ teaspoons dried oregano
- ¾ teaspoon fine sea salt
- ¾ teaspoon ground cumin
- ½ teaspoon turmeric
- ½ teaspoon cayenne
- 1 tablespoon olive oil
- 1 yellow bell pepper, seeded and cut into ½-inch dice
- 1 red onion, peeled, cut into ½-inch dice
- 1 (15-ounce) can chick peas, rinsed and drained
- 1 (15-ounce) can tomato sauce
- ¼ cup water

COUSCOUS

- 1 cup reserved tea
- 3 cups water
- 1 teaspoon fine sea salt
- 4 cups dry couscous
  chopped fresh cilantro, for garnish

1. Place the tea bags into a small pot with 2 cups water. Over high heat, bring to a boil, then turn down to a simmer. Turn off the heat and allow the tea bags to steep for 5 minutes. Remove the tea bags and add the raisins to the water to soften and become infused with the tea flavor. Reserve the tea.

2. Place the lamb into a medium bowl. Set aside.

3. In a small bowl, combine the oregano, salt, cumin, turmeric, and cayenne. Toss with the lamb, rubbing it in to coat all the cubes.

4. Heat the olive oil in a large (12-14-inch) skillet over medium to high heat. Add the lamb cubes in a single layer. Using tongs, turn the cubes so they brown on all sides, 4-5 minutes per side. Remove the lamb as it is done. Repeat until all the lamb is browned.

5. In the same pan sauté the yellow pepper and red onion, scraping up the fond or browned bits from the bottom of the pan. Return the lamb to the pan along with the chick peas, tomato sauce, raisins, and ¼ cup water. Cover and cook for 20 minutes, stirring every 5 minutes.

6. Meanwhile prepare the couscous: Place 1 cup of the reserved tea, plus 3 cups water, and 1 teaspoon salt into a medium pot. Bring to a boil. Add the couscous. Stir, cover, and remove from heat. Allow to stand for 5 minutes. Fluff with a fork.

7. Transfer the couscous to a serving bowl or dish. Top with the lamb and garnish with cilantro.

BULGOGI

Bulgogi is Korea's most famous street food. It is also served in homes and restaurants, prepared on tabletop hibachi-style grills.

The key to this dish is slicing the meat paper-thin so it absorbs all the flavors of the marinade and cooks quickly. If you freeze the meat for 30-45 minutes out of its packaging in a piece of foil or parchment, it will be much easier to slice thinly.

8 cloves fresh garlic, sliced

2 tablespoons soy sauce

2 teaspoons dark brown sugar

2 teaspoons rice vinegar

1 teaspoon Worcestershire sauce
see note on p. 166

$\frac{1}{4}$ teaspoon cayenne

$1\frac{1}{2}$ pounds filet split, cut into paper-thin $\frac{1}{16}$-inch slices

canola oil

1 head Bibb or Boston lettuce, separated into leaves

DIPPING SAUCE

$\frac{1}{4}$ cup soy sauce

2 tablespoons honey

2 teaspoons fresh ginger, peeled and minced

$\frac{1}{2}$ teaspoon roasted or toasted sesame oil

$\frac{1}{4}$ teaspoon red pepper flakes

1. In a medium bowl, mix the garlic, soy sauce, brown sugar, vinegar, Worcestershire, and cayenne. Add the sliced steak. Toss and stir to separate the slices and make sure they are well coated. Allow to marinate at room temperature for 15-20 minutes.

2. Heat 1 tablespoon canola oil in a large skillet over medium heat. Remove the meat from the marinade and discard any remaining marinade. Sear the meat, in a single layer, allowing room between slices; you may need to do this in batches. If so, wipe out the pan between each batch and heat a bit more oil. Don't move the meat around. Get some good caramelization and then, using tongs, turn each slice over and repeat on the second side, 3-5 minutes in total cooking time.

3. Roll $\frac{1}{2}$ cup meat in a Bibb lettuce leaf. Repeat until all the meat is rolled. Transfer to a plate or platter.

4. In a small bowl, prepare the dipping sauce: Whisk together the soy sauce, honey, ginger, sesame oil, and red pepper flakes. Serve with the bulgogi.

MARINATED VEAL ROAST WITH POTATOES AND MUSHROOMS

- 6 cloves fresh garlic
- 1½ cups white wine, divided
- 3 tablespoons dark brown sugar
- 3 tablespoons tomato paste
- 2 tablespoons balsamic vinegar
- 2 tablespoons Worcestershire sauce *see note on p. 166*
- 2 tablespoons coarse grain Dijon mustard
- 1 tablespoon capers, rinsed and drained
- 1 tablespoon dried oregano
- 1 tablespoon dried rosemary
- 1 tablespoon coarse sea salt or kosher salt
- ½ teaspoon freshly ground black pepper
- 4 pounds shoulder veal roast, rolled and tied to hold shape
- 2 tablespoons canola oil
- 1 onion, peeled, cut in half, thinly sliced
- 2 shallots, peeled, thinly sliced
- 6 ounces sliced cremini mushrooms
- 5 ounces sliced shiitake mushrooms, stems discarded
- 4 Yukon Gold potatoes, unpeeled, each cut into 8 chunks
- 1 cup beef stock

If you have a cast-iron Dutch oven, use it for this recipe. It holds the heat in better and allows for less evaporation of the pan juices. This recipe, like other meats or poultry roasts, benefits from selecting a pan that the roast fits snugly, because roasts shrink dramatically as they cook, and an oversized pan requires excess liquid to adequately keep the meat moist. This can compromise the end results.

1. In the bowl of a food processor fitted with the metal "S" blade, process the garlic until chopped. Add 1 cup white wine, brown sugar, tomato paste, balsamic vinegar, Worcestershire sauce, Dijon, capers, oregano, rosemary, salt, and pepper. Pulse until combined. Pour into large heavy-duty ziplock bag. Add veal. Marinate 8 hours or overnight in refrigerator.

2. Preheat oven to 350°F. Allow the veal to come to room temperature, 15-20 minutes. Remove from marinade, reserving marinade. Pat the roast dry with paper towels.

3. Heat the oil in an ovenproof pot or roasting pan over medium-high heat. Sear veal on all sides, about 5 minutes per side, for a total of 20 minutes. Remove the meat. Add the onion and shallots to the pan with remaining ½ cup white wine. Using a wooden spoon, scrape the brown bits from the bottom of the pan while the onion and shallots soften, 4-5 minutes. Add the mushrooms and stir. Allow the wine to cook out, about 3 minutes.

4. Return the veal to the pan, laying it over the mushrooms and onions. Surround with the potatoes. Drizzle on the reserved marinade and beef stock. Cover the pot and place into the oven. Cook for 1½-2 hours, depending on thickness of veal. The meat thermometer should register 145-150°F. Allow to stand for 10 minutes. Slice and transfer to platter.

BEEF STEW

2 pounds beef cubes, chuck or shoulder

2-3 tablespoons all-purpose flour

2 tablespoons canola oil

2 cups beef stock

1 cup water

1 tablespoon balsamic vinegar

1 tablespoon Worcestershire sauce
see note on p. 166

5 cloves fresh garlic, peeled

3 bay leaves

2 medium onions, peeled and sliced

1½ teaspoons paprika

1½ teaspoons black pepper

1 teaspoon sugar

½ teaspoon garlic powder

⅛ teaspoon ground allspice

3 large carrots, peeled and sliced

3 ribs celery, root ends trimmed, sliced

1 cup frozen peas

1½ pounds whole baby white creamer potatoes with skin, each cut in half

¼ cup cold water

2 tablespoons cornstarch

Beef stew — comfort food at its best. Beef stew has hundreds of variations; my recipe is among the traditional sort but feel free to put your own spin on it. I do stand in praise of this braise as it is inexpensive, and once the beef has browned, it is almost entirely hands-off till dinner.
I worked on this one on a snow day when my whole family was home. The aroma slowly brought my family out of their rooms as they gathered around the cast-iron pot.
The stew was so good that they ate it from bowls standing around the stove; we never even made it to the table.

1. Sprinkle the beef cubes with flour, shaking off the excess. Heat the oil in a heavy pot, cast iron if possible, over medium-high heat. When the oil is very hot but not smoking, add the beef and brown on all sides, using tongs to turn the pieces as they brown. Do this in batches as necessary. Return all beef cubes to pot.

2. Add the beef stock, water, balsamic, Worcestershire sauce, garlic cloves, bay leaves, onions, paprika, black pepper, sugar, garlic powder, and allspice. Bring to a boil. Reduce heat, cover, and simmer 1 hour, 45 minutes.

3. Remove and discard bay leaves. Add carrots, celery, peas, and potatoes. Cover and cook 40 minutes longer, stirring occasionally, until potatoes are pierced easily with a fork.

4. Combine ¼ cup water and cornstarch until smooth; add to pot. Stir and cook until bubbly.

5. Transfer to serving bowls. Serve over egg noodles or with crusty hunks of bread, if desired.

KANSAS CITY RIBS

½ cup water

20 large (5-inch long) beef spare ribs, 5-6 pounds

DRY RUB

2 tablespoons dark brown sugar

4 teaspoons paprika

2 teaspoons garlic powder

1 teaspoon fine sea salt

½ teaspoon celery seed

½ teaspoon cayenne

½ teaspoon ground coriander

½ teaspoon dry mustard powder

Mop sauce ingredients on facing page

This dish is an ode to my beloved brother-in-law Clint, who hails from Kansas City and whose "grub" I often rave about. A feature of Kansas City barbecue is the liberal use of a sweet, spicy, tangy tomato-based BBQ sauce, as in his famous food. The other feature is the dry rub, which gets the flavor going in the oven.

I am often asked about how to make ribs that stay on the bone, and not fall off after the long cooking period. I went to a real authentic source, my food stylist's Aunt Irene from Johnson City, Tennessee, who explained the difference is in cooking procedures. For ribs that fall off the bone, pat them with the dry rub and put them right into the pan in a single layer. Cover the pan tightly with foil and bake for 2½ hours, until ribs are very tender. Most will be off the bone when you "wet mop" them with the sauce. For ribs that stay attached to the bone, follow the recipe instructions and cooking time as written below. Either way, grab a stack of napkins!

1. Preheat oven to 300°F. Place a cookie cooling rack into a jellyroll pan. Pour ½ cup water in the pan, below the ribs; this will help them steam. Arrange the ribs in a single layer on the rack. Set aside.

2. Prepare the dry rub: In a small bowl, mix the brown sugar, paprika, garlic powder, salt, celery seed, cayenne, coriander, and mustard powder.

3. Sprinkle dry rub evenly on the ribs. Rub in with your fingers. Cover the pan tightly with heavy-duty aluminum foil and bake for 2 hours, until ribs are tender but still attached to the bone. Drain off the fat and liquid.

4. Meanwhile, prepare the mop sauce: Heat the oil in a medium pot over medium heat. Add the onion and garlic; sauté for 4-5 minutes, until the onion is shiny; do not allow it to brown.

Add the ketchup, brown sugar, molasses, vinegar, mustard, Worcestershire, salt, mustard powder, smoked paprika, and cumin. Stir well to combine. Bring to a boil. Reduce heat; simmer for 15 minutes.

5. Heat an oiled grill or grill pan to make the surface nonstick. Add the ribs, basting 2-3 times with the sauce until the ribs are charred and crisp, about 5 minutes per side. Serve ribs with any remaining sauce.

MOP SAUCE

- 1 tablespoon olive oil
- 1 small onion, peeled, minced
- 2 cloves fresh garlic, minced
- 1 cup ketchup
- ¼ cup dark brown sugar
- ¼ cup molasses
- 2 tablespoons red wine vinegar
- 1 tablespoon yellow mustard
- 1 teaspoon Worcestershire sauce
  see note on p. 166
- ½ teaspoon fine sea salt
- ¼ teaspoon dry mustard powder
- ¼ teaspoon smoked paprika
- ⅛ teaspoon ground cumin

1 large onion, peeled

5 carrots, peeled,
   cut into chunks

2 parsnips, peeled,
   cut into chunks

3½ pounds brisket, first cut

1 cup dark brown sugar,
   packed

3 tablespoons instant
   decaffeinated coffee
   granules

1 tablespoon chili powder

1 tablespoon garlic
   powder

1 teaspoon ground white
   pepper

1 teaspoon coarse sea salt
   or kosher salt

2 (12-ounce) bottles beer

SPICED COFFEE-BRAISED BRISKET

What sets this brisket apart is that by cooking it uncovered, the brisket stays firm and a crusting of the spices forms. It slices beautifully; just make sure to slice it thinly and serve with plenty of the pan juices. If you prefer a softer brisket, the kind you can pull apart with a fork, use a second-cut brisket and cook it covered.

1. Preheat oven to 350°F.

2. Cut the onion in half and then cut each half into 4 chunks. Separate the onion layers and arrange the onions in a layer in the center of a 9 x 13-inch oven-to-table casserole or roasting pan. Arrange the carrots and parsnips around the onion.

3. Place the brisket on top of the onions. In a small bowl, mix the brown sugar, coffee granules, chili powder, garlic powder, white pepper, and salt. Rub all over the top of the brisket, patting it into the surface to coat it evenly.

4. Pour the beer around the brisket, not over it, so as to not wash away the spice coating.

5. Bake, uncovered, for 2 hours.

6. Allow the brisket to cool; slice against the grain. Serve with the vegetables.

3 tablespoons canola oil, divided

3 leeks, roots trimmed, cut into ½-inch slices

1 (2-pound) California, shell, or French roast

fine sea salt

½ cup thin barbecue sauce, like Bone Sucking Sauce

½ cup duck sauce

½ cup chili sauce

⅓ cup balsamic vinegar

¼ cup Cabernet Sauvignon, or other good red wine

8 cloves fresh garlic, minced

1 tablespoon molasses

1 large Spanish onion, thinly sliced

20 cherry tomatoes, stems removed

½ teaspoon cracked black pepper

TOMATO-LEEK CALIFORNIA ROAST

When my husband Kal tastes a new dessert of mine and the verdict is that it tastes "parve," then I know I have more work to do. When he samples a meat dish and I ask his opinion and the verdict is that it tastes like "Shabbos meat," I know it tastes too traditional and it is back to the drawing board for me. This one passed the test with flying colors.

1. Preheat oven to 350°F.

2. In a large (12-14-inch) skillet, heat 2 tablespoons of the oil over medium heat. When the oil is hot, add the leeks. Sauté until shiny and caramelized, 4-5 minutes. Transfer to a roasting pan or oven-to-table casserole that is just a little bigger than the roast.

3. Season the meat with salt. In the same skillet, heat remaining tablespoon canola oil over medium heat. Add the roast and sear until caramelized on each size, about 5-6 minutes per side. Place over the leeks.

4. Meanwhile, in a medium bowl, whisk the barbecue sauce, duck sauce, chili sauce, balsamic vinegar, red wine, minced garlic, and molasses. Pour over the roast.

5. Scatter the sliced onion, cherry tomatoes, and black pepper over the top. Cover and roast for 2 hours. Allow the roast to cool. Using a sharp or an electric knife, slice across the grain. Return to the roasting pan; top with the sauce. Reheat, covered, before serving.

3 pounds shoulder London broil

1 tablespoon plus ¼ teaspoon ground cumin, divided

¼ teaspoon chili powder

8 cloves fresh garlic, minced

1 (12-ounce) bottle beer, light colored, divided

1 tablespoon olive oil

3 small onions, peeled, halved, cut into very thin slices

3 cups sliced carrots

1 teaspoon dried rosemary, crumbled

½ cup orange juice

2 tablespoons canola oil, divided

fresh rosemary, for garnish

CUMIN-MARINATED LONDON BROIL

Don't use filet split in this recipe, it is too thin. If that is all you have, cook the carrots for just as long but the meat for just 5 minutes per side. You can use pre-sliced carrot coins from the supermarket or peel and thinly slice your own.

1. Score the meat, criss-crossing both sides of the London broil. Rub 1 tablespoon of cumin, chili powder, and garlic into both sides of the meat. Place into large (2-gallon) heavy-duty ziplock bag. Pour in 1 cup of beer. Massage it all into the meat. Place into the refrigerator to marinate for 2 hours or up to overnight. When ready to cook, remove the meat from the refrigerator and allow to come to room temperature for 20 minutes.

2. Preheat oven to 400°F.

3. In a large (12-14-inch) skillet heat the olive oil over medium heat. Add the onions, carrots, remaining ¼ teaspoon ground cumin, and rosemary. Sauté until the onions are shiny, about 4-5 minutes. Add orange juice and remaining ½ cup beer. Bring to a simmer. Simmer 5 minutes, until the carrots are slightly soft. Transfer to an oven-to-table casserole and bake, uncovered, for 30 minutes or until the carrots are fork-tender.

4. Rinse and dry skillet. Over medium heat, heat 1 tablespoon canola oil. Remove meat from marinade; discard the marinade. Sear the meat for 10-15 minutes per side, depending on thickness. Heat the remaining tablespoon canola oil before searing the second side. Use tongs to turn meat. Do not move the meat around while searing. Cook until very medium-rare. Place the London broil on the carrots and return pan to the oven, cooking uncovered, for another 10 minutes, until the steak is medium and just slightly pink in the center.

5. Allow the meat to rest for 10 minutes. Transfer to a cutting board. Thinly slice on the diagonal. Serve with the carrots and onions and garnish with fresh rosemary.

LAMB SHANKS WITH CHERRIES AND PORT

Cherries, Port, lamb, and rosemary make for a perfect flavor profile. But can a dish so elegant really incite bad manners? It sure can when you find yourself licking your plate clean of this delectable sauce.

6 lamb shanks; have butcher trim bones

fine sea salt

freshly ground black pepper

1 tablespoon olive oil

½ medium onion, peeled, cut into very small dice

1 rib celery, minced

1 carrot, peeled, minced

1 sprig fresh rosemary

3 sprigs fresh thyme, chopped, leaves and sprigs

1 cup dried cherries, divided

1 (750 ml) bottle Port wine (Ruby if possible)

4 cups chicken stock

½ cup plus 2 tablespoons, divided, good-quality black cherry preserves; I like Hero brand

2 cinnamon sticks

1. Season the lamb shanks with salt and pepper. Heat the olive oil in a large heavy pot or Dutch oven over medium-high heat. In batches, so you don't crowd the pan, add the lamb shanks and brown, 3-4 minutes per side, turning to sear all sides. Remove to a jellyroll pan.

2. Add the onion, celery, and carrot to the pot, stirring to scrape up browned bits from the bottom. Add the rosemary, thyme, and ½ cup dried cherries. Remove from heat. Pour in the Port and chicken stock. Stir. Return to medium heat. Whisk in the ½ cup black cherry preserves to dissolve. Drop in the cinnamon sticks. Return the lamb shanks to the pot. Raise heat, bring to a boil, then turn down to a simmer. Cover and cook for 2 hours. Check after 1 hour and see if the shanks need rotating if they are not completely submerged.

3. Remove the shanks from the pot. Remove and discard the cinnamon sticks and rosemary sprig. Using an immersion blender, blend the sauce, then simmer for 20 minutes over medium heat, uncovered, to reduce, skimming any impurities from the surface. Whisk in remaining 2 tablespoons black cherry preserves. Return the shanks to sauce and sprinkle with remaining ½ cup dried cherries. Cook for 10 minutes; serve with sauce. Can be made in advance and reheated.

FALL HARVEST SILVER TIP ROAST

- 1 pound sunchokes, aka Jerusalem artichokes, unpeeled, rinsed
- 1 large (1 pound) turnip, rinsed, unpeeled, cut into 1½-inch chunks
- 3 yellow beets (¾-pound), rinsed, ends trimmed, quartered
- 1 teaspoon fine sea salt
- ¼ teaspoon black pepper
- 1 tablespoon olive oil
- 8 cloves fresh garlic, minced
- 2 teaspoons dried tarragon, crumbled
- ½ cup fresh dill sprigs, packed, chopped
- 2 tablespoons coarse grain Dijon or Country Dijon mustard
- 1 (3-4 pound) silver tip roast, tied
- 1 heaping cup red seedless grapes, each cut in half
- 2 large shallots, peeled, cut into small dice
- 1½ tablespoons red wine vinegar
- 1½ cups chicken stock

This is a stunning dish. Save it for a special occasion or holiday meal.

If you can't find sunchokes, you can substitute 1 pound of fingerling or baby Yukon Gold potatoes, each also cut in half.

1. Preheat oven to 375°F.

2. Cut each sunchoke in half lengthwise, and then the bigger pieces into fourths. Place the sunchokes, turnip, and beets in a single layer in a heavy metal roasting pan. Sprinkle with salt, pepper, and olive oil. Toss to coat.

3. In a small bowl, mix the garlic, tarragon, dill, and mustard. Pat evenly over the top and sides of the roast. Set aside.

4. Place the roast over the vegetables. Bake, uncovered, 1 hour 45 minutes.

5. Remove the roast from the pan. Add the grapes, shallots, vinegar, and chicken stock to the pan, stirring or swirling to pick up the fond that the meat left behind. Return the uncovered pan with sauce and vegetables to the oven for 5 minutes. Slice the meat, place on platter, surround with the vegetables. Spoon the pan sauce over the meat.

HANGER STEAK WITH RED WINE SHALLOT SAUCE

2 tablespoons olive oil, divided

6 (6-8 ounce each) hanger steaks, split by butcher

freshly ground black pepper

3 large or 4 medium shallots, peeled and sliced

¼ teaspoon dried thyme leaves

1 cup Cabernet Sauvignon, or other good red wine

1 cup beef stock or broth, divided

1½ teaspoons all-purpose flour

Hanger steak is also known as the butcher's steak because butchers used to keep this formerly little-known part for themselves. Hanger steak has long been popular in Europe. In French, it is known as the onglet. It is highly flavorful, but isn't perfectly tender, so it responds well to quick cooking with searing heat, perfect for outdoor grilling if the season is right. Medium-rare is a must, as is thin slicing against the grain to serve. You can use it in Bulgogi and fajitas. If you can't find hanger steak, you can substitute with filet split or skirt steak.

1. Heat oil in a medium skillet over high heat. Pat the steaks dry with a paper towel and season them with pepper. When the pan is hot, add the steaks, and allow them to sear, getting good caramelization. Do not move the steak pieces until they have browned on one side. Using tongs, continue to turn them until they are cooked on all sides, about 18 minutes in total for medium-rare (the steaks will continue to cook as they rest). Transfer the steaks to a warm dish; cover with foil and let them rest while you prepare the sauce.

2. Reduce the heat to medium. Add the remaining tablespoon of oil and the shallots. Season with pepper and thyme. Cook, stirring frequently, until the shallots are softened, about 3 to 5 minutes. Do not allow them to brown. Add the wine and bring to a boil. Let the wine reduce by half, about 5 minutes.

3. In a small bowl, whisk ¼ cup beef broth with the flour and ¼ teaspoon black pepper until smooth. Add to the wine and whisk. Add the remaining ¾ cup beef broth. Cook at a low simmer for 10 minutes until sauce thickens slightly.

4. To serve, cut each steak against the grain into thin slices. Fan the slices out on a warm dinner plate. Serve with the warm shallot sauce.

CHILI BURGERS

If you are bored by plain old burgers, switch up the spices for a whole new take. These burgers get a Mexican transformation using very simple additions. Serve these yummy burgers with tortilla chips.

- 2 pounds ground beef
- ¼ cup chili sauce
- 2 teaspoons chili powder
- 2 teaspoons Worcestershire sauce
  see note on p. 166
- ½ teaspoon ground cumin
- ½ teaspoon garlic powder
- ¼ teaspoon fine sea salt
- 2 teaspoons canola oil
  hamburger buns
- 1 (15-ounce) can refried beans
  ripe Haas avocado, peeled, pitted, sliced
- 1 beefsteak tomato, very thinly sliced
- 2 limes
  freshly ground black pepper

1. Place the ground beef into a medium bowl. Add the chili sauce, chili powder, Worcestershire sauce, cumin, garlic powder, and salt. Mix, kneading the beef to distribute the spices. Divide into 8 equal balls. Form patties 3½ inches in diameter.

2. Heat the oil over medium in a grill pan or skillet. Sear the burgers, 3-4 minutes per side.

3. Toast the buns, cut-side-down, in the same skillet. Remove from heat.

4. Heat the refried beans in a small pot. Spread 2 tablespoons of the beans on each burger, top with a few slices of avocado, 1 slice tomato, a squeeze of lime juice, and a tiny pinch of black pepper. Place each burger into a bun. Serve on a plate or platter.

»> 27

FISH

GAME PLAN

One of the healthiest and quickest meals you can make is fish. We should all be eating fish a few times a week. Once you become familiar with fish and how to work with it, my bet is that it will become a go-to favorite in your menu planning.

BUYING FISH

FISH STORE

The most important decision regarding fish that you will make is where you buy it. Shop in a popular, clean, well-lit store that has a lot of turnover and where the fishmonger is knowledgeable and forthcoming. Don't be afraid to ask when a fish had come in and by when it needs to be cooked. If fish is truly fresh, you can keep it for 2 days in the coldest part of your refrigerator. Trust what your fishmonger tells you is at its best. Be prepared to switch your menu based on what is freshest. Ask for the best way to prepare a fish that is unfamiliar. Whole fish should be buried right in the ice crystals, fillets on parchment or other paper and then on ice, to keep the ice from damaging them.

SIGNS OF FRESHNESS

Whole fish should have clear bulging eyes, firm shiny flesh, and moist fins. Older fish will have cloudy eyes and dry fins that stand away from the body. The gills, right behind the head, should be pinkish-reddish. If you touch the flesh and your finger leaves an indentation, the fish is not fresh. With fillets, the flesh should look moist and the color should not darken around the edges. A fresh fish should smell like clean water, or a touch briny like the sea. Under no circumstances should you buy a smelly fish. Cooking will only make it smell worse and it will stink up your kitchen. If you can, take an insulated bag and some ice packs to keep the fish fresh on its journey from the store. Fresh fish is my preference, but if not available, let's discuss the frozen option.

+ *Place ice packs into a pan or on a plate to catch drips. Store your fish on the ice packs in the coldest part of your refrigerator.*

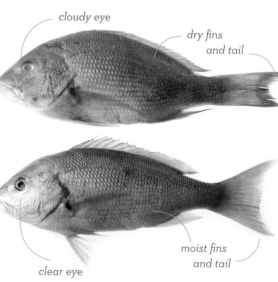

cloudy eye

dry fins and tail

clear eye

moist fins and tail

FRESH VS. FROZEN

The answer used to be obvious, with fresh the clear winner, but that is not necessarily so anymore. Today, fresh catches can be processed and flash-frozen immediately, at their peak of freshness, to very low temperatures right on the boat. This freezes without the damaging ice crystals that would form in a home freezer and result in freezer burn and texture changes. I think this works best with fatty fishes like salmon and sea bass. I am more hesitant about leaner fish. However, frozen seafood can spoil if the fish thaws during transport and is left at warm temperatures for too long. The texture also suffers if you defrost it quickly on the counter at home. Defrost fish gently, overnight in the refrigerator. To help ensure that the flash-frozen fish you're buying is safe, follow these guidelines: Don't buy frozen seafood if its package is open, torn, or crushed on the edges. Avoid packages that are positioned above the "frost line" or top of the freezer case in the store's freezer. Look for signs of frost or ice crystals or blood. These could mean the fish has been stored a long time or thawed and refrozen. Frozen fish should meet the fresh-smell test. Freezing fish at home is not recommended, as the texture and flavor are altered.

PREPPING

PIN BONING

If your fishmonger did not remove the pin bones, it is easy to do yourself. Run your finger down the spine of the fish starting at the head end. You will feel small bones protruding about every half inch. Using pliers or tweezers, gently pull the bones out at a 45° angle.

SKINNING

STEP 1 To remove skin from a fish fillet, place it skin-side-down on your cutting board. Using a thin, sharp, flexible knife, at a 45° angle, make a diagonal cut through the fish on the tail end but don't cut through the skin.

STEP 2 Grab the skin with your other hand, like a handle. Run your knife between the fish and the skin all the way to the end of the fillet.

STEP 1

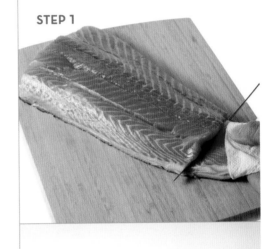

STEP 2

UNDERSTANDING TYPES OF FISH

When selecting fish for a recipe, understanding each fish's texture, thickness, and fat content will make it simple to select a cooking method and to find appropriate substitutes when a particular fish is not available.

THIN/FRAGILE FISH

> Delicate in flavor.
> Great starter fishes for people who are not used to eating fish.
> Too fragile for grilling but are perfect for sautéing, pan-frying, shallow poaching, or baking.

Tilapia

Sole

Flounder

SLIGHTLY FIRM FISH

> Stand up to every cooking method. Poach, sauté, roast, bake, grill, or broil.

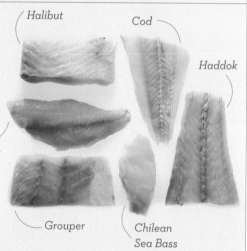

Halibut

Cod

Haddok

Red Snapper

Grouper

Chilean Sea Bass

DENSER FISH

> Dense fish, like mahi-mahi and striped bass, also withstand any cooking method and grill well.
> Salmon and halibut are wonderful prepared in any way and respond very well to poaching.
> Tuna should be served rare.

Salmon Fillet

Tuna

Salmon Steak

COOKING

Always bring fish to room temperature before cooking. Fish is delicate. Do not overcook it or it will be dry. The general rule is 10 minutes total cooking time per full inch, measuring at the thickest part. If a fillet is ³/₄-inch thick, it will be done in 7 minutes — that is counting both sides. Exceptions are cases like tuna, where you want the inside to be rare. Thin fillets do not need to be turned. To cook them evenly, tuck the thin tapered end under the fillet to make an even thickness.

tail tuck

For thicker fillets, use a flexible fish turner or your widest spatula and a quick flipping motion to flip the fillet in one piece. Another way to avoid breaking a fillet when flipping is to coat it in flour or cornmeal before adding it to a hot, greased, nonstick pan.

To check for doneness, cook your fish until an instant-read thermometer registers 145°F. The flesh should be opaque and the fish should be moist but flake cleanly when separated with a fork at its thickest part. Fish continues to cook for 5 minutes after removed from its heat source so cook it just under where you want it to be done.

SERVING SIZE

whole fish ››› 1lb. ››› per person
fillets ››› 4-8ounces ››› per person

4-ounces is the healthy portion range
8-ounces is a restaurant portion size

COOKING TECHNIQUES

BAKING/ROASTING

I find baking to be one of the easiest and most reliable methods of cooking fish. Bake from 350-375°F. Individual fillets will cook faster than whole sides. Salmon, for example, will cook in 15-20 minutes at 375°F if cut into fillets but will take closer to 30 minutes for a side of salmon.

BROILING

Intense heat cooking is good for robust, white-fleshed fish such as bass and halibut.

GRILLING

Grilling is fine for dense fillets or steaks like tuna, mahi-mahi, or salmon steaks. Delicate fish may fall through the grates. Experiment with cedar planks; they are a great tool in grilling seafood.

PAN-FRYING OR SAUTÉING

All fish respond well to this simple method. The goal is to get the fish colored to an even brown and remain juicy.

DEEP FRYING

White-fleshed types of fish that have been battered or breaded are good for frying. Make sure your oil is at the correct 355-375°F before adding the fish.

OVEN-POACHING

Poaching is a gentle method that keeps fish moist. Enclosed in a poacher, fish can be poached easily in the oven. If you do not have a fish poacher, create one out of large sheets of heavy-duty foil.

A 2-3-pound side of salmon cooks in 35-40 minutes at 350°F. Individual fillets will cook in less time.

metal fish poacher

MAKING A FOIL POACHER

STEP 1 Lay the fish and aromatics and liquids (like white wine) in the center of the foil.

STEP 2 Seal the foil packet, leaving room at the top for the liquid to help steam the fish. Place the packet on a jellyroll pan to catch any leaks.

PARVE
YIELD: 6-8 SERVINGS

SOY-POACHED SALMON WITH CHIVE OIL

2 pounds salmon fillet, with skin, pin bones removed

1/4 cup soy sauce

1/4 cup mirin, rice cooking wine; I like the Eden brand

1/4 cup white wine

1 tablespoon light brown sugar

2 teaspoons roasted or toasted sesame oil

1/8 teaspoon red pepper flakes

1-2 lemons, thinly sliced

2 cloves fresh garlic, quartered lengthwise

2 inches fresh ginger, peeled, thinly sliced into rounds

6 sprigs fresh cilantro

CHIVE OIL

1 bunch fresh chives

1/4 teaspoon fine sea salt

1/2 cup extra-virgin olive oil

>> If you do not have a poacher, create one from wide-roll heavy duty aluminum foil. See note on p. 209

Although poaching salmon in the dishwasher is an old party trick, I much prefer using an oven. You can't beat poaching for turning salmon into a delicacy that is so moist, it can even be made a day in advance, a usual fish faux pas. During poaching, the flavorings in the liquid seep into the salmon, so in this recipe Asian flavors, although light and subtle, really make the fish delectable. The chive oil is a visual wow, and tastes delicious, but honestly I added it to this recipe to take your eye away from the brown tinge that the soy sauce puts on the salmon.

1. Preheat oven to 350°F.

2. Place the salmon in a fish poacher.

3. In a small mixing bowl, whisk the soy sauce, mirin, white wine, brown sugar, sesame oil, and red pepper flakes. Pour the soy mixture over the fish.

4. Arrange the lemon slices, garlic, ginger, and cilantro over the top of the fish.

5. Cover or seal the poacher. Bake for 30 minutes.

6. Meanwhile, prepare the chive oil: Fill a medium skillet with water and bring to a boil (see blanching technique on page 255). Fill a bowl with ice and cold water.

7. Add the chives to the boiling water and blanch for 30 seconds. Remove immediately and plunge into the ice water to stop the cooking and retain the chives' bright green color.

8. Remove chives from the ice water, drain, wrap in a towel and squeeze out all the moisture. With scissors, cut the chives into 1-inch pieces and place in a blender or food processor. Add the salt. With the machine running, add the olive oil through the feed tube and process until completely smooth.

9. Strain into a bowl through a fine mesh strainer, pressing against any solids with the back of a spoon to extract as much oil as possible. Discard solids.

10. Transfer chive oil to a squirt bottle or other container.

11. Open the poacher. Remove and discard the cilantro, lemons, ginger, garlic, and liquid. Transfer the salmon to a platter. Garnish with chive oil. Serve warm or at room temperature.

DAIRY
YIELD: 6 SERVINGS

LEMONY GROUPER

This simple presentation will appeal to kids and adults alike. Grouper belongs to the sea bass family. It is high in oil and moisture, making it a moist fish and an easy one to cook. It is popular in the Caribbean; I first ate blackened grouper in Florida and fell in love.

- 3 tablespoons butter, plus additional for greasing pan
- 6 (4-ounce) grouper fillets, pin bones removed
- 1/3 cup homestyle breadcrumbs or cornflake crumbs
- 1/4 teaspoon ground white pepper
- 3 tablespoons grated Parmesan or Romano cheese
- 1 lemon, divided
- 2 1/2 tablespoons white wine, divided

1. Preheat oven to 375°F.

2. Select a round or square Pyrex or oven-to-table baking dish that holds the fish snugly. Rub butter all over the bottom and sides of the pan. Place fillets into prepared pan. Set aside.

3. In a small bowl, combine breadcrumbs, white pepper, and cheese. Mix well. Set aside.

4. Place 3 tablespoons butter, juice from 1/2 lemon, and 1 1/2 tablespoons wine into a microwave-safe bowl. Microwave 40 seconds, or until the butter is melted.

5. Brush the butter mixture over the grouper. Top with the cheese/breadcrumb mixture, patting the crumbs to form a crust.

6. Squeeze the remaining lemon half over the fish. Drizzle remaining tablespoon wine around the fish, but not on the breadcrumbs.

7. Bake, uncovered, for 15-20 minutes, depending on the thickness of the fillet. The fish will flake easily and be opaque in the center when it is done.

CUBAN HALIBUT

- 1 cup vegetable stock, divided
- 6 (4-6-ounce) thick halibut or grouper fillets, skin and bones removed
  fine sea salt
  freshly ground black pepper
- 1 tablespoon olive oil
- 1 medium onion, peeled, and cut into 1/4-inch dice
- 1 small-medium green bell pepper, seeded and cut into 1/4-inch dice
- 1 cup heavy cream
- 3 tablespoons white wine
- 1 (15-ounce) can black beans, rinsed and drained

Halibut is a nice firm fish, which makes it perfect for grilling as long as your grates are well-oiled, but this preparation is the hands-down favorite in my house. In fact, there was one week last year when it was the requested meal 3 nights in a row. The flakey fish in the decadent cream with the pop of the black beans ... maybe Castro would have been in a better mood if someone had served him this dish.

If using grouper, cut the cooking time from 30 minutes to 10-15 minutes since it is a thinner fish.

1. Preheat oven to 375°F.

2. Place 1/2 cup stock into an oven-to-table casserole dish or ovenproof skillet. Add the fish. Season with salt and pepper. Cook, uncovered, for 30 minutes.

3. Meanwhile, in a large (12-14-inch) skillet, heat the oil over medium heat. Sauté the onion and green pepper until onion is translucent and soft; do not allow to brown, 5-6 minutes. Add the heavy cream and remaining 1/2 cup vegetable stock. Bring to just a boil; reduce heat and simmer until heated through. Stir in the wine and black beans and heat through.

4. Transfer the fish to plates or a platter. Spoon the sauce over the fillets and around the plate.

CHILEAN SEA BASS WITH COCONUT-MANGO SALSA

1 mango, peeled, pitted, cut into ¼-inch dice

½ red onion, peeled, cut into ¼-inch dice

1 tablespoon lime juice, fresh or bottled

⅓ cup sweetened flaked coconut

2 teaspoons chopped fresh cilantro leaves

¼ cup blanched slivered almonds

fine sea salt

freshly ground black pepper

olive oil

6 (4-5 ounce) portions center cut Chilean sea bass or mahi mahi fillets, skin removed

1 lime, halved

This refreshing quick dish is perfect for outdoor summer dining. Chilean sea bass is a nice fish for grilling since its high fat content makes it very hard to overcook. There are some sustainability issues involving sea bass, so when it is hard to find or too pricey, mahi mahi can stand in very well in this recipe.

1. Prepare the salsa: Place the mango, red onion, lime juice, coconut, cilantro, and almonds into a large bowl. Season with ¼ teaspoon salt and ¼ teaspoon pepper. Mix well. Set aside.

2. Season the sea bass with a light sprinkle of salt and pepper. Brush with olive oil on both sides.

3. Brush a grill or grill pan with olive oil. Heat over medium heat. Add the fish and cook for 7 minutes. Flip each fillet over and cook for an additional 3-4 minutes on the second side.

4. Remove the fish to a platter and top with Coconut-Mango salsa. Squeeze the lime halves over the dish.

SOLE WITH PEACH-BASIL REDUCTION

Dover Sole meunière is a classic French dish that Julia Child made famous here in America by promoting it as the first meal she ate in France. I took liberties with the basic recipe and added other dimensions with the fruit and basil. In the right season, you could grill fresh peach slices and use them in place of the canned.

6 (4-6 ounce) fillets sole, flounder, or tilapia

fine sea salt

freshly ground black pepper

juice of ½ lemon

4 large eggs, beaten with a whisk or an immersion blender

1 cup all-purpose flour

2 tablespoons canola oil, plus additional as needed

2 cups orange juice

1 tablespoon parve chicken consommé powder

handful fresh basil leaves, stems discarded, stacked, sliced into ribbons

1 (15-ounce) can peach halves, drained, each sliced into 6 slices

1. Season both sides of each fillet with salt and pepper.

2. Drizzle the lemon juice on the fish.

3. Place the beaten eggs into a shallow pan and the flour in a second one. Dip the fish into the flour and then into the egg.

4. Heat the canola oil in a large (12-14-inch) skillet over medium heat. Add the fish in a single layer and lightly sear until golden brown. Flip and cook for 3 minutes longer on the second side. This will need to be done in batches. Add more oil as needed. Transfer to a platter as each is done.

5. Meanwhile, pour the orange juice and consommé powder into a small pot. Cook, whisking, over medium-high heat until reduced by half. It will have a slightly thickened consistency.

6. Add the basil and peach slices.

7. Pour the sauce over the fish. Serve hot.

SALMON NIÇOISE BURGERS

Good for your brain and a snap to prepare. A winning combination and a real no-brainer for a great lunch or dinner.

1½ pounds salmon fillet, skin and pin bones removed

1½ tablespoons chopped fresh dill

1½ tablespoons capers, rinsed and drained

1½ tablespoons mayonnaise

8 kalamata or niçoise olives, pitted and chopped

juice of ½ lemon

½ teaspoon fine sea salt, plus more for sprinkling

¼ teaspoon freshly ground black pepper, plus more for sprinkling

1 tablespoon olive oil, plus more for drizzling

6 hamburger buns

½ small red onion, peeled, thinly sliced

2 plum tomatoes, thinly sliced

1. Slice the salmon into 2-inch strips. Place into the bowl of a food processor fitted with a metal "S" blade. Using on-off pulses, chop the salmon; don't pulse too many times or you will grind the salmon too finely. Transfer the salmon to a medium bowl. Mix in the dill, capers, mayonnaise, olives, lemon juice, ½ teaspoon salt, and ¼ teaspoon pepper. Form into 6 (heaping ⅓-cup) patties.

2. Heat the oil in a nonstick skillet or grill pan over medium-high heat. Cook the salmon burgers for 3-4 minutes per side, until just cooked through.

3. To serve, place each burger on a bun. Top with red onion, a slice or two of tomato, a drizzle of olive oil, and a light sprinkling of salt and pepper.

OLIVE OIL-POACHED HERBED HALIBUT

olive oil (2-3 cups, or more, depending on size of dish)

3-4 lemons, very thinly sliced

leaves from 2 parsley sprigs, thinly sliced

leaves from 2 sprigs cilantro, thinly sliced

leaves from 2 stems basil, thinly sliced

4 (6-ounce) portions skinless halibut fillets; cut into large squares if possible

fine sea salt

freshly ground black pepper

1½ tablespoons capers, drained and finely chopped

>> *After the fish is cooked, use the poaching oil to sauté green beans or to fluff mashed potatoes – both would be great side dishes to this recipe.*

Poaching fish in oil results in exceptionally tender fish. It melts in your mouth and, due to the low cooking temperature, actually absorbs less fat than fried fish. The quality of oil is very important, so buy a good fruity olive oil – and you must use thick fillets such as salmon, tuna, cod, mahi mahi, grouper, and, of course, halibut.

For an Asian twist, blend canola and toasted sesame oil; then follow the same technique.

Pair this dish with a crisp salad or vegetables for a great contrast in textures.

1. Preheat oven to 300°F.

2. Select a small Pyrex or oven-to-table casserole dish that fits the fish perfectly and snugly without the fillets overlapping, such as an 8 x 8-inch dish.

3. Pour 1 cup of olive oil into the dish.

4. Arrange a layer of lemon slices in the dish. Toss on half of the parsley, cilantro, and basil.

5. Pat the fish dry. Season with salt and pepper on both sides. Place into the dish in a single layer without overlapping fillets. Top with remaining herbs.

6. Sprinkle on the capers and rub them into the fish. Cover with overlapping slices of lemon. Add enough oil to submerge everything. Press down on the lemons to compact everything into the dish.

7. Bake, uncovered, for 45 minutes. Using a slotted spoon, remove the halibut from the oil. Serve with some of the lemon and capers. Can be served hot or room temperature. If serving at room temperature, remove from the oil right after cooking.

3 ears corn on the cob,
in their husks

6 (6-ounce) tilapia fillets
fine sea salt
freshly ground black
pepper

1½ cups fine cornmeal

4 teaspoons dried
oregano, crushed

½ teaspoon cayenne

1 cup all-purpose flour
canola oil

½ jalapeño pepper, seeded
and minced
see p. 260

½ cup loosely packed fresh
cilantro leaves, chopped
zest and juice of 1 lime

1 cup black beans (from
a 15-ounce can), rinsed
and drained

2 teaspoons sweetened
flaked coconut

1 firm, ripe plum tomato,
cut into ¼-inch dice

CRISPY TILAPIA WITH CORN SALSA

Tilapia is the most popular farm-raised fish in America; make sure yours is from the US, not from China or Taiwan. The mercury in these imported fish is at unsafe levels. Tilapia is mild and has no fishy taste, making it perfect for kids or people who are new to fish dinners. The cornmeal in the recipe gives it nice crunch and complements the corn in the salsa.

1. Preheat oven to 425°F. Using scissors, cut off the tips of each ear of corn, including the silky tops. Leaving on the husks, wet thoroughly. Place on a cookie sheet and roast for 15-20 minutes until the husks are dark and brown. Remove from oven and set aside.

2. Season the tilapia fillets with salt and pepper.

3. In a shallow pan mix the cornmeal, oregano, and cayenne.

4. Place the flour into a second shallow pan.

5. Dredge one side of each tilapia fillet in the flour, shaking off excess, and then the other side of each in the cornmeal mixture.

6. Pour a coating of canola oil into the bottom of a nonstick skillet. Heat over medium until hot but not smoking. Add the fish, cornmeal-side-down, and cook for 3 minutes until golden. Shake the pan to make sure the fish is not sticking and there is enough oil. Flip each fillet and cook for 3 minutes on the second side. Re-oil as needed between batches and wipe out any cornmeal bits if they start to burn.

7. Remove and discard the corn husks and silks. Cut the corn from the cobs into a large bowl. (See head note on page 78 for an easy way to do this.) Add the jalapeño, cilantro, lime zest and juice, black beans, coconut, and tomato. Mix well.

8. Serve each portion of fish with some of the corn salsa.

PARVE
YIELD: 6 SERVINGS

6 (6-ounce) red snapper fillets, with skin, or lemon sole, skinless

fine sea salt

freshly ground black pepper

all-purpose flour

3 tablespoons olive oil

½ cup white wine

15 Gaeta or kalamata olives, (⅓ cup) pitted, coarsely chopped

2 teaspoons capers, rinsed well, chopped

1 large beefsteak tomato, cut into ½-inch dice

8 fresh basil leaves, stemmed, finely chopped

juice of ½ lemon

1 teaspoon dried oregano

¼ teaspoon red pepper flakes

2 handfuls fresh baby spinach

pine nuts, for garnish

RED SNAPPER WITH WARM OLIVES, CAPERS, AND TOMATO

Although red snapper is hard to find these days, buy it when you do, and try it with this recipe. Purchase it with skin.

It is fun and easy to pit the olives, just press each one on your cutting board with your palm and the pit pops right out.

1. Cut diagonal score marks in the skin side of the red snapper fillets. Skip this step if using lemon sole.

2. Season the fish on both sides with salt and pepper. Dust both sides with flour, shaking off excess.

3. Heat the olive oil in a large (12-14 inch) skillet over medium heat. Add the red snapper, skin-side-down, in a single layer; you will need to do this in batches. Cook 2-3 minutes until golden brown. Flip each fillet to finish on the other side. Remove to platter and cover with foil to keep warm. Cook remaining fillets.

4. Add the wine to the pan, allowing it to bubble. Add the olives, capers, tomato, basil, lemon juice, oregano, red pepper flakes, and spinach. Cook until the spinach has wilted, about 2 minutes. Spoon this mixture over the fish. Sprinkle with pine nuts. Serve hot.

TANDOORI SALMON

nonstick cooking spray

2 pounds salmon fillet, with skin, pin bones removed

1/2 cup plain yogurt or nondairy yogurt

1 tablespoon lemon juice

2 cloves fresh garlic, minced

1 teaspoon grated fresh ginger

3/4 teaspoon curry powder

1/2 teaspoon paprika

1/2 teaspoon fine sea salt

1 tablespoon chopped fresh cilantro leaves

My family is timid about the Indian spices but if yours isn't, you can go heavier on the curry powder.

1. Spray a nonreactive dish with nonstick cooking spray. Place the salmon into the dish.

2. In a medium bowl, whisk the yogurt, lemon juice, garlic, ginger, curry, paprika, salt, and cilantro. Pour the marinade evenly over the fish. Cover and marinate in the refrigerator for 4 hours.

3. Preheat oven to 450°F. While preheating, remove the fish from the refrigerator.

4. Bake in marinade, uncovered, until the fish is opaque when tested with a knife, about 20 minutes. Transfer to platter.

PASTA/EGGS

GAME PLAN

There are hundreds of pasta shapes; here is a sampling.

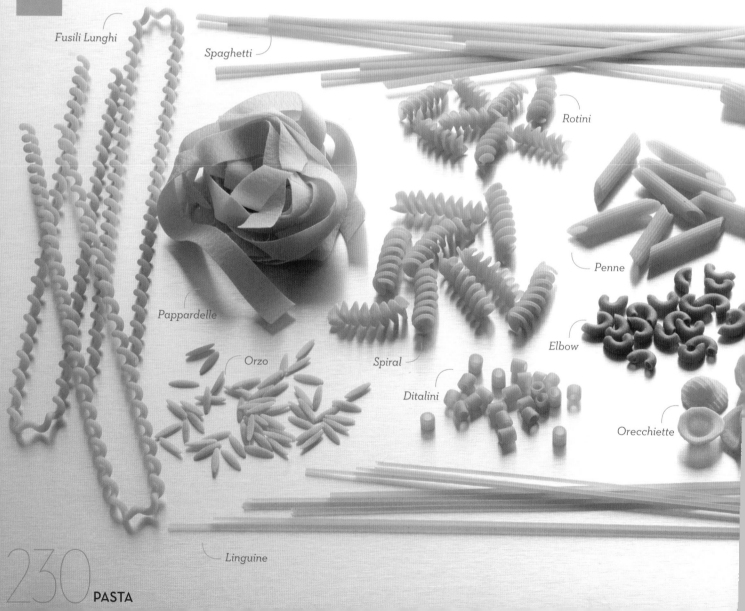

Fusili Lunghi

Spaghetti

Rotini

Pappardelle

Penne

Orzo

Spiral

Elbow

Ditalini

Orecchiette

Linguine

» *Flat pastas are best with thin sauces; other shapes have nooks and crannies to catch chunkier sauces. Think about the kind of sauce being used when selecting a pasta shape.*

» *Most dried pasta doubles in volume when cooked. The general rule is that one pound of dry pasta or freshly made pasta will serve six as an appetizer or four as a main course.*

Ziti

Farfalle

Angel Hair

Pasta is the world's favorite food; some sort of noodle is served in almost every country in the world. It is cheap, easy to prepare, and the ultimate comfort food. Pasta is versatile. It can be dressed up with vegetables and homemade sauces or dressed down with simple additions like butter, Parmesan, or jarred sauce. Either way, it always tastes good and fills your stomach. It produces energy in the form of carbohydrates, which is why athletes eat pasta regularly. Pasta can also be stored for a long time, so a box or two should always be in your pantry.

Pasta should be cooked al dente. The phrase is Italian and means "to the tooth," which comes from testing the pasta's consistency with your teeth. Pasta cooked al dente should be fully cooked, but not overly soft or mushy. You want the pasta to be a bit on the firm side, but not chewy or crunchy. This is especially important when you're using it in a recipe that requires further cooking.

Follow these simple tips for perfect results every time.

› Cook pasta in a large pot of boiling salted water.

› Use a large pinch of kosher salt to flavor the water; it will bring out the best flavor in the pasta.

› If the water is not at a full boil when the pasta is added, the starch in the pasta dissolves and the pasta will turn out gummy. The intense heat of boiling hot water "sets" the starch.

› If there is not enough room for the pasta to cook and move around, it will clump together.

› Stir with a long-handled spoon, wooden or otherwise, right after you add the pasta and then again every few minutes.

› Never add oil to the pasta water. Oil will prevent sauces from adhering to the pasta.

› Don't cover the pot once the pasta is added.

› Pasta overcooks quickly. Don't rely solely on the times on the box. Boxes will give you a range for al dente results. Always take a sample bite at the lower end of the time estimate. The pasta should have a slight resistance when biting into it, but should not be soft, overdone, or have a hard center. Pasta will continue to cook after it is removed from the heat and drained.

GAME PLAN

Eggs are a low-cost protein that are packed with nutrients. Eggs can be used in any meal, from omelettes to frittatas, scrambled eggs, shakshouka, quiches, fried rice dishes, desserts and more. Eggs should be a staple that you always have on hand.

Egg shell and yolk colors vary based on the breed of hen that laid the egg. They have no effect on quality or nutrition. Hens with white feathers and ears lay white eggs. Breeds with red feathers and ears lay brown eggs. The yolk colors vary based on the diet of the hen.

The ropey strands of egg white that anchor the yolk in place in the center of the thick white are called the chalazae. They are not imperfections. In fact, the more prominent the chalazae, the fresher the egg. Chalazae does not interfere with the cooking or beating of the white and do not need to be removed.

Eggs come in various sizes. They are measured by weight. The 3 most common supermarket sizes are large, extra large, and jumbo. Although any size egg may be used for poaching, scrambling, or frying, most recipes (including all of mine) for baking dishes and desserts are based on the use of large eggs.

Eggs need to be kept cold to maintain health and safety. Store them in their cartons so that you know the expiration date, and keep them in the coldest part of your refrigerator. A cold egg left out at room temperature can sweat, facilitating the growth of bacteria that could contaminate the egg. After eggs are refrigerated, it is important to keep them that way. In baking, room temperature eggs beat better. However, remember that refrigerated eggs should not be left out more than two hours, so keep your eye on the amount of time they are left out, especially in a warm kitchen.

Use older eggs to make hard-boiled eggs, as the shells will come off more easily after being cooked.

Liquid egg whites are pasteurized egg whites. This product contains no fat or cholesterol or any of the essential nutrients found in the yolk. To substitute for egg whites fresh from the shell, 2 tablespoons of product equals 1 large egg white.

» *If you don't know if an egg is raw or hard-boiled, spin it on a hard surface. If the egg spins quickly without taking off or flying off in one direction, the egg is hard-boiled. Raw eggs will have a wobbly and unsteady spin.*

» *If you are making Deviled Eggs, place the carton of eggs on its side for a day. The yolk will then center itself directly in the middle of the white. This is aesthetically pleasing for this recipe.*

jumbo   extra large   large

HARD-BOILED AND SOFT-BOILED EGGS

› Select eggs that don't have any cracks.

› If your eggs are at room temperature for 20-30 minutes, they will need 1 minute less of cooking time than eggs right out of the fridge.

› For even cooking, select a pot big enough to hold the number of eggs you are making in a single layer, but small enough so that they don't have too much room to knock into each other.

› Cover with cold water by an inch.

› Do not add salt; it will make the eggs rubbery.

› If you are hard-boiling them, use eggs that are a few days old; they will be easier to peel. There is a simple way to test the freshness of an egg: Place the egg in a bowl of water; if it lies on its side, it is very fresh. As it ages, the air pocket inside the egg grows, which buoys the egg so it stands on one end. If the egg floats to the top, it is past its prime and should be tossed out.

STEP 1 Bring the eggs in a pot of water to just a boil on high heat. Immediately remove the pot from the heat.

STEP 2 Cover the pot and allow the eggs to stand in the hot water.

soft-boiled

For soft-boiled: Allow to stand for 4-6 minutes.

For hard-boiled: Allow to stand for 15-16 minutes. Do not overcook or a green layer will form around the yolk.

STEP 3 Once the cooking time is over, use a slotted spoon to transfer the eggs to a bowl of ice water for 10 minutes to stop the cooking.

› Peel hard-boiled eggs by rolling on your work surface and using the weight of your palm to crack the shell all over instead of cracking in one spot against the side of a bowl, which may break into the white.

hard-boiled

WHIPPING EGG WHITES

Start with a clean bowl and beaters. Make sure there are no traces of grease in the bowl and on the beaters or any yolk in the whites. Bring the whites to room temperature for 15 minutes.

STEP 1

Whip the egg whites right before using them so they don't deflate. Beat at a medium speed until foamy. At this point, you can add a pinch of cream of tartar for stability.

STEP 2

Raise the speed. As more air is incorporated the foam will begin to thicken. When you raise the beater you will see soft peaks that fall over to one side.

STEP 3

If you keep beating, you will see that the beater can leave distinct tracks in the whites. The peaks formed when you lift the beaters will be stiffer and retain their shape longer. Don't go beyond these stiff peaks or the foam may collapse and separate.

BUTTERNUT SQUASH BROKEN LASAGNA

2 (12-ounce) boxes frozen cooked winter squash

5 ounces frozen chopped spinach see p. 254

2 cups ricotta cheese

2 cloves fresh garlic, minced

1/2 teaspoon onion powder

1/2 teaspoon fine sea salt

1/4 teaspoon garlic powder

1/4 teaspoon freshly ground black pepper

12 fresh sage leaves (about 1/4 cup loosely packed), chopped

1 (16-ounce) box standard lasagna noodles, not the no-bake kind

1 cup heavy cream

2 (10-ounce) bags frozen butternut squash cubes

1/4 cup pumpkin seeds, shelled

1/3 cup Parmesan cheese

Many of us are familiar with Southland butternut squash from old squash kugel recipes. Do not use it in this recipe. If you read the nutritional information, you will see that it is a prepared product with other ingredients, including margarine and oils. This recipe needs plain, pure squash. The value of fat should be zero and a serving should have 45 calories and 2 grams of sugar.

Rigatoni can substitute for the broken lasagna noodles.

1. Preheat oven to 425°F.

2. Place the frozen winter squash in a pot over medium heat. Cook until it is defrosted. Add the spinach and cook until it defrosts as well.

3. In a large bowl, mix the ricotta, garlic, onion powder, salt, garlic powder, pepper, and chopped sage leaves. Set aside.

4. Break the lasagna noodles into 3-4 pieces each and cook noodles according to package directions, until al dente.

5. Drain the noodles and rinse with plenty of cold water. Drain very well.

6. Mix the noodles into the ricotta. Add the winter squash and spinach. Stir well. Mix in the heavy cream and butternut squash cubes. Transfer to 9 x 13-inch oven-to-table casserole or baking dish. Smooth the top with a spatula. Sprinkle on the pumpkin seeds and Parmesan.

7. Bake, uncovered, for 30 minutes. Serve hot.

olive oil

1 large Italian eggplant
(1½ pounds), with skin,
ends trimmed, cut into
½-inch dice

1 red onion, peeled,
cut into ½-inch dice

3 cloves fresh garlic,
thinly sliced

1 (6-ounce) can tomato
paste

½ teaspoon paprika

½ teaspoon smoked
paprika

⅛ teaspoon cayenne
zest from ½ large
or 1 medium orange

⅓ cup golden raisins (can
rehydrate in mint tea)

1 cup white wine, divided

1 cup water

1 (16-ounce) box rotini
pasta

1 teaspooon mint leaves,
finely chopped

1 teaspoon 2-4 parsley
sprigs, chopped

fine sea salt

freshly ground black
pepper

ROTINI WITH EGGPLANT CAPONATA

Feel your tastebuds come alive with this wonderful dish. Caponata has a long list of ingredients, but don't let that scare you off. The payoff is like a Sicilian ratatouille that has layers of flavors and textures.

1. Heat ¼-cup olive oil in a large, high-sided skillet over medium heat. Make sure the oil is hot or the eggplant will soak it up. Add the eggplant in batches. Don't over-crowd the pan so the eggplant won't steam and can caramelize, 3-4 minutes, stirring occasionally. Add another tablespoon or two of oil for the second batch if the pan is dry. Remove from the pan. Set the eggplant aside.

2. Add 2 tablespoons olive oil to the pan and heat over medium-high. Add the diced onion and sweat them, so they cook but don't turn brown, 6-7 minutes. Add the garlic and cook for 5 minutes longer. Add half of the tomato paste, stirring for 3-4 minutes. Add second half of the tomato paste. Cook for another 2 minutes.

3. In a small bowl, mix the paprika, smoked paprika, cayenne, and orange zest. Stir in the raisins. Add the spiced raisins to the pan with ½ cup wine. Scrape the bottom of the pan to pick up bits of flavor. Raise the heat; cook for 1 minute so the wine can reduce a little. Add remaining ½ cup wine along with 1 cup water. Return the eggplant to the pan. Reduce heat to medium-low and cook the caponata for 5-6 minutes, stirring every few minutes, till bubbly and slightly thickened.

4. Cook pasta in salted water according to package directions until al dente. Drain, rinse, and toss with a drizzle of olive oil. Mix in the mint and parsley. Season with salt and pepper. Transfer to serving bowl. Top with Eggplant Caponata. Serve hot or at room temperature.

1 (16-ounce) box orecchiette pasta

1 bunch (about 1 pound) broccoli rabe

4 tablespoons olive oil, divided

6 cloves fresh garlic, thinly sliced, then chopped

1/4 teaspoon red pepper flakes

1/4 teaspoon fine sea salt

grated Parmesan cheese, if using for dairy

ORECCHIETTE WITH BROCCOLI RABE

This pasta, pronounced, "oh-reck-ee-ET-tay" means "little ears" in Italian, as they are shaped like tiny ears or bowls.

Broccoli rabe is also called broccoli raab, rapini, and Chinese broccoli. It is a relative of the turnip and cabbage families. The leaves, stems, and flower heads are cooked (broiled, stir-fried, braised, sautéed, or steamed) and eaten just like regular broccoli; they have a flavor similar to broccoli but much more pungent. The nutty flavor and slightly bitter taste may take some getting used to but once you acquire the taste, it's addictive and really healthy.

1. Cook pasta in salted water according to package directions until al dente.

2. While the pasta is cooking, trim off the bottom 4-6 inches from the broccoli rabe and discard, leaving the stems and florets. Chop into 2-inch pieces.

3. Heat 2 tablespoons olive oil in a large (12-14-inch) skillet over medium heat. Add the broccoli rabe and stir. Cover the pan and cook for 2 minutes.

4. Uncover pan and add the garlic, red pepper flakes, and salt. Stir; shake the pan to keep the garlic from burning. Add remaining 2 tablespoons olive oil. Re-cover the pan and cook for 6 minutes longer.

5. Toss with the pasta. For dairy meals, sprinkle with grated Parmesan.

GNOCCHI

4 large Idaho or Russet potatoes

1 tablespoon extra-virgin olive oil

1³⁄₄ cups all-purpose or "OO" flour, divided, plus more for kneading

1 large egg

kosher salt

>> You can freeze the uncooked shaped gnocchi on a floured baking sheet. Once frozen, store in sealed container in freezer for up to 1 month.

Gnocci, small dumplings originating in Italy, are treated like pasta: top with creamy mushroom, tomato-based, or cheese sauces, meat ragu, bolognaise sauce, etc. Add cooked gnocchi to tomato or chicken soup instead of noodles.

Gnocchi dough can be prepared a day ahead. Cover with plastic wrap and store in fridge. Cook right before serving to keep them light and fluffy.

Making gnocchi together is a great family activity! Get everyone involved, helping rice, knead, and form the gnocchi — and then watch them eat!

Authentic gnocchi flour is very fine "OO" Italian flour; the gnocchi will be light and delicate. Although hard to find, it's worth the effort. Ask your supermarket manager to stock "OO" flour.

A ricer makes lighter gnocchi than mashing the potatoes; having one is worthwhile, as it can be used for many recipes. A bench cutter helps form the gnocchi without crushing them, and it's handy for scooping them up to drop into the pot.

1. Preheat oven to 375°F. Wash and dry the potatoes. Wrap each in foil. Bake for 60 minutes, until you can pierce them with the tip of a knife. Allow to stand until cool enough to handle.

2. Peel and discard the skin. Push the potatoes through a potato ricer or food mill into a large bowl. Add the oil. Sprinkle in 1 cup flour and add the egg. Knead the mixture until it starts to form a dough, adding in the remaining flour a little at a time, until the dough is slightly sticky but not sticking. You may have a bit of flour left or you may need 1 tablespoon or so more, depending on the time of year, humidity, etc. Go by feel; result should be a smooth dough that has layers of flour.

3. Lightly dust your work surface with flour. Divide the dough into 16 balls. Roll one ball into a long, thin, 13-inch log, and sprinkle the log with flour. Using a bench cutter, cut the log into small ¹⁄₂-³⁄₄-inch pillow-shaped pieces. Roll each into a ball the size of a small gumball.

4. Place a ball of dough onto the back of a fork, pushing gently into the tines. Using your thumb, roll it down gently and allow it to fall off the fork. Sprinkle the gnocchi with flour. Continue until all the dough is used and all the gnocchi are rolled.

5. Fill large pot ³/₄-full of water. Add salt until the water tastes salty. Bring to a gentle simmer; don't allow to boil vigorously.

6. To keep them from sticking together, cook gnocchi in batches. Gently scoop up some of the gnocchi with the bench cutter so you don't smush them. Add to the pot. Stir the perimeter of the pot to create a swirling motion in the water without touching the gnocchi. In 1-2 minutes they will float to the surface. Allow them to cook for 1 minute longer. Scoop the gnocchi out with a slotted spoon and serve with sauce of choice.

SPINACH-ARTICHOKE FARFALLE

5   tablespoons butter

4   tablespoons all-purpose flour

4   cups milk

$^1/_2$ teaspoon garlic powder

2   teaspoons fine sea salt

1   (16-ounce) box farfalle pasta

1   (12- 14-ounce) can or ($8^1/_2$-ounce) jar artichoke hearts, rinsed, roughly chopped

6   ounces fresh baby spinach leaves

$^1/_2$ cup shredded mozzarella cheese

$^1/_4$ cup grated Parmesan or Romano cheese

    freshly ground black pepper

If you can't find canned artichoke hearts with proper kosher certification, you can use $8^1/_2$ ounces of the jarred marinated ones; just wash them very well to remove the oil and spices and then quarter them.

1. In a medium saucepan, heat the butter over medium-low heat until just melted. Add the flour and whisk until smooth. Cook until the mixture turns a light golden color, about 6-7 minutes. This will cook out the floury taste.

2. Meanwhile, heat the milk in a separate small pot until just starting to bubble. Add the hot milk to the butter mixture, 1 cup at a time, whisking continuously, until very smooth. Whisk in the garlic powder. Bring to a boil. Simmer for 10 minutes, whisking constantly. Whisk in the salt.

3. Meanwhile, in a large pot of boiling salted water, cook the pasta until al dente according to package directions. When you drain it, reserve 1 cup of cooking water, which you may need to thin the finished sauce with. Return the drained pasta to the pot. Add the chopped artichokes and the spinach. Pour the white sauce into the pasta and cook over medium heat until the spinach is wilted and the artichokes are warmed through. If the sauce is too thick, thin with some of the reserved pasta water. Sprinkle in mozzarella and Parmesan cheeses. Cook until the mozzarella is melted. Transfer to a serving bowl. Serve hot. Sprinkle with freshly ground black pepper.

POACHED EGGS WITH HOLLANDAISE

POACHED EGGS

- water
- 1 tablespoon white vinegar
- 6 large eggs

HOLLANDAISE SAUCE

- 2 tablespoons apple cider vinegar
- 2 large egg yolks
- ½ teaspoon cracked black pepper
- ½ teaspoon fine sea salt
- 12 tablespoons butter, melted, warm

- 6 pieces of toast or English muffins

The vinegar helps keep the egg from separating and floating out into the water. If your whites are floating too far, try this trick shared by my food stylist Melanie Dubberley. Remove the top and the bottom from an empty 8-ounce can of water chestnuts and clean it well. (A water chestnut can is taller than a tuna can, so it works best, as it will be above the water line when placed in the skillet. Any 3½-inch-wide by 2⅛-inch-high can will work if both ends can be removed). Spray inside of can with nonstick cooking spray. Place it into the skillet. Pour the egg into the can. Once the form is set, remove can and finish poaching the egg.

1. Fill a large skillet a little more than halfway with water. Add the vinegar. Over medium heat, bring it to just below a simmer. You should see bubbles forming on the surface but not hear bubbling and popping.

2. Crack each egg into its own small ramekin or teacup. Using a silicone spatula or slotted spoon, gently swirl the water in the pot. Getting as close to the water as possible, gently pour the egg in, using a spoon to push the white in toward the middle as it initially sets. The white may float away; push it back gently toward the center. If it sticks to the bottom, carefully slide your spoon or a spatula under it to loosen. Repeat with remaining eggs. Cover and cook for 4 minutes, or less time for a much runnier result. It should wobble a little when nudged.

3. Using a slotted spoon, remove the poached eggs from the water and set each on a piece of toast or English muffin.

4. Prepare the hollandaise sauce: Place the apple cider vinegar, egg yolks, pepper, and salt into a blender. Run the blender for 10 seconds. Very slowly, with the blender running, slowly dribble the butter through the opening in the top of the blender; the sauce will thicken immediately. If it is too thick, thin with a few drops of warm water. Drizzle over eggs.

THE PERFECT OMELETTE

prepared filling of choice

3 large eggs

1 tablespoon milk

⅛ teaspoon fine sea salt

⅛ teaspoon freshly ground
black pepper

2 teaspoons unsalted
butter

Make sure all of your fillings are pre-cooked. For special Sunday brunches, I set out a nice assortment of various fillings, including sautéed mushrooms, caramelized onions, cooked spinach, steamed asparagus, goat cheese crumbles, feta cheese, chopped tomatoes, and fresh herbs. Each guest takes a small bowl and selects the desired fillings. With 2-3 skillets going at once and everyone's fillings already portioned, my guests can then customize their omelettes quickly and efficiently, so we all eat together.

1. In a small bowl, whisk the eggs, milk, salt, and pepper. You can use a fork, but get some wrist action into it. Set aside.

2. Over medium-low heat, melt the butter in a nonstick 8-10-inch skillet, swirling it to coat the sides and bottom of the pan.

3. **A** Pour the eggs into the skillet and cook until just starting to set at the edges. Watch the heat — you don't want the eggs to burn. **B** Using a silicone spatula, push eggs toward center of pan. Swirl and tilt the pan so that egg flows onto the exposed surface. Once the omelette starts to set, turn off heat. **C** Add filling to one half of omelette. Allow to stand for 45-60 seconds. Turn heat to medium to be sure filling is melted or set; the eggs should still be yellow.

4. **D** Flip the second half over the filling **E** as you slide the omelette out of the pan onto a plate.

SHAKSHOUKA

1/4 cup olive oil

1 onion, peeled,
cut into 1/4-inch dice

1 jalapeño pepper, with
seeds, finely chopped
see p. 260

1/2 green pepper, seeds
removed, cut into
1/4-inch dice

6 cloves fresh garlic,
minced

1 (28-ounce) crushed
tomatoes

3/4 cup water, plus more
for thinning sauce

1/4 cup tomato paste

2 teaspoons sweet
or hot paprika

1/2 teaspoon fine sea salt

1/4 teaspoon freshly ground
black pepper

1/2 cup crumbled feta
cheese, optional for
dairy meals

8 large eggs

chopped parsley
for garnish

warm pita bread or
challah for serving

*I ate shakshouka on my last trip to Israel and have been
obsessed ever since. You'll love the dish as much as you'll
love saying the name. It can be served at any time during
the day, not just at breakfast. You can make it as mild or
spicy as you want by varying the kind of paprika you use.
This dish is especially nice for a brunch since it serves 8.*

1. Heat the oil in a large (14-inch) frying pan over medium heat. Add
the onion and sauté until shiny and transluscent, 4-6 minutes.
Add the jalapeño, green pepper, and garlic. Sauté for 5 minutes
or until fragrant.

2. Add the crushed tomatoes, 3/4 cup water, tomato paste, paprika,
salt, and pepper. Bring to a boil. Turn heat down; simmer for 15
minutes, adding water one tablespoon at a time if the sauce is
too thick, stirring occasionally.

3. Sprinkle in feta, if using. Make 8 wells, spaced evenly in the
sauce, and drop an egg into each well. Cover and poach for 6-8
minutes on medium heat, until egg whites are just set and yolks
are slightly runny.

4. Sprinkle with parsley. Serve with warm pita bread or challah.

PECAN PIE FRENCH TOAST BAKE

nonstick cooking spray

8 tablespoons (1 stick) unsalted butter, cut into chunks

¾ cup packed dark brown sugar

½ cup light pancake syrup

1 cup chopped pecans

1-2 (15-ounce) egg challahs, with crusts, ends trimmed, cut into ¾-inch thick slices

8 large eggs

1½ cups half and half

1 cup milk

¼ teaspoon freshly ground black pepper

Breakfast in bed is the worst-kept surprise of every Fishbein birthday. Everyone knows it is coming and the cat is certainly out of the bag when days before your birthday, siblings or kids start asking you about your dream breakfast meal. Pecan Pie French Toast played a starring role this year.

1. Preheat oven to 350°F. Spray a 9 x 13-inch baking dish with nonstick cooking spray; set aside.

2. Melt the butter and brown sugar in a small pot over medium heat. Whisk in the pancake syrup. Stir in the pecans. Set aside.

3. Tightly arrange the challah in slightly overlapping slices in the dish. A few slices may not fit; press the challah down to compact it.

4. In a medium bowl, whisk the eggs, half and half, milk, and pepper. Pour evenly over the challah. Press the challah down to soak in the egg mixture. Allow the bread to absorb the egg mixture for at least 20 minutes. You can prepare up to this step the night before; just cover with plastic wrap and store overnight in the refrigerator. Press the bread again to soak up more liquid. Pour the pecan mixture evenly over the top. Bake, uncovered, for 30-35 minutes, or until the bread is light brown and puffed. Serve warm.

TUNA QUICHE

Pair this with a big salad and you have a quick and easy weeknight meal.

- 1 (9-inch) deep-dish frozen pie crust, at room temperature for 15 minutes
- 4 ounces canned French fried onions, such as French's
- 3 large eggs
- 1 cup milk
- 1 cup sour cream, not fat-free
- 1 teaspoon fine sea salt
- 1/2 teaspoon Worcestershire sauce
- 4 ounces shredded cheddar cheese
- 1 (7-ounce) can white tuna, packed in water, drained

1. Preheat oven to 350°F. Set pie crust on cookie sheet to catch drips.

2. Place half of the fried onions into the pie crust.

3. In a medium bowl whisk the eggs. When lightly beaten, whisk in milk, sour cream, salt, Worcestershire sauce, cheese, and tuna. Pour into crust. You may have a little extra filling, depending on the brand of crust. Top with remaining fried onions.

4. Bake, uncovered, for 45-50 minutes, until set. Don't overbake. Cool slightly. Cut into wedges.

SIDE DISHES

GAME PLAN

Nothing heralds the changing of the seasons better than vegetables. Each year I eagerly await asparagus, artichokes, and peas in spring; peaches, berries, tomatoes, and corn in summer; pumpkins, pears, and apples in autumn; sunchokes, squashes, kale, and cabbages in winter. The vegetables and fruits themselves almost dictate what is on my menus.

In this country it can be confusing, since almost everything is available all year round, flown in from far corners of the world. The whole "eat locally" philosophy centers around buying what local farmers raise. This can mean only in their proper season. It emphasizes cutting out the global trek that out-of-season veggies flown in from far-off places are forced to take. Not only do they lack in flavor, they have a negative effect on local farming economies as well as on the environment. Educate yourself about what is in season in your local area and try to find local sources for the vegetables and fruits.

Out-of-season produce benefits from roasting to intensify its flavors. When a vegetable or fruit is out of season, head over to the freezer case. You will do better budget-wise, and in some cases frozen can mean nutritionally healthier, since the veggies are frozen at their peak of freshness.

When you need only 5 ounces of frozen spinach, defrost the box (usually 10 ounces) for 15 minutes, then, using a serrated knife, cut right through the box. You can refreeze the other half or defrost it fully and use it in a rice dish, pasta sauce, or your next omelette.

STORING FRESH PRODUCE

› Keep produce in perforated plastic bags in the produce drawer of the refrigerator. Use scissors to snip holes in the bag.

› Keep fruits and vegetables separated, in different drawers, because ethylene can build up in the fridge, causing spoilage.

› Discard vegetables that show signs of rotting, because they tend to spread rot quickly to other vegetables in the bin.

› Tomatoes, potatoes, onion, whole heads of garlic, and winter squash store best at room temperature.

› Before using, wash your produce to rid it of pesticides, grit, dirt, and germs from being handled.

VEGETABLE TECHNIQUES

BLANCHING

Blanching is a technique used to capture the freshest flavor and brightest color of vegetables.

STEP 1 Briefly cook the vegetables in boiling water until they are no longer raw, then, **STEP 2** quickly transfer to a bowl of ice water to "shock" them, stopping the cooking and setting the color. This is a great way to retain vitamins. This technique also works well for vegetables that need to be partially cooked or parboiled and then finished in another way.

ROASTING

Roasting is my favorite way to coax great flavor out of veggies by naturally caramelizing their sugars and starches. This results in crisp exteriors and moist interiors. Just make sure you cut the veggies into uniform pieces so they cook evenly. One of my favorite sides that has no set amount and varied ingredients is roasted root veggies. Cover a big cookie sheet with parchment. Toss on cut up carrots, parsnips, acorn and butternut squashes (which I don't even peel, just chunk up and seed), sunchokes, sweet potatoes, and leeks. Make sure all are about the same size. If you are short on time, cut them smaller; if not, I like them in medium chunks. I either drizzle with olive oil, rosemary, and coarse sea salt or toss with regular or date honey, olive oil, and a little thyme. I toss well with gloved hands to coat everything evenly, and roast uncovered at high heat until golden, sticky, sweet, and fabulous.

When roasting vegetables, make sure your oven is fully preheated and that you select the proper pan. One of the most popular recipes that I have ever written was for Cauliflower Popcorn, in ***Kosher by Design Entertains***. When I eat it at other people's homes, I immediately know what kind of pan they used for roasting. In the photo on the right you see cauliflower that was roasted on a cookie sheet with low sides, and the same amount of florets in a high-sided roasting pan. The florets roasted on the cookie sheet are crisp and caramelized. Each

STEP 1

STEP 2

floret is a delicious morsel. Heated air is able to reach the cauliflower on all sides, giving a perfectly roasted result. By leaving room between florets, there is no steaming, so no mushy cauliflower. In the roasting pan, the heat is reflected from the sides of the pan, heating the florets, causing them to give off their water content. The overcrowding causes steaming and a mushy result.

SOME SIDE DISH COMPONENTS

Whether you braise, stir fry, purée, bread, roast, grill, or fry, there are endless side dishes you can produce using vegetables. Some of my favorites include:

SPAGHETTI SQUASH

Spaghetti squash is a fun, low-calorie vegetable that can be seasoned in dozens of ways. It can be cooked in the microwave, boiled, or baked. My preferred method is to roast it whole, right on the grates in a preheated 350° F oven for 1 hour (a few minutes more for a very large one). It is done when you can depress the sides. Just do this gently so you don't puncture the squash, plunging your finger into hot squash flesh. The color may turn a bit deeper as well. I then let it cool, cut it in half horizontally, and pull out the seeds. Using a fork, I scrape the spaghetti-like strands into a bowl and use them in recipes or simply season with some olive oil and spices or marinara sauce.

spaghetti squash

SUMMER SQUASH

Summer squashes, such as yellow squash and zucchini, are great for stir fries, grilling, or steaming. They are mild in flavor and cook pretty quickly. The blossoms are a Tuscan delicacy; if you can find them, they can be battered and fried.

SUNCHOKES

Sunchokes, also called Jerusalem artichokes, are the root of the sunflower plant. They are knobby-looking. Purchase ones that look firm and unshriveled. Peel them for soups, but for roasting, just wash very well, cut in half, season, and roast as you would a potato.

sunchokes

EGGPLANTS

Eggplants come in all sorts of shapes and sizes. I am a big fan of the deep purple, skinny Asian eggplants usually sold in Asian markets. They have no bitter seeds and require no salting. I use them in stir fries, in pasta sauces, and for roasting.

Italian eggplants are great for baked dishes and grilling. Look for firm, unblemished eggplants. The greener the stem, the fresher the eggplant. Slice them into $1/2$–1-inch-thick rounds, with or without the peel, or cut into cubes. Before cooking, sprinkle with salt to remove bitterness. Let rest in a colander for up to an hour; then rinse, pat dry, and use as needed in the recipe. When sautéing, keep extra oil on hand because they really soak it up.

PORTOBELLO MUSHROOMS

Portobello mushrooms are oversized creminis. Select ones that are firm and plump, not slippery or dried. They have a nice texture and a deep flavor that makes them perfect for roasting, grilling, and using in salads. The gills have a bit of a muddy flavor and will turn anything you cook with it dark, so remove them. Trim the stem and edges. Use a melon baller or a round-ended knife to scrape out the gills and discard.

GREENS

Greens such as kale, swiss chard, and bok choy are all great in big stir fries or steamed. Just remember to remove the thick stems before cooking.

BEANS AND LEGUMES

Beans are great as side dishes or as meatless main dishes. They are a source of high-quality protein, fiber, and complex carbs. Beans don't spoil, but they do get old and lose their moisture. This may cause them to require longer cooking times, and they will fall apart more readily when cooked. Store them in a cool dry place in closed packages. Always pick through and rinse beans, looking for pebbles and debris. Soak them with enough cold water to cover, in order to cut down on cooking time and to make them easier to digest. Six to eight hours at room temperature should suffice. Add

Italian Eggplant

Asian Eggplant

Portobello Mushrooms

Red Lentils   *French Lentils*

Yellow Split Peas   *Green Split Peas*

more water if the level gets too low. To see if beans have soaked long enough, cut one bean in half; it should be the same color throughout. Drain and rinse before cooking.

Do not add any salt or acid to the water in which you cook beans as it affects the way the skins break down and how they absorb water. You can add salt once the beans become tender.

When you are short on time, canned beans, which are fully cooked, are a fantastic way to make a quick soup, chili, or grain dish. To reduce sodium, rinse the beans before using.

Lentils and split peas do not need soaking and do not need as much cooking time as beans. They are done in about 30-45 minutes.

RICE

There are two main types of rice. **LONG-GRAIN** rices produce fluffy and separate grains when cooked. Examples are basmati and jasmine. **SHORT-GRAIN** rices are fatter rices that are stickier when cooked, such as Arborio and Carnaroli, used in sushi and risotto.

BROWN RICE is superior nutritionally to white rice and I like the taste and texture better. Rice usually cooks in one part dry rice to 2 parts water plus 1-2 teaspoons fat, like butter or oil. Bring to a boil, turn down to a simmer, and cook covered for the amount of time it states on the package. Once the rice is cooked, leave it in the covered pot for a few minutes to steam.

Rice dishes can also be made in the oven. They will need a little less water, since there is less evaporation. If I am making 1$\frac{1}{2}$ cups dry rice, I put it in an 8 x 8-inch casserole. I add 2$\frac{1}{2}$ cups boiling water or stock and the butter or oil. I then cover the dish tightly, and bake for about an hour at 375°F. Short-grain brown rice will take a little longer than white rice. Boxed **RICE PILAF** mixes, such as Near East brand, work beautifully using this method and you can make lots of boxes at once for a big crowd; an hour in the oven does it for these mixes. Always make more rice than you need and use the leftovers for another meal, like a giant stir fry or a rice-and-beans side dish. Cooked brown rice and jasmine rice freeze well.

>> *Cooked beans can keep for up to 5 days in an airtight container in the refrigerator or up to six months in the freezer. Thaw them slowly in the refrigerator.*

>> *After bringing to the initial boil, never let beans or legumes cook above a simmer, or they will become mealy.*

SIDE DISHES

GRAINS

When you strip away the bran and germ from a grain of wheat, you are left with a soft white interior that is ground into white flour. This makes for soft nice flour, but in the stripping process you lose most of the fiber and nutrients. Whole grains are the way to go for a healthy diet — and as far as taste and texture, they win hands-down over white rice or couscous.

WHEATBERRIES, **BULGUR**, **MILLET**, **SPELT**, **FARRO**, and **BARLEY** are some of my favorite whole grains. All can serve as blank canvases to be used as grainy salads, molded into bundt pans for pretty side dishes, or seasoned with Asian sauces such as teriyaki or ponzu for a quick side. Sauté onions and other vegetables to bulk up the grains or make a full hearty meal. Add chopped cooked chicken or turkey and use in a wrap. By changing the seasoning and add-ins, you completely change the taste.

While **QUINOA** is not technically a grain (it's a seed), it is often lumped with whole grains. Quinoa is a protein. It cooks quickly, in less than 15 minutes; it can be used in any way that you would use couscous or rice. Be sure to rinse it in a fine mesh strainer before cooking it to remove a soapy coating. My kids love it with Parmesan. I use it in burritos and have even seen it used as a rice substitute in sushi during Pesach.

ONIONS

When you cut into an onion, you cut into the cell walls and release a sulfuric compound. This chemical reacts with the saline in your eyes and produces a mild sulfuric acid. Your eyes create tears to rinse the acid away. Refrigerating for about an hour slows down the release of the compound, but my favorite way to fight tears is to wear onion goggles that form an air-tight seal around my eyes. Haven't shed a tear in years.

hard red winter wheatberries

Soft white spring wheatberries

Barley

Kasha / Buckwheat

Spelt   Millet   Farro

onion goggles

mince

dice

chunk

slice

» See note on p. 9 for instructions and illustrations on how to cut onions into even dice.

CHILIS AND CHILI SAUCES

A fantastic way to spice up your cooking is to work with chilis. They are great in salsas, marinades, and dressings. The chilis sold in most markets range in heat levels from somewhat mild to very hot. Going from milder to hot are **JALAPEÑOS,** which can be green or red, **SERRANOS, HABANEROS,** and crazy hot **SCOTCH BONNETS** (not pictured). Start with mild and work your way up. Always wear gloves when working with chilis, even jalapeños. Make sure to remove the gloves before touching any open membranes, like your mouth or eyes. Wash anything that touched the chilis. Pictured also are red pepper flakes, which are great in soups, stews, and on pizza. Chile de arbol can be stored in a cool dry cabinet for up to 6 months and lends nice heat to stir fries, soups, and stews.

Jalapeño peppers that are smoked and dried are called **CHIPOTLE. CHIPOTLE IN ADOBO** is the chipotle canned in a tomato sauce. I have seen this kosher but it is hard to find.

CHILI GARLIC SAUCE is a recent entrant to the kosher marketplace. It is made by a number of companies, but each brand makes it in its own way. Chili garlic sauce is not the same thing as ketchup chili sauce like Heinz, or sauce that looks like duck sauce that has visible chili flakes, even if the name is the same. Authentic chili garlic sauce is a blend of coarsely ground chilies and garlic. It is bright red with chili flakes visible in it. You can add some to your meat marinades for kick or to add heat to chilies, soups, and salsas. My family likes the duck saucy versions as a dip for chicken, but the real stuff is used to add heat to recipes. You can also use **SAMBAL OELEK** or **SRIRACHA,** the smooth version, which is a great hot sauce to shake over any food.

Jalapeños • Habaneros • Chiles de arbol • Serranos • Red pepper flakes

>> *If you have eaten a pepper that was too hot, don't grab for water. Capsaicin, the chemical that makes a hot pepper hot, doesn't dissolve in water, so even ice water won't help remove the heat. Your best bet is milk to relieve some of the burn. If you have eaten meat, eat bread or rice to absorb the heat. Cucumber can also have a cooling effect.*

Sweet or Duck Sauce-Based Chili Garlic Sauce

Authentic Chili Garlic Sauce

Sriracha

CAJUN QUINOA

I like the Ancient Harvest brand of quinoa because it is pre-washed. If you can't find that, just rinse the quinoa well in a fine-mesh strainer to remove the soapy coating.

I have a small, 6-cup bundt pan that works nicely with this recipe. I spray it heavily with nonstick cooking spray and then pack in the quinoa once it has cooked. To unmold, I just hold a plate over the top and invert. You can also do this in individual bundt pans or silicone molds.

1. Place the red and plain quinoa into a medium pot. Add the stock. Bring to a boil over high heat. Turn the heat down and simmer for 15-18 minutes, until all the water is absorbed.

2. Heat the canola oil in a large (12-14-inch) skillet over medium heat. Add the onion, squash, garlic, and thyme. Sauté until the vegetables are shiny and soft, about 6-8 minutes. Add the Cajun seasoning, salt, pepper, tomatoes, and scallions. Sauté for 3 minutes. Remove from heat. Stir the quinoa into the vegetables. Toss to combine. Transfer to serving dish or mold as per headnote.

- 1 cup red quinoa
- 1 cup quinoa
- 4 cups chicken or vegetable stock
- 1 tablespoon canola oil
- 1 small red onion, cut into ½-inch dice
- neck of 1 small butternut squash, peeled, cut lengthwise, cut into ¼-inch dice (1½ cups)
- 3 cloves fresh garlic, minced
- ½ teaspoon dried thyme
- 1 tablespoon Cajun seasoning blend
- ¼ teaspoon fine sea salt
- ¼ teaspoon freshly ground black pepper
- 2 plum tomatoes, seeded, cut into ¼-inch dice
- 2 scallions, roots trimmed, sliced thinly on diagonal

SWEET SPAGHETTI SQUASH KUGEL

nonstick cooking spray

1 large spaghetti squash, 4-5 pounds

4 large eggs

1/3 cup sugar

1 large Granny Smith apple, peeled, cored, cut into 1/4-inch dice

1 (15-ounce) can diced peaches, syrup drained and discarded

1 teaspoon ground cinnamon

2 tablespoons margarine

1/2 cup packed dark brown sugar

3/4 cup cornflake crumbs

1/2 cup chopped pecans

If you love sweet noodle kugel, this dish will be love at first bite!

1. Preheat oven to 350°F. Spray a 9 x 13-inch casserole or oven-to-table dish with nonstick cooking spray. Set aside.

2. Place the whole spaghetti squash onto a cookie sheet or directly on the grate of the oven. Bake for about 1 hour, until slightly darker in color and a little soft when you gently squeeze the sides. You are looking for obvious depressions but be careful not to puncture the skin, as the flesh will be really hot. The time may vary based on the size and weight of the squash; it may need an extra few minutes but don't overcook the squash or it will come out mushy. Do not turn off oven. Remove from oven and allow to cool until it is easy enough to handle. Once the squash is cool, cut it in half lengthwise. Scoop out and discard the seeds. Use a fork to scrape the flesh into spaghetti-like strands and place them into a large mixing bowl.

3. Whisk the eggs with the sugar and add to the squash. Pick out any loose seeds and discard. Mix in the apple, peaches, and cinnamon. Transfer to prepared baking dish.

4. In a medium pot, heat the margarine and brown sugar, stirring often. When they are melted and smooth, remove from heat. Add the cornflake crumbs and pecans. Mix well. Sprinkle over the squash. With a sweeping motion, spray the top of the kugel lightly with nonstick cooking spray. Bake, uncovered, for 45 minutes, until the top is golden brown and the kugel does not jiggle when shaken.

PARVE

YIELD: 6-8 SERVINGS

2 large, long Italian eggplants, or 8 Asian eggplants, unpeeled

canola oil

4 ounces blond or barley miso

½ cup orange juice

1 tablespoon mirin, rice cooking wine; I like the Eden brand

2 teaspoons fresh ginger, peeled, grated on a microplane

2 tablespoons honey

1 tablespoon dark brown sugar

fresh cilantro leaves, chopped, for garnish

MISO-GLAZED EGGPLANT

If you are watching calories, there is a way to skip the frying part of this recipe. Just use Asian eggplants. They are dark purple, long and skinny, similar in shape to a zucchini. If you can find those (Asian markets always have them), just cut them in half lengthwise, skip the pan-frying, and put them right on the baking sheet to be glazed. They are not bitter or hard like their Italian counterparts, so do not need the softening that the frying provides — but they may need a few extra minutes in the oven.

1. Preheat oven to 400°F.

2. Line a large cookie sheet with parchment paper. Set aside.

3. Slice the eggplants in half lengthwise. Cut into ½-inch thick slices.

4. Heat ¼-inch canola oil over medium heat in a large skillet, nonstick if possible. Add the eggplant in a single layer and sear, 3-4 minutes per side. Remove the eggplant and drain on paper towels. Transfer to the prepared sheet as the slices are done; this may need to be done in batches and more oil may be needed, as the eggplants tend to soak up oil.

5. Place the miso, orange juice, mirin, ginger, honey, and brown sugar into a quart-sized container. Using an immersion blender, emulsify the mixture. This can also be done in a food processor fitted with a metal "S" blade.

6. Brush the miso glaze onto both sides of each eggplant slice. Bake for 5 minutes.

7. Sprinkle some chopped cilantro onto the serving plate. Arrange the eggplant. Brush with some of the remaining miso, if desired. Sprinkle with remaining cilantro.

SILAN-ROASTED SWEET POTATOES AND LEEKS

6 large sweet potatoes, half of them peeled, each cut into 1½-inch chunks

2 large leeks, root end and top 4 inches trimmed, sliced into ½-inch thick rounds, cleaned well

⅓ cup extra-virgin olive oil

⅓ cup silan date honey

>> *The silan may caramelize and become hard if the potatoes are left too long on the pans before serving. If this happens, return to the hot oven for a few minutes until the silan liquifies, then transfer immediately to serving bowl.*

Silan is date honey or date syrup. Available online, it can also easily be bought anywhere Israeli products are sold, particularly in Syrian and kosher markets. This versatile ingredient is sweet, sticky, and will do wonders for any vegetable that you can roast. It has a unique flavor, deeper and richer than honey. I have seen it used in everything from cookies, Passover charoset, dressings, chicken and meat dishes, to topping off an ice cream sundae. Track down a bottle — it is so worth it.

1. Preheat oven to 400°F.

2. Cover 1-2 jellyroll pans with aluminum foil. Set aside.

3. Place the sweet potatoes and leeks into a large bowl. Toss with the oil to coat all the vegetables. Pour in a single layer onto prepared pans. Roast, uncovered, for 30 minutes. Remove from oven and drizzle on the silan. Be careful — the pan will be hot. Coat the vegetables well. Return, uncovered, to the oven and roast for an additional 15-20 minutes, until the sweet potatoes are fork-tender and sticky. Toss once during the roasting time.

4. Immediately transfer to serving bowl.

MUSHROOM ARRABBIATTA OVER SPAGHETTI SQUASH

1 whole medium spaghetti squash, about 3 pounds

extra-virgin olive oil

fine sea salt

freshly ground black pepper

3 tablespoons canola oil

½ small green pepper, seeded, cut in half horizontally and then into very thin strips

½ medium Spanish onion, peeled, thinly sliced

12 ounces button mushrooms, cleaned and quartered

12 ounces cremini mushrooms, cleaned and quartered

2 teaspoons red pepper flakes

1 (15-ounce) can tomato sauce

The word "Arrabbiata" means angry or enraged. In Italy, this sauce is a standard for pasta. You won't be either angry or enraged after tasting this easy and delicious dish, but you will notice the very spicy kick the red pepper gives it. The mushrooms are great as a side for steak or grilled tuna.

1. Preheat oven to 350°F.

2. Place the whole spaghetti squash onto a cookie sheet or directly on the grate of the oven. Bake for about 1 hour, until slightly darker in color and a little soft when you squeeze the sides. The time may vary based on the size and weight of the squash; it may need an extra few minutes, but don't overcook the squash or it will come out mushy. Remove from oven and allow to cool until it is easy enough to handle. Once the squash is cool, cut it in half lengthwise. Scoop out and discard the seeds. Use a fork to scrape the flesh into spaghetti-like strands and place them into a large mixing bowl. Drizzle with olive oil, then season with salt and pepper to taste.

3. Meanwhile, heat the canola oil in a large (12-14-inch) skillet over medium-high heat until almost smoking. Add the green pepper and onion. Sauté for 1 minute. Add the mushrooms, sauté 4-5 minutes until liquid is released from the mushrooms and starts to cook off. The mushrooms should start to caramelize. Sprinkle in the red pepper flakes and ¾ teaspoon salt. Cook for 2 minutes. Add in the tomato sauce. Stir well. Simmer, uncovered, for 10 minutes, stirring every few minutes. Drizzle with 2 tablespoons olive oil and ¼ teaspoon freshly ground black pepper.

4. Transfer the squash strands to a serving dish; top with the mushrooms. Serve hot.

PARVE
YIELD: 12 SERVINGS

1 (14-ounce) can coconut milk, well shaken, opened, and stirred

4 cups water

3 cups short-grain brown rice

1 (8-ounce) can crushed pineapple with its juice

10-12 dried apricots, thinly sliced to equal ½ cup

2 teaspoons fine sea salt

¼ cup sweetened or unsweetened flaked coconut

¼ cup blanched slivered almonds

BAKED COCONUT-BROWN RICE PILAF

We keep hearing from doctors and nutritionists that we need to be eating more whole grains. Well, here is a fabulous, painless, delicious way to get some in the form of short-grain brown rice. When rice is milled, and the bran and germ are removed to convert brown rice into white rice, there is destruction of most of the vitamins and minerals. Fully milled and polished white rice must be "enriched" with vitamins and iron since it has been made so nutritionally poor. The process that produces brown rice removes only the outermost layer, the hull, of the rice kernel and is the least damaging to its nutritional value.

Short-grain brown rice is pleasing texturally. The kernels are so plump, they are almost round. They have a high starch content, which keeps the rice moist.

1. Preheat oven to 375°F. Pour the coconut milk and water into a 9 x 13-inch oven-to-table casserole dish. Stir in the raw rice.

2. Stir in the pineapple, apricots, and salt. Sprinkle the coconut and almonds over the top. Cover tightly with foil. Bake for 1 hour and 40 minutes until the rice is soft. Serve hot.

- 4 large eggs, whisked well
- 1³/₄ cup panko breadcrumbs
- 1 pound green beans, stem ends sliced off
- 1 bunch (20-28 spears) medium-thick asparagus, bottom 2 inches cut off
- nonstick cooking spray
- ½ cup mayonnaise
- 1 tablespoon yellow mustard
- 1 tablespoon finely chopped dill or Israeli pickles
- 2 teaspoons pickle juice from jar or can of pickles

GREEN BEAN AND ASPARAGUS FRIES WITH DIPPING SAUCE

Speed green-bean-eating contests, created by my ingenious sister-in-law Sarah, were a clever way to get my kids and their cousins to competitively eat their veggies while at the same time satisfying their mothers' desire for veggie consumption. There will be no need for contests with these fun "fries." Just make sure to have plenty of the dipping sauce on hand.

1. Preheat oven to 425°F.

2. Set up a 2-part breading station. Place the whisked eggs in one part and the panko in the second part.

3. Working with a small handful of green beans at a time, dip into the eggs and then into the panko, patting to adhere the panko to the vegetables. Place in a single layer, with space between the coated "fries," on 1-2 jellyroll pans. Repeat with remaining green beans and the asparagus. Using a sweeping motion, spray nonstick cooking spray over the green beans and asparagus. Bake, uncovered, for 12 minutes, until crisp and light golden brown.

4. In the meantime, prepare the dipping sauce: In a medium bowl, whisk the mayonnaise, mustard, chopped pickle, and pickle juice.

5. Serve the "fries" with the dipping sauce.

HERB-ROASTED BABY PEPPERS

2 pounds mini sweet peppers, assorted colors

10 cloves fresh garlic

2 teaspoons dried oregano

1 teaspoon dried rosemary

½ cup extra-virgin olive oil

¼ teaspoon coarse sea salt or kosher salt

I started buying these beautiful little peppers at Costco but now I see them popping up in regular supermarkets too. I always roast a whole bag since they are great as a side dish to steak or chicken.

1. Preheat oven to 400°F.

2. Spread the peppers in a single layer on a jellyroll pan. Roast, uncovered, for 15 minutes.

3. Meanwhile, place the garlic, oregano, and rosemary into the bowl of a food processor fitted with a metal "S" blade. Pulse a few times to chop the garlic. With the motor running, drizzle the oil through the top of the machine into the garlic. Process until combined, 3-4 seconds. Remove the peppers from the oven. Pour the garlic mixture over the peppers and use a spoon to toss and coat them all. Return the pan to the oven and roast for an additional 20 minutes.

4. Sprinkle the salt over the peppers. Transfer the peppers to a bowl or platter. Serve hot or at room temperature.

CHEESY GIGANTE BEANS

- 1 pound (2 cups) gigante beans or other large white bean, soaked overnight in a bowl with plenty of room-temperature water to cover by 6 inches, leaving room for expansion

  water
- 1 large onion, peeled, root end left on, halved
- 1 large or 2 small carrots, peeled and halved
- 2 ribs celery, ends trimmed, each cut in half
- 3 cloves fresh garlic
- 3 bay leaves
- 1 teaspoon dried crushed rosemary, divided
- 1/2 teaspoon ground sage
- 2 tablespoons olive oil
- 1 cup grape tomatoes, each cut in half
- 1/2 teaspoon fine sea salt
- 1/4 teaspoon freshly ground black pepper
- 1 cup grated Parmesan cheese

I met and fell in love with gigante beans at a farmers market two summers ago. I made them cheesy and dairy and served them with fish. I made them parve and served them with steak. I think I made a batch almost every week of that summer. Gigante beans are large (about an inch in length!), rich, buttery, and a nutritional powerhouse. They are of Spanish origin and are used in Greek and Mediterranean cooking. They are worth seeking out and the internet or gourmet stores come in handy here. However, other large white beans, such as Italian butter beans, cannellini, runner, and flageolet beans would be good substitutes. You want a bean that will hold its shape and doesn't fall apart after cooking.

If you forgot to soak the beans overnight, do a quick soak: Put beans into a heavy pot. Cover with water by about 2 inches. Bring them to a boil, then turn off the heat. Cover with the lid and let them soak for 1-3 hours. Beans that were soaked overnight will cook more quickly.

1. Using a strainer, rinse beans and check for any stones or debris. Place rinsed beans into a medium bowl, cover with water by 6 inches, and soak overnight.

2. Drain the beans and rinse. Transfer the beans to a large pot and cover with water by 4 inches. Add the onion, carrots, celery, garlic cloves, bay leaves, 1/2 teaspoon rosemary, and sage. Stir. Bring to a boil, skimming any foam that rises to the surface. Reduce heat to low and simmer. Check after 1 hour 10 minutes to see if beans are tender; they may need as much as 1 1/2 hours. You will need less time if using a smaller bean than a gigante.

3. Drain beans, reserving 2 cups of the cooking liquid. Discard onion, celery, carrots, bay leaves, and garlic if possible.

4. When ready to serve, heat the olive oil in the pot over medium heat. Add remaining $1/2$ teaspoon dried rosemary. Return the beans to the pot along with 1 cup of the reserved cooking liquid (saving the other cup in case you want to heat up leftovers), tomatoes, salt, and pepper. Stir. Cook until hot and soupy. Add the Parmesan and toss to combine. Remove from heat. Serve hot.

PARVE
YIELD: 10-12 SERVINGS

MEDITERRANEAN BARLEY TIMBALES

1½ cups pearled barley

½ teaspoon dried oregano

¼ teaspoon dried basil

water

1 English hothouse cucumber with skin

1 cup grape tomatoes, sliced into ¼-inch rounds

¾ cup kalamata olives, pitted, chopped

¾ cup marinated artichoke hearts, rinsed, roughly chopped

6 mint leaves, chopped

3 tablespoons extra-virgin olive oil

1 tablespoon rice vinegar

½ teaspoon fine sea salt

½ teaspoon freshly ground black pepper

nonstick cooking spray

large basil leaves

Grains such as barley work very well as molded side dishes, as in this timbale. It allows for pretty presentation as well as portion control. You can use ring molds, aluminum muffin tins, ceramic ramekins, or silicone molds for endless sizes and shapes of timbales. If there is not a lot of oil in the recipe, just spray the mold with nonstick cooking spray for easy release.

1. Heat an empty large (12-14-inch) skillet over medium-high heat. Add the barley and toast until you begin to smell it, 6-7 minutes. Shake the barley every few minutes. Add oregano and dried basil. Add water to cover the barley by ½-inch; the amount will vary depending on the size of your skillet. Simmer, uncovered, for 20-30 minutes, or until soft. Add water 1 tablespoon at a time if it has cooked out.

2. Slice the cucumber in half lengthwise, remove and discard seeds, and then cut each half into 3 long strips, then into ¼-inch dice. Place into a large bowl.

3. Add the tomatoes, olives, artichokes, mint, olive oil, vinegar, salt, and pepper. Add the barley and mix well.

4. Spray a 4-ounce ramekin with nonstick cooking spray. Pack the ramekin with the barley mixture. Lay a basil leaf on top of the barley and invert the timbale onto a plate or platter, with the basil serving as a base. Repeat with remaining barley. Can be served hot or at room temperature.

KALE CHIPS

olive oil-flavored nonstick cooking spray

1 large bunch curly kale, thick ribs removed and discarded, washed, dried very well

3 tablespoons olive oil

1/2 teaspoon garlic powder

1/8 teaspoon smoked paprika

1/8 teaspoon ground white pepper

fine sea salt

I remember from my pregnancy days that kale is one of the healthiest foods around. After a few misses with recipe ideas, this one was a pleasant surprise for my kids. If you start with bone-dry kale, you will end up with a crispy, potato-chip like result that is surprisingly addictive. My kids were snacking on them right off the cookie sheet — the first batch never even made it to the dinner table.

If you have leftovers, which I doubt, you can re-crisp them, uncovered, the next day in the oven.

1. Preheat oven to 375°F. Cover a jellyroll pan with aluminum foil and spray with nonstick cooking spray. Place the pan into the oven as it preheats.

2. Roughly cut the kale into large pieces. Place the dried kale into a large bowl. If the kale is wet it will steam rather than crisp in the oven. Drizzle on the olive oil and, using your hands, toss to coat the leaves well. Sprinkle on the garlic powder, smoked paprika, and white pepper. Toss well.

3. Carefully remove the hot pan from the oven once it is fully heated. Place the kale onto the pan. It is okay if some overlap slightly. Spray the tops with one more sweep of nonstick olive oil cooking spray.

4. Roast, uncovered, for about 10-12 minutes until the kale is deeper in color, crisp, and a little brittle. Go by color more than by time, so keep checking. Remove individual leaves as they are done. Don't overcook or the leaves will taste burnt. Immediately sprinkle with a pinch of fine sea salt.

CHILI GARLIC CAULIFLOWER

PARVE

YIELD: 8-10 SERVINGS

10 tablespoons canola oil, divided

1 tablespoon soy sauce

1 tablespoon cooking sherry or marsala wine

2 large egg whites

2 heads cauliflower, cut into florets (2½-3 pounds cauliflower florets)

1 cup cornstarch

nonstick cooking spray

6 dried chilies (chili de arbol), or ¼ teaspoon red pepper flakes

3 cloves fresh garlic, minced

sesame seeds, for garnish

SAUCE

½ cup water

¼ cup tomato paste

¼ cup soy sauce

2 tablespoons rice vinegar

2 teaspoons hoisin sauce

2 teaspoons chili garlic sauce

2 teaspoons sesame oil

2 tablespoons dark brown sugar

2 teaspoons cornstarch

There are two unusual ingredients in this recipe but they are absolutely worth looking for. The dried chilies or chili de arbol are long skinny red chilies and can usually be found in small packages in the produce department. I must have passed them in my Shoprite a million times, but never noticed until I asked the produce manager. I was told that they do not require a hechsher as long as there are no other ingredients added. The chili garlic sauce is made by a number of companies that have certification. See p. 260 to make sure you are buying the right type.

1. Cover 2 large jellyroll pans with foil. Pour 4 tablespoons of the canola oil into each pan. Place them into the oven while it preheats to 425°F.

2. In a very large bowl, whisk the soy sauce, sherry, and egg whites until foamy. Add the cauliflower florets. Transfer to a second large bowl or aluminum tin and pass back and forth between the two bowls to coat all the florets evenly. Wipe one of the bowls dry and place the cup of cornstarch into it. Pass the cauliflower back and forth between the 2 bowls to coat the florets evenly in the cornstarch. Set aside.

3. When the oven is up to temperature, carefully remove the jellyroll pans, being aware that the oil will be very hot. Carefully transfer the cauliflower to the pans; don't crowd the pans or the cauliflower will steam. Spray the tops well with nonstick cooking spray. Roast, uncovered, for 30-35 minutes, until crisp and somewhat golden. Toss the cauliflower once during the cooking time.

4. Toward the end of the roasting time, prepare the sauce: In a bowl or quart-sized container, whisk the water, tomato paste, ¼ cup soy sauce, rice vinegar, hoisin, chili garlic sauce, sesame oil, brown sugar, and cornstarch.

5. Heat remaining 2 tablespoons canola oil in a 14-inch frying pan. Add the dried chilies and the 3 cloves minced garlic. Cook until just fragrant, about 20 seconds. Add the sauce to the pan and allow it to simmer and thicken. Add in the cauliflower and toss to coat and warm through.

6. Transfer to a serving dish and garnish with sesame seeds.

PARVE
YIELD: 6 SERVINGS

RANCH-ROASTED POTATOES

- ¹/₃ cup plain, unsweetened soymilk, not vanilla flavored
- 1 lemon

  nonstick cooking spray
- ¹/₂ cup regular mayonnaise
- ¹/₂ teaspoon dried dill
- ¹/₂ teaspoon dried parsley
- ¹/₂ teaspoon dried chives
- ¹/₂ teaspoon garlic powder
- ¹/₂ teaspoon onion powder
- ¹/₂ teaspoon coarse sea salt or kosher salt
- ¹/₄ teaspoon freshly ground black pepper
- 2 pounds baby red potatoes, each cut in half

If making for a dairy meal, you can use ¹/₂ cup sour cream in place of the soymilk and lemon juice. Just whisk it in with the mayonnaise.

1. Pour the soymilk into a small bowl. Add the juice of the lemon. Set aside.

2. Preheat oven to 400°F. Cover a cookie sheet with aluminum foil, spray the foil with nonstick cooking spray, and set aside.

3. In a large bowl, whisk the mayonnaise, dill, parsley, chives, garlic powder, onion powder, salt, and pepper. Whisk in the soymilk. Remove half of the dressing and reserve. Place the potatoes into the bowl with remaining dressing and toss to coat. Place in a single layer on the prepared pan and roast, uncovered, for 40-45 minutes, until fork tender.

4. When the potatoes are done, remove to a serving bowl and toss with the remaining dressing to coat. Serve hot.

VEGETABLE FRIED RICE

- 2 tablespoons butter or margarine
- 1 medium onion, peeled, minced
- 4 cups water
- 2 teaspoons vegetable consommé powder
- 2 cups white basmati rice
- 2 tablespoons canola oil
- 2 cloves fresh garlic, minced
- 1 red bell pepper, seeded, cut into 1/4-inch dice
- 1 carrot, peeled, minced
- 6 stalks asparagus, bottom cut off, sliced on diagonal into 1/4-inch slices
- 2 large eggs, beaten well
- 1/4 cup soy sauce
- 1 tablespoon roasted or toasted sesame oil
- 1/4 cup frozen green peas
- 1/4 teaspoon freshly ground black pepper
- 3 scallions, roots trimmed, sliced thinly on diagonal

In the time it takes to have your Chinese food delivered, you could whip up a big batch of this favorite.

1. Melt the butter or margarine in a medium pot over medium heat. Add the onion and sauté until shiny, about 4-5 minutes; do not allow it to brown. Add the water, consommé, and rice. Bring to a boil. Reduce to a simmer and cook for 15 minutes, uncovered.

2. Meanwhile, heat the oil in a large (12-14-inch) skillet over medium heat. Sauté the garlic, pepper, carrot, and asparagus. Cook until shiny and brightly colored, about 4-5 minutes. Add the beaten eggs, stirring vigorously while shaking the skillet. Add the rice to the pan along with the soy sauce and sesame oil. Mix well. Add the green peas and season with pepper. Toss on the scallions. Serve hot.

DESSERT

GAME PLAN

Although dessert ends a meal, for most, it is far from an afterthought. The hallmark of a good homemade dessert is starting with simple ingredients and using simple techniques to turn out something inspired, desired, and sublime.

For some this is easier said than done. I am in that camp. I am excited to cook anything new and use my creative input to improvise, substitute ingredients, and play around. Desserts, however, are more of a science; there is no playtime, but therein lies the magic. A bowl of powders mixes with a bowl of liquids and you end up with something you will be dreaming about and craving the next day. Directions must be followed exactly, as in all scientific endeavors. Pan sizes matter, temperature matters.

The key is to start with the best quality ingredients: perfectly ripe fruit; good-quality chocolate; fresh eggs, butter, and cream at the stated temperatures. Proper measurement is a must; there is no "a little of this a little of that." The reward is that once you've mastered the different dessert techniques, you will be able to produce dozens of spectacular sweets.

Everybody's budget and space constraints are different, but the photo on the facing page represents most of the pans that you will need to produce a variety of desserts.

EQUIPMENT

OVEN THERMOMETER

An inexpensive oven thermometer is a must for baking. I even keep 2 in one oven because even within a single oven, the temperatures can vary. I adjust the oven temperature based on what those thermometers tell me the temperature is, not what my oven controls read.

PASTRY BRUSH

I like silicone pastry brushes for basting on the barbecue, but in a baker's kitchen I use a standard pastry brush. It is much more delicate.

SIFTER

If a recipe calls for sifting dry ingredients, don't skip this step. Fine ingredients like cocoa powder can have clumps and sometimes a sifter is also used to thoroughly distribute ingredients. If you don't have a sifter, you can improvise with a fine sieve and whisk.

OFFSET SPATULA

A small metal offset spatula is useful for loosening the edges of a cooled cake before turning it out. It is what I use for spreading most frostings and bar cookie doughs.

» *Always preheat before placing a dessert in the oven to bake and keep your oven door closed during the entire baking time, or you can destroy a cake.*

Muffin Pan

Bundt Pan

PAREVE

Loaf Pans

Jellyroll Pans

Silicone Mixing Bowl

Square Baking Pan

Oven-to-Table Casserole

Springform Pan

Tube Pan

Sifter

Thin Metal Spatula

Tart Pans with Removable Bottoms

Cooling Rack

Cookie Sheet

Pastry Brush

Small Offset Spatula

Silicone Spatula

Silicone Spatula

JELLYROLL PANS AND COOKIE SHEETS

If you can, multiple jellyroll pans and cookie sheets are useful so that you don't have to clean and cool a pan between batches. If you are starting out, begin with the basics and build from there, but buy heavy-duty aluminum so it does not warp. Thin cookie sheets are less sturdy and don't bake as evenly. Buy the largest cookie sheets that your oven can handle so that you can get more cookies in a batch. **SQUARE** or **RECTANGULAR BAKING PANS** are used for bars and some cakes. I like shiny metal as opposed to dark, as it reflects heat away from the contents so they are less likely to overbake. Always use the size pan that a recipe calls for; spreading the volume of an 9 x 9-inch cake into a 9 x 13-inch pan will cause it to overbake; if the pan is too small, the cake will not be done in the center. If you use Pyrex to bake a recipe that asks for a metal pan, check for doneness earlier than indicated on the recipe and you may even need to turn your temperature down by 15-25 degrees.

TUBE PAN OR BUNDT PAN

When a recipe calls for a tube pan or bundt pan, use it. Some heavier cakes need this center tube to transfer heat to the center of the cake for more even baking.

In some lighter cakes, like angel food, a tube pan is needed for structure and the way the tube comes out of the pan makes for easy unmolding.

The green bowl in the photo on page 289 is a **FLEXIBLE SILICONE BOWL**. This works great for cakes and cookies, when you mix the dry ingredients first and then add them to the stand mixer bowl.

COOLING RACKS

Wire cooling racks are important for when cookies come out of the oven. When cookies are placed on these elevated racks, air circulates on all sides, allowing them to cool evenly and not steam on the bottom as they would if left on the pan. They are also useful for glazing, as the excess glaze drips through, leaving a cleaner decorated look.

TAPE MEASURE

Measure the diameter of a round pan across the top. I find that keeping a clean tape measure around comes in handy for this and also when I am rolling dough to a certain length.

PAN LINERS

I always have parchment paper, heavy-duty aluminum foil, and nonstick aluminum foil on hand. Parchment makes a surface nonstick without marring it the way nonstick cooking sprays do, as they build up over time.

BENCH SCRAPER

A bench scraper is very useful for scraping dough off the counter, portioning out doughs, and helping to move ingredients.

INGREDIENTS

FLOUR

The main difference among flour types is in the gluten content, which varies depending on whether the flour is made from hard wheat or soft wheat. Gluten is the protein that helps yeast stretch and rise, so the more gluten, the more elasticity. This is important for bread, less so for cake. The flour you use will affect the appearance and texture of your finished dessert. Make sure you use the flour that the recipe calls for.

ALL-PURPOSE FLOUR

All-purpose flour is a balance of hard and soft flours. It is a type of flour that lets you make a wide variety of baked goods from cookies, cakes, and muffins to quick breads and pie crusts. It is available bleached or unbleached. Bleached flour has been treated with bleaching chemicals after milling to make it whiter. You can use them interchangeably unless a recipe is specific.

There are about 3½ cups of flour per pound, so a five-pound bag contains approximately 17½ cups.

CAKE FLOUR

Cake flour is a fine-textured flour that has a high starch content. It has the lowest protein content of any wheat flour, 8% to 10% protein (gluten). It gives cakes and pastries good texture. This flour is excellent for baking fine-textured cakes that don't need to rise much. If you cannot find cake flour, substitute all-purpose flour, but subtract 2 tablespoons of flour for each cup used in the recipe.

BREAD FLOUR

Bread flour is white flour that has more gluten strength and protein content than all-purpose flour. It is unbleached and sometimes conditioned with ascorbic acid, which increases volume and creates better texture. Bread flour has 12% to 14% protein (gluten). This is the best choice for yeast doughs like challah, babka, or cinnamon buns.

» *The most accurate way to measure flour is to use a scale*

ALL-PURPOSE FLOUR
1 cup weighs 4.25 ounces
CAKE FLOUR
1 cup weighs 4 ounces
BREAD FLOUR
1 cup weighs 4.25 ounces

Without a scale, to measure flour properly, spoon it into the measuring cup until it is overflowing then use a flat edge to level the flour.

WHOLE-WHEAT FLOUR

Whole-wheat flour is made by grinding or mashing the whole grain of wheat, also known as the wheatberry. It is more nutritious than all-purpose flour but yields heavy, dense results in baking. If you are looking to swap out white flour in your desserts, in general, you won't be able to substitute the full amount of all-purpose flour for whole wheat. Try starting with ¼ whole wheat, ¾ all-purpose flour and see how the recipe behaves. Breads will respond better than cakes and cookies. Another option is whole wheat pastry flour, which is ground finer, will weigh less and will perform better in a cake recipe. Whole wheat will be less noticeable in cakes that have other strong flavors, such as chocolate.

EGGS

Eggs whip better at room temperature. If you forgot to bring them to room temperature, place them into a bowl of warm water to get the chill out. It is easier to separate eggs when they are cold.

» *The easiest way to separate an egg is right through your fingers, allowing the whites to slip through and leaving the yolk in your hand.*

BUTTER

Always use the freshest unsalted butter in sticks. Different brands use differing amounts of salt, so unsalted butter allows you to control the salt in the recipe. Salt is added to butter to preserve it and mask inferior ingredients.

Most baking recipes call for butter at room temperature because it is easier to cream. This is an important step, as it creates air pockets that affect the texture of the final product in baked goods. The way to know if it is at the right texture is to simply bend the stick in its wrapper. It should bend slightly. If it snaps, it is still too cold. If it depresses too much, it is too warm.

If you are in a rush, take the butter out of the wrapper and cut it into small cubes; it will reach room temperature quicker.

just right

too cold

HEAVY CREAM AND NONDAIRY CREAM

Cream is the thick, fat-rich part of milk, which rises to the top when milk is fresh and is skimmed off. Heavy cream, or whipping cream, has a fat content between 36% and 40% and will double in volume when whipped. Heavy cream adds tenderness and moisture to baked goods. The fat in the cream is what helps stabilize it after it is whipped. It makes mousses light and creamy and it also prevents the cream from freezing too hard when it is used in ice cream, leading to a creamier finished product. I love it just whipped and served with berries.

There is no real substitution for heavy whipping cream. There are nut-based creams on the market but I dislike the taste. The best current option when baking parve is nondairy whipped topping. Although full of chemicals, it gets the job done. For use in recipes, make sure you don't buy parve whipped cream that is already whipped. Use the pourable kind; I like Rich Whip brand nondairy topping.

SUGARS

SUGAR is a refined product of sugar cane. It sweetens and moistens baked goods and gives a rich color.

CONFECTIONER'S SUGAR or **POWDERED SUGAR** is sugar that has been ground to a powder and has cornstarch added in to prevent clumping. Since the texture and sweetness are different from that of granulated sugar, it cannot be substituted in equal amounts.

SUPERFINE SUGAR is also known as **CASTER SUGAR** or **BAKER'S SUGAR**. It is granulated sugar that has been ground to make fine, uniform crystals that dissolve easily in liquids, making it perfect for drinks. It is also great in light baked goods like angel food cakes. If a recipe calls for superfine sugar and you don't have any, you can process regular sugar in a food processor for about 1 minute per cup.

LIGHT and **DARK BROWN SUGARS** are granulated sugar with molasses added. Dark has more molasses and a bit stronger flavor. Brown sugar is always measured in packed cups (7 ounces to a cup on the scale).

soft peaks

firm peaks

*over-whipped,
cream becomes butter*

*light brown
sugar*   *dark brown
sugar*

CHOCOLATE

Always use the best quality chocolate that you can. Inferior chocolate is waxy and sometimes made of liquor, not cocoa beans. The key things to look for are cocoa solids and cocoa butter. The more cocoa solids a chocolate contains, the deeper and more intense the chocolate flavor. The wrapping must list the quantity of cocoa solids; bars containing less than 50% will have little real chocolate taste. One with 70% or more will have a much stronger, finer chocolate flavor.

The amount of cocoa butter listed on the packet will also help you to determine the quality of the chocolate. The more cocoa butter the chocolate contains, the softer it is, making for a real melt-in-your-mouth quality. Cocoa butter does not have to be listed on the packet by percentage, but you can figure about how much is present by its position in the ingredients list, since these are shown in order of volume. If vegetable oil comes higher on the list than cocoa butter, the chocolate is inferior.

By definition, **WHITE CHOCOLATE** is not technically chocolate, since it has no cocoa solids, which is what give dark and milk chocolate their flavor and color. It is a confection made of cocoa butter, sugar, milk solids, and milk fat. Beware of parve white chocolate, most contain vegetable oil instead of cocoa butter and obviously contain no milk solids or milk fat. The taste and quality are waxy and inferior.

VANILLA BEANS AND EXTRACT

There are many types of vanilla, but the three main types are: **MADAGASCAR BOURBON** (named after the Bourbon islands, not the liquor; it is sweet and fruity and has a hay-like aroma), **TAHITIAN** (which is floral or fruity), and **MEXICAN** (which is spicy or woody). Good vanilla beans, regardless of where they come from, should have a rich aroma, be oily to the touch, and be sleek in appearance. Avoid beans that have very little scent, are brittle or dry, or are mildewed.

To cut open a vanilla bean, lay it flat on a cutting surface. Holding one end of the bean to the surface, carefully slice the bean open lengthwise. When you separate the bean, thousands of tiny seeds are exposed. Use the tip of a sharp knife to scrape them out and use them in a recipe. It is usually a good idea to rub them with sugar through your palms to disperse the seeds.

Pure vanilla extract is expensive. To make the product more affordable, imitation vanilla was developed. Unfortunately, imitation vanilla extracts are made with synthetic vanilla that lacks flavor and leaves a bitter aftertaste. When buying vanilla extract, spend the extra money if you can and make sure it is labeled "pure."

COCOA POWDER

Cocoa beans are slightly acidic and therefore cocoa powder is as well. This can give cocoa a somewhat harsh flavor. There are two main types of cocoa powder:

DUTCH-PROCESS COCOA POWDER, like Droste, is made from cocoa beans that have been washed with a potassium solution to neutralize their acidity. The process makes the cocoa darker, reddish-brown, and mellows the flavor somewhat. **NATURAL COCOA POWDER** is made from cocoa beans that are simply roasted, then pulverized into a fine powder, like Hershey's. Because natural cocoa powder hasn't had its acidity tempered, it's generally paired with baking soda (which is alkali) in recipes. Dutch-process cocoa is frequently used in recipes with baking powder, as it doesn't react to baking soda like natural cocoa does.

If a recipe calls for either, the main difference is that Dutch-process cocoa will give a darker color and a more complex flavor, whereas natural cocoa powder tends to be fruitier tasting and lighter in color.

When baking, you should always use unsweetened cocoa powder, not sweetened cocoa powder, sweet ground chocolate, or hot cocoa mix, because doing so allows you to control the amount of sugar in the final product.

Cocoa powder is very fine and tends to clump in the container. Recipes will generally tell you to sift or whisk the cocoa to break up the lumps and disperse it into other dry ingredients.

When making a chocolate cake or gluten-free cake, you can dust the pan with cocoa powder instead of flour. Simply add a spoonful of cocoa powder to the greased pan and roll it around, shaking the pan to ensure an even layer of powder, then tap out any excess.

BAKING POWDER AND SODA

Both baking powder and baking soda are chemical leaveners that help a baked good rise by releasing carbon dioxide into the baking process.

BAKING SODA produces carbon dioxide when mixed with an acidic ingredient and a liquid. This includes lemon juice, yogurt, vinegar, and buttermilk, but also includes cocoa powder (which requires another liquid to be added to combine the two ingredients) and chocolate. Baking soda begins to react immediately when moistened, so batters and doughs made with baking soda should be placed in the oven shortly after mixing.

BAKING POWDER is a combination of baking soda plus an acidic ingredient that is added to produce carbon dioxide when baking. The most common type of baking powder in the US is double-acting baking powder, which releases some gas when a liquid is added and releases more gas when exposed to heat in the oven. Be sure yours is fresh — old baking powder produces inferior baked goods.

NUTS

Make sure your nuts are fresh. The only real way to know is by smelling them; you should smell nothing. If you smell anything, toss them — they are rancid and will only smell worse after being intensified when baked or roasted in your recipe. Store nuts in your freezer to prolong their life.

PHYLLO DOUGH/PUFF PASTRY DOUGH

Although they are both dough and are sold side by side in the freezer section of the supermarket, puff pastry dough and phyllo dough are not related. **PUFF PASTRY DOUGH** is made by placing chilled butter (or margarine) between layers of pastry dough. It is then rolled out and folded, again and again until there are many layers of dough and butter/margarine. When placed in a hot oven, the dough puffs to a light airy result, buttery and soft, as in croissants. **PHYLLO** (also spelled filo) **DOUGH** is tissue-thin pastry dough. It is used in many Greek and Middle Eastern dishes like Spanikopita, baklava, and Moroccan cigars. The result is crisp and flaky. Phyllo dough can be used as a substitute for strudel dough or for other pastry wrappers, such as for spring rolls. It needs to be brushed with fat, like melted butter or margarine, and stacked in layers. For a lower fat option, you can lightly spray the layers with nonstick cooking spray. For best results, store your phyllo sealed, in the refrigerator. It can stay for months and will always be ready to use. When kept at this constant state of defrost and if you work quickly with it, you should not have any problems with it drying out. Opened phyllo becomes brittle, so use up whatever has been unsealed.

TESTING FOR DONENESS

In general, a cake is done when a toothpick inserted in the center comes out clean.

1. If you insert the toothpick (or piece of raw spaghetti) and remove it and it's sticky and moist like this, your cake isn't done yet.

2. If it comes out looking more solid but still moist or with moist crumbs, the cake is almost done but isn't done yet.

3. When the toothpick comes out clean, or with a few crumbs (that look like regular cake crumbs) clinging to it, it should be done.

» But look for other cues as well. The top should feel springy, be evenly browned, and pull away slightly from the sides of the pan.

» In some cakes, a toothpick test will never work, like on a molten chocolate cake, which is moist in the center even when it's done.

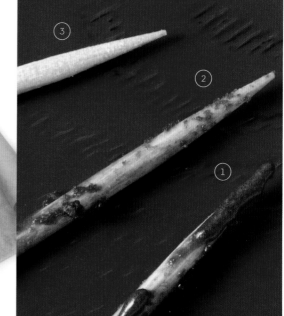

FRUIT

Always use fresh, ripe fruit in baking. To core an apple or pear, cut the fruit in half and then use a melon baller to scoop out the seed packet.

GRILLING or **ROASTING** fruit really intensifies the flavors. Whether you are using up a surplus, have some banged-up bruised fruit, or just want an easy and healthier dessert, fruit can be your ticket to a show-stopping dish.

In summer, when your grill is out, use it for dessert! Brush peeled pineapple slices or unpeeled pitted peach halves with a little canola oil. Sprinkle the cut side of peaches or both sides of pineapple slices with brown sugar and cinnamon; or brush with rum and then sprinkle with brown sugar. Place the slices on a hot grill, peaches cut-side-down, and grill for 5 minutes to caramelize the sugar and to make nice grill marks. Turn the fruit over and grill 5 minutes for a pineapple slice or 10-15 for the peach halves, until the fruit is tender. The peaches should be almost custardy, like peach pie. Serve plain or top with vanilla ice cream and granola or mascarpone cheese.

Fruit is great **OVEN-ROASTED** as well. Place halved apricots, nectarines, peaches, plums, or figs into an oven-to-table casserole dish in a single layer. Add white wine (red wine for figs), a drizzle of honey or maple syrup, and the herb of your choice. I like to use fresh rosemary, mint, or thyme. Cover the dish and bake for 20 minutes at 400°F. Serve in a pretty glass or spoon over angel food cake, sponge cake, or ice cream.

》 *Don't forget to try berries as well. Roasted strawberries, blueberries, blackberries, and cherries are fantastic! Place the berries in a single layer in a baking dish. Sprinkle with sugar. For strawberries, I add a splash of balsamic. Roast at 350°F for 30-40 minutes until the juices thicken; the cherries may take a little longer. Allow fruit to cool before serving.*

billberryphotography/bigstock.com

DAIRY OR PARVE
YIELD: 2 PIES (10 SERVINGS EACH)

6 tablespoons butter or margarine, melted

1 cup dark brown sugar, packed

1/2 teaspoon fine sea salt

3/4 cup light corn syrup

2 teaspoons pure vanilla extract

3 large eggs

2 cups shelled walnut halves

1 (19.9-ounce) package chewy brownie mix and ingredients listed on the box for fudgy, not cakey result (I like Duncan Hines brand)

2 frozen deep dish pie shells

GOOEY WALNUT BROWNIE PIE

There is a deep dark secret in the Fishbein house: we all (except for my husband, who was brought up on his Mom's brownies and thus is a brownie snob) love Duncan Hines brownies.

I love the ease of using it as a base in this decadent pie. This recipe calls for a box of brownie mix but a pie needs only half of the batter, so this recipe is written to make 2 complete pies so as to not waste the brownie mixture. You can store the second one, covered in the fridge for up to 5 days — or make a friend's day!

1. Preheat oven to 350°F.

2. In the bowl of a stand mixer, beat the melted butter or margarine with the brown sugar and salt until smooth.

3. Pour in corn syrup and vanilla. Beat until thoroughly combined. Add eggs, one at a time, mixing between each addition. Stir in walnuts and set aside.

4. Prepare brownie batter as instructed on package for a chewy, not cakey result, if it gives you that option.

5. Remove two frozen pies shells from freezer and divide brownie batter evenly between the two. Spoon walnut mixture evenly over the brownie batters.

6. Bake, uncovered, for 50-55 minutes, until golden brown and slightly puffy. The centers will still be a little jiggly. Cover with foil if the crusts start to brown toward the end of the baking time.

7. Store in refrigerator and serve cold.

BLUEBERRY RIPPLE SEMIFREDDO

12 ounces fresh blueberries

3 large eggs
plus 2 egg yolks

1 teaspoon pure
vanilla extract

1 cup superfine sugar

1³⁄4 cups heavy whipping
cream or 2 (8-ounce)
containers parve
whipping cream;
I like Rich Whip brand

Semifreddo means semi-frozen. Semifreddo desserts are part custard, part ice cream, with a texture like a frozen mousse. The big advantage of this wonderful summer dessert is that it's the perfect way to make a frozen treat without an expensive ice cream maker. It does use raw eggs so if you intend to serve this to someone who is expecting or who has a compromised immune system, make sure to use pasteurized eggs.

In place of a hand mixer, I have a whisk attachment for my immersion blender and it works well here.

1. Place the blueberries into the bowl of a food processor fitted with a metal "S" blade. Process until smooth. Set aside.

2. Place the eggs, egg yolks, vanilla, and sugar into a large glass or metal heatproof bowl. Set the bowl over a pot of simmering water over medium-low heat. Make sure the bottom of the bowl is not touching the surface of the water and that the heat is not too high or the eggs will scramble. The bubbles of simmering water should just break the surface. Using a hand mixer, beat the eggs at medium speed until thick and pale, like softly beaten cream, about 5 minutes. Remove from heat and continue beating for another 5 minutes until the mixture cools down.

3. In the bowl of a stand mixer, beat the cream until soft peaks form; do not overbeat or the cream will be too stiff. Gently fold into the whipped egg mixture. Remove ¹⁄2 cup of this mixture and set aside.

4. Pour the remainder of the cream mixture into a pretty, freezer-safe casserole dish. You can use a 9 x 9-inch square or a dish that has an 8-9 cup capacity. Hold a fine mesh strainer over the reserved cream. Pour the blueberries through the strainer, pressing them against the mesh so the skins are caught but the blueberry pulp goes through. Stir the cream to get a consistent purple color. Swirl decoratively into the semifreddo. Cover with plastic wrap. Place into the freezer for 4-6 hours or until set.

CHOCOLATE-GLAZED CREAM PUFFS

CREAM PUFF PASTRY

$3/4$ cup bread flour

$2/3$ cup water

4 tablespoons unsalted butter or margarine, softened, cut into 10 pieces

1 teaspoon sugar

$1/2$ teaspoon fine sea salt

2 large eggs, room temperature

1 large egg white, room temperature

1 teaspoon pure vanilla extract

$1/2$ teaspoon almond extract

CHOCOLATE GLAZE

$1^{1}/_{2}$ cups powdered sugar

$1/4$ cup Dutch-process cocoa powder

$1^{1}/_{4}$ teaspoons pure vanilla extract

about 3 tablespoons boiling water

about $1^{1}/_{2}$-2 cups whipped cream or prepared vanilla pudding

1. Make the puffs: Preheat oven to 425°F. Line a jellyroll pan with parchment paper and set aside. Place bread flour into a small bowl; set aside. Place $2/3$ cup water, butter or margarine, sugar, and sea salt into a 3-quart heavy-bottomed sauce pot. Heat over medium just until margarine is melted, no more. Whisk occasionally to mix well.

2. Immediately add the flour all at once. The mixture should form quite readily into a nice ball and clean the sides of the pot. Stir and mash this ball around with a flat-bottomed wooden spoon or stiff spatula. A slight film may form on the bottom of the pot. Total cooking time for the flour mix should be about 3 minutes.

3. Transfer dough to the bowl of an electric mixer. Using the paddle attachment, beat for about 40-60 seconds to cool dough slightly. Add one whole egg and beat on high for about 10 to 20 seconds or until the egg is fully incorporated. Repeat with the second egg and scrape the sides of the bowl. Add the egg white and beat again for about 10 to 20 seconds or until batter is smooth, scraping sides as needed. Add vanilla and almond extracts; continue beating for another 5 or 10 seconds.

4. Divide the batter into eight balls by dropping dough onto the prepared pan using a 1-ounce spring-action ice cream scoop, a well-rounded 2 tablespoon measure, a scant $1/4$-cup measure, or a large spoon (about 3 tablespoons batter for each puff); leave at least 3 inches between each ball. Bake at 425°F for 15 minutes. Then without opening the oven door, reduce temperature to 375°F and bake an additional 8 minutes. Working quickly, remove puffs from the oven and use a sharp knife to cut $1/2$- to $3/4$-inch slits in their sides and tops to let the steam escape. Return vented puffs to the oven, then turn the oven off and prop the door open with a wooden spoon. Let the puffs dry for 40 minutes. Transfer from the parchment paper to a cooling rack and allow to cool completely.

302

5. Once the puffs are completely cool, make the chocolate glaze: Set a cookie cooling rack on top of a jellyroll pan. Sift together powdered sugar and cocoa powder into a small bowl. Combine vanilla extract with 2 tablespoons of boiling water. Stir vanilla water into the powdered sugar and cocoa mix. Mix well, pressing the glaze against the sides of the bowl to dissolve the sugar and cocoa lumps. Add more hot water in 1 tablespoon increments until the glaze is at desired consistency. It should take about 3-4 tablespoons total of hot water (including the first 2). If drizzled from a spoon into the bowl, the zigzags should hold their shape only briefly, then melt away, but still be shadows of themselves.

6. Holding the bottom of a puff, dip the top into the chocolate glaze and swirl it around to cover the surface well. Shake off excess and set it right side up onto the prepared cooling rack. The glaze should adhere in a nice even coat and be shiny and smooth. (If it is too thick, add more water; if it is too thin, add a touch of sifted powdered sugar. Mix well after either addition.) Repeat with remaining puffs. Set aside to let glaze harden a bit, about 15 minutes. The glaze will dull slightly.

7. With a serrated knife, slice horizontally most of the way through and fill with whipped cream or prepared vanilla pudding. Alternatively, filling can be piped into the puff before glazing.

》 *Puffs can be made ahead and stored unfilled in an airtight container at room temperature for up to 1 day or frozen for up to 3 weeks. Reheat in a 325°F for 5 minutes if at room temperature or 8 minutes for frozen puffs. Or fill ahead and keep in an airtight container in the refrigerator for up to 1 day, though this will result in a softer puff.*

》 *This batter can also be used for éclairs. Smaller puffs can be filled with pesto & sun-dried tomatoes to make an appetizer. Once the technique for the puff is learned, the options are limitless.*

CARAMEL APPLE CAKE

CARAMEL SYRUP

4 tablespoons (1/2 stick) butter or margarine

3/4 cup light brown sugar, packed

1/4 teaspoon ground cinnamon

1/2 cup light corn syrup

APPLE CAKE

nonstick cooking spray

2-3 Granny Smith apples, peeled

2 1/2 cups all-purpose flour

1 teaspoon baking soda

1/2 teaspoon salt

3/4 cup canola or vegetable oil

1/2 cup (1 stick) butter or margarine

1 1/2 cups sugar

3 large eggs

1/2 teaspoon pure vanilla extract

2 Macintosh, Braeburn or honeycrisp apples, peeled, grated on a box grater, using the bigger holes, to make 1 1/2 cups grated apple

This beautiful, moist cake is stunning. With its apple slices peeking out and its wonderful caramel glaze, serve this one at High Holiday season; it will surely earn you high praise.

1. Preheat oven to 350°F. Using nonstick cooking spray, grease the bottom and sides of a 9 x 13-inch glass or metal baking pan. Cut a piece of parchment paper to fit the bottom of the pan. Spray the parchment. Cut the Granny Smith apples through the belly into a total of 12 (1/2-inch thick) slices; you should see the star in the center of most of the apple slices. Pick out seeds if desired. Place into the pan in rows of 3, overlapping slightly if needed. Set aside.

2. Prepare the caramel syrup: In a medium pot, heat the 4 tablespoons butter, brown sugar, cinnamon, and corn syrup over low heat, stirring until the sugar is dissolved and the butter is melted. Remove from heat. Pour 1/2 cup of the syrup over the apples in the prepared baking pan. Reserve the rest in the pot.

3. In a medium bowl, whisk the flour, baking soda, and salt. Set aside.

4. In the bowl of a stand mixer fitted with the paddle attachment, cream the oil, butter, and sugar, on medium-high speed. Add the eggs one at a time, mixing after each addition. Mix in the vanilla. On low speed, beat in the flour mixture until a smooth batter forms. Using a spatula or wooden spoon, fold in the grated apples. Pour the batter evenly over the apples in the pan. Smooth with a small offset spatula. Bake for 40-45 minutes, until toothpick inserted in center comes out clean.

5. Allow the cake to stand for 5 minutes or until the pan is cool enough to touch. Run a knife around the edge of the pan to loosen the cake. Turn the cake out onto a very large platter. Remove and discard the parchment paper.

6. Allow to cool completely. Heat the remaining caramel in the pot or in the microwave. Drizzle over the cake and platter in a decorative fashion.

DOUGH

²/₃ cup milk or unsweetened soymilk

2 large eggs

¹/₃ cup butter or margarine, melted but not too hot

¹/₄ cup water

¹/₄ cup sugar

1¹/₂ teaspoons fine sea salt

2¹/₂ teaspoons active dry yeast or bread machine yeast

4 cups bread flour

nonstick cooking spray

CHOCOLATE FILLING

12 ounces good-quality semisweet chocolate

1 cup sugar

2¹/₂ teaspoons ground cinnamon

¹/₂ stick butter or margarine, melted

CRUMB TOPPING

1¹/₂ cups confectioner's sugar

1¹/₂ cups all-purpose flour

1 stick butter or margarine, melted

CHOCOLATE BABKA MELTAWAY

One for this week, and one to freeze for up to a month. You can make this recipe as one big batch in a 9 x 13-inch baking pan, you just won't get to see the pretty sides as you do when you release the spring on the springform pan.

1. In the bowl of an electric mixer fitted with the paddle attachment, or in the bowl of a Magic Mill or Bosch mixer, beat the milk or soymilk, eggs, butter or margarine, water, sugar, salt, and yeast, until combined. If using a stand mixer, switch to the dough hook. On low speed, incorporate the flour and mix until a smooth, shiny dough is formed, about 6-7 minutes. If using a bread machine, add the ingredients to the pan according to manufacturer's directions and set to dough cycle. You can also knead all the ingredients by hand until a smooth satiny dough is formed. Cover the bowl with plastic wrap. Set aside in a warm place to rise until doubled in bulk, about 1 hour.

2. Meanwhile prepare the chocolate filling: On a cutting board, with a sharp knife, preferably serrated, very finely chop and shave the chocolate. Transfer it along with any of the shavings from the cutting board to a large bowl. If you don't have good knife skills, you can transfer moderately-sized chunks to the food processor to pulse until finely chopped. Return the chocolate to the large bowl. Mix in the sugar and cinnamon. Pour the warm melted butter or margarine over the mixture and stir until chocolate is coated and it looks like wet sand.

3. Preheat oven to 350°F. Spray 2 (9-inch) springform pans with nonstick cooking spray.

4. Turn the dough out onto a lightly floured surface. Roll the dough into a large 17- x 21-inch rectangle. Sprinkle on the chocolate filling in an even layer to cover all the dough. Starting with the long side of the rectangle, roll up the dough, jellyroll fashion. You can use a bench scraper or thin metal spatula to help ease it off the counter and to help roll. Using a sawing motion, cut into 1-inch-thick slices.

5. Place the rolls flat into the prepared springform pans. It's okay if the rolls don't completely fill the pan; they will expand as they bake.

6. Prepare the crumb topping: Place the confectioner's sugar and all-purpose flour into a medium bowl. Add the melted butter or margarine and pinch to form large crumbs. Make sure they look moist, but don't over-pinch: leave most of the crumbs nice and big — about 1 inch.

7. Bake, uncovered, for 25-30 minutes, until the crumbs look dry, the chocolate looks melty, and the dough is baked and starting to brown in some spots. Do not overbake or the cake will be dry, especially if making in advance and reheating.

8. When ready to serve, release the spring on the pan and remove outside ring. Serve warm or at room temperature.

DAIRY OR PARVE
YIELD: 8 SERVINGS

1/2 cup honey roasted peanuts

2 cups sugar, divided

nonstick cooking spray

2 tablespoons confectioner's sugar

6 tablespoons creamy peanut butter

1/2 cup (1 stick) plus 2 tablespoons unsalted butter or margarine at room temperature for 10 minutes, divided

4 ounces good-quality semisweet chocolate, such as Schmerling Noblesse

4 large eggs, at room temperature

1/2 teaspoon fine sea salt

3/4 cup all-purpose flour

1 teaspoon pure vanilla extract

8 (4-ounce) ramekins

CHOCOLATE PEANUT BUTTER MOLTEN CAKES

Is there any more legendary combination than chocolate and peanut butter? As if just the combination wasn't enough, I've added to the legend, by creating this rich, gooey warm dessert. I apologize in advance if you can't get it off your mind once you've tasted it; addiction is a real possibility here.

1. Preheat oven to 425°F.

2. Place the peanuts and 1/2 cup sugar into the bowl of a food processor fitted with a metal "S" blade. Use on-off pulses to finely chop the peanuts. The texture will be like sand, but with a few larger peanut grains. Don't let the motor continuously run or they may become creamy. Spray 1 (4-ounce) ramekin very well with nonstick cooking spray. Sprinkle in 1 heaping tablespoon of the peanut mixture. Hold the ramekin on its side over the open food processor to catch the excess as you tap the sides, turning the ramekin to coat the sides with the chopped peanuts. Repeat with remaining ramekins. Add 1 more teaspoon of the mixture to the bottom of each ramekin. Set aside, reserving any excess crumbs to decorate the plate if you desire.

3. In a small bowl, using a spoon, mix the confectioner's sugar, peanut butter, and 2 tablespoons margarine until creamy. Place in freezer to chill. Set aside.

4. Break the chocolate into small pieces; place it and the remaining 1/2 cup (1 stick) butter or margarine into a microwave-safe dish. Microwave on medium power for 30-second intervals, stirring in between, until the chocolate is completely melted.

5. In the bowl of an electric stand mixer with the paddle attachment, beat the eggs and salt on high speed until foamy. Slowly pour in the remaining 1 1/2 cups sugar and continue beating until very fluffy and pale yellow. On low speed stir in the flour and vanilla until thoroughly combined. Scrape down the sides as needed.

6. Increase speed to high. While beating slowly, drizzle in the melted chocolate mixture. Once added, continue to beat for 1 minute, scraping down the sides of the bowl.

7. Pour the chocolate batter to come halfway up on each ramekin. Remove peanut butter mixture from freezer and roll into 8 balls. Drop a peanut butter ball into each. Cover with remaining batter, coming almost to the top of each ramekin.

8. Place ramekins on a cookie sheet. Bake for 14-15 minutes, until the tops are puffed and cake-like but the centers are still molten.

9. Serve immediately. Be cautious, as the ramekins will be hot. Garnish with reserved crumbs, if desired.

nonstick cooking spray

1 (8-ounce) block cream cheese, NOT whipped, at room temperature

½ cup sugar

2 large eggs

½ cup heavy cream

½ teaspoon pure vanilla extract

zest of 1 lemon

6 sheets phyllo dough

4 tablespoons butter, melted

ground cinnamon, for garnish

raspberries, for garnish

CHEESE DANISH GALETTE

This simple tart is part cheese Danish, part cheese cake, and part strudel. What a great mix! Have the phyllo defrosted in the refrigerator for at least a day, and up to 3 months.

1. Preheat oven to 350°F. With nonstick cooking spray, coat a 9-inch tart pan with removable bottom. Place on a cookie sheet. Set aside.

2. In the bowl of a stand mixer with the paddle attachment or in a mixing bowl with a hand mixer, on high speed, cream the cream cheese and sugar until fluffy. Lower the speed to medium, add the eggs, one at a time, and beat until incorporated. Mix in the heavy cream, vanilla, and lemon zest. Set aside.

3. Open the package of phyllo dough. Lay one sheet in the pan, allowing to overhang on all sides. Brush with some melted butter. Lay the second sheet of phyllo rotating it so that the corners of the second sheet are angled slightly away from points of the first. Repeat with 4 more sheets of phyllo, laying each at an angle so all the corners form a design.

4. Pour the cheese filling into the tart.

5. Fold the edges of the galette in toward the middle of the pan,. Filling will be visible. Brush undersides of the dough with any remaining butter.

6. Bake for 30-35 minutes, until the phyllo is golden brown. The cheese filling will be slightly puffed and the center won't jiggle. Remove the galette from the oven and allow to cool completely before storing in the refrigerator. Serve cold, sprinkled with ground cinnamon and garnished with raspberries.

cooking spray

1½ tablespoons unsalted butter, softened

½ teaspoon pure vanilla extract

¼ teaspoon fine sea salt

1 cup heavy whipping cream

3½ ounces semisweet chocolate, very finely chopped, almost shaved; I like Schmerling brand

⅔ cup Dutch-process cocoa powder; I like Droste brand

1⅓ cups sugar

⅓ cup light corn syrup

¾ cup roasted salted whole almonds with skin

CHOCOLATE ALMOND SMOOCHES

When I was a kid I went to HALB, and every year the PTA would sell Bartons candy for Passover. I remember scouring the catalogue with my siblings, looking for the black can of Almond Kisses that was a seasonal treat only available at Passover. The creamy, fudgy caramel enrobed whole almonds and made up for any chametz snacks that were off-limits.

I promise, this version, a divine dairy rendition, will not disappoint.

1. Line an 8 x 8-inch baking pan with nonstick or heavy-duty foil so it overhangs the sides; gently fit it to the pan, being careful not to poke holes in the corners. Spray with cooking spray; set aside. Have ready 1 cup of very cold water (ice cold, but without ice), 1 cup of hot water with a clean pastry brush, and measured butter, vanilla extract, and fine sea salt (for step 5). Also, have ready a clean silicone spatula and a candy thermometer.

2. Heat cream in a heavy-bottomed, 6-8-quart pot over medium heat until it just boils. Remove from heat and immediately add finely chopped chocolate and cocoa powder. With a flat-bottomed wooden spoon or a stiff silicone scraper, stir until chocolate and cocoa are mostly melted, about 1-2 minutes. Be sure to scrape the bottom and sides well. The mixture will be shiny but grainy.

3. Return to heat and quickly stir in sugar and corn syrup. Stirring constantly, bring the chocolate mix to a boil; this will take about 3-4 minutes. Scrape sides occasionally. The mixture will be shiny and look smooth on the surface, but when stirred will look spotty and have small bubbles.

4. As soon as the chocolate boils, scrape the sides with a silicone spatula. Using a clean pastry brush dipped in hot water, rinse the chocolate residue from the pot sides; this prevents the sugar from

crystallizing. Clip the candy thermometer to the side of the pot. Stirring and scraping the bottom of the pot constantly, bring to a boil. It will boil quickly at first; lots of steam will be produced, and the bubbles will be large and thickened. Eventually, around 230-240°F, the mixture will boil a bit less vigorously and be very thick. Watch closely; once the mixture gets close to target, the temperature rises quickly. Boil until the candy thermometer reads 257-260°F (hard ball stage), about 8 minutes.

5. Immediately, remove the thermometer and take the pot off heat. Add butter and stir for about 20 seconds; then add measured salt and vanilla. Rapidly stir the caramel until butter is fully dissolved and then for a few seconds more.

6. Instantly, pour chocolate caramel into the prepared baking dish. Do not scrape the bottom of the pan into the mold; that caramel will be hotter than the rest and have a different texture. Working fast, press almonds gently onto the surface of the caramel. Be careful — the caramel is very hot! Let cool completely, at least 3 hours. Using the foil edges, lift chocolate caramel out of the pan; fold down the foil edges. Spray a large knife with cooking oil and use a sawing motion to slice into 40 rectangles. They will be pliable and chewy. Spray knife as needed to keep caramels from sticking. Wrap candies individually in parchment paper squares or candy wrappers (ends twisted) or layer between parchment paper. Keep in an airtight container at room temperature for up to 2 weeks.

DAIRY
YIELD: 28-30 COOKIES

2 cups all-purpose flour

$^3/_4$ cup bread flour

1 teaspoon baking powder

1 teaspoon baking soda

$^1/_2$ teaspoon fine sea salt

2 sticks (1 cup) unsalted butter, at room temperature for 15 minutes

1 cup sugar

1 cup light brown sugar

2 large eggs

1 teaspoon pure vanilla extract

1 cup best-quality semisweet chocolate or a mix of white chocolate chips and semisweet

coarse sea salt

ULTIMATE SEA SALT CHOCOLATE CHIP COOKIES

Ever since the 1930's when Ruth Wakefield invented the Toll House cookie, chocolate chip cookies have been an American favorite. Everyone has a version; most are a variation of her original, from the back of the chip bag. I have tinkered over the 20 years of my marriage to find the perfect cookie that would appeal to both my (crunchy) and my husband's (chewy) likings.

1. Preheat oven to 350°F. Cover 2 cookie sheets with parchment paper. Set aside.

2. In a medium bowl, whisk the all-purpose flour, bread flour, baking powder, baking soda, and salt. Set aside.

3. In the bowl of a stand mixer fitted with a paddle attachment, beat the butter, sugar, and brown sugar until light and creamy.

4. Add the eggs, one at a time, mixing after each addition. Mix in the vanilla.

5. With the mixer on low, beat in the dry ingredients until the batter is just combined. Mix in the chocolate chips.

6. Using a small ice cream scoop or 2-tablespoon measuring spoon, scoop uniform balls of dough onto the cookie sheets. Leave at least an inch of room between them for spreading. Sprinkle with a small pinch of coarse sea salt, pat slightly to keep the salt from rolling off. Bake 13-15 minutes until golden brown. The shorter bake time will yield a chewier cookie, the longer time a crisper cookie. Remove cookie sheet from oven and transfer the cookies to a rack to cool. Repeat with remaining dough. Serve warm.

DAIRY OR PARVE
YIELD: 24 BARS

1¼ cups old fashioned oats, NOT the quick-cooking kind

1¼ cups all-purpose flour

¾ cup sweetened, flaked coconut

¼ cup plus ⅔ cup sugar

¼ cup almond paste

½ teaspoon fine sea salt

¾ cup (12 tablespoons) butter or margarine, melted

1 cup strawberry preserves or jelly

3 large egg whites, at room temperature

¼ teaspoon cream of tartar

STRAWBERRY MERINGUE BARS

Always start making meringue with clean, dry bowls and beaters. Any grease or water will stop your whites from whipping. You can use a little white vinegar on a dish towel to make sure all traces of grease are wiped away. Also, if possible, use superfine sugar for making the meringues and when making meringues in general, to yield a shinier, less grainy meringue.

1. Preheat oven to 325°F. Use parchment paper to line a 9 x 13-inch metal pan, leaving some overhang for easy removal of the finished recipe.

2. In a large bowl, with a wooden spoon or silicone spatula, combine the oats, flour, coconut, ¼ cup sugar, almond paste, and salt. Use your fingers to break up the almond paste and rub it into the mixture. Stir in the butter until blended and flour is no longer visible. Press dough evenly into pan. A small offset spatula is useful to get the crust in evenly. Bake for 18-20 minutes, until edges are lightly golden. Remove from oven. Reduce oven temperature to 300°F. Cool the crust for 5 minutes. Spread the preserves in a thin even layer over the crust.

3. In the bowl of a stand mixer fitted with a whisk attachment, beat the egg whites and cream of tartar on medium until thick and foamy. Gradually add the remaining ⅔-cup sugar, scraping down the sides of the bowl as necessary. Beat on high until stiff peaks form. Use a spatula to dollop the meringue over the preserves. Spread in an even layer, using a small metal offset spatula.

4. Return the pan to the 300°F oven for 45-50 minutes, until the meringue is pinkish-brown and looks dry. It should feel dry when lightly tapped. Remove from oven. Let cool for 5 minutes. Run knife around the edges of the pan without parchment overhang. Using the parchment, pull the Strawberry Meringue out of the pan to a cutting board or countertop. Cut into 24 bars. Let cool completely.

CHOCOLATE MINT COOKIES

1 cup all-purpose flour

¼ cup Dutch-process cocoa powder

¾ teaspoon baking powder

¼ teaspoon fine sea salt

½ cup sugar

3 tablespoons unflavored vegetable shortening

1 large egg

1¼ teaspoons peppermint extract, NOT mint extract

1-3 tablespoons ice-water

GLAZE

6 ounces good-quality semisweet chocolate, finely chopped

3 tablespoons unflavored vegetable shortening

⅛ teaspoon peppermint extract

Channel your inner Girl Scout. If you loved their mint cookies you will find these unbelievable. If your chocolate is taking too long to set, place the cookies in the refrigerator. I actually serve them right from the fridge. Peppermint extract and mint extract are not the same flavor. Mint is too strong a spearmint flavor for this recipe. Stick with peppermint. If you bought peppermint oil instead of extract, use just a few drops, it is very potent.

1. For the cookies: In a medium bowl, whisk together the flour, cocoa, baking powder, and salt. Set aside.

2. In the bowl of a stand mixer, beat the sugar and shortening until well creamed. Add the egg and peppermint extract; continue to beat until smooth, lighter in color, and fluffy. Stir in the dry ingredients. Mix until dough starts to form large lumps, then add ice-water as needed, 1 tablespoon at a time, stirring well after each addition just until a nice dough ball forms when the mixture is pressed between cupped hands.

3. Preheat oven to 400°F. Line 2 cookie sheets with parchment paper.

4. On a lightly floured surface, roll half of the dough to ¼-inch thickness. With a pastry brush, clear away the excess flour on top and around edges. Cut into 2-inch rounds and place 1-inch apart on prepared sheets. Work the dough scraps into remaining dough and roll out to ¼-inch thickness. Cut into 2-inch rounds as well. With a fork, poke holes into cookies in a decorative pattern. Bake for 10 minutes. For crunchier cookies bake 12 minutes. Remove from oven. Let cookies rest 1-2 minutes, then transfer to cooling racks. Cool completely.

5. For the glaze: Line a cookie sheet with parchment paper; set the cooling rack with the cookies onto the cookie sheet.

6. In a microwave-safe small bowl, melt together the chocolate, shortening, and extract in 15-second intervals, stirring well between each, until the chocolate is smooth and thoroughly melted.

7. With two forks, dip each cookie totally into the chocolate and shake vigorously to remove excess chocolate. Return cookies to the cooling rack, allowing excess chocolate to drip onto parchment paper. Let stand for 2-5 minutes, then press fork tines on to the chocolate and lift. Repeat a couple of times to make a rippled effect. Let cookies set until chocolate is firm. The chocolate takes longer to set in a warm kitchen. Store in an airtight container at room temperature — or they are very yummy eaten cold, out of the refrigerator or freezer.

PEANUT BUTTER CAKE

nonstick baking spray with flour in the can

2 cups all-purpose flour

2 cups sugar

1 teaspoon fine sea salt

1 teaspoon baking soda

1 cup (2 sticks) butter or margarine, cut into chunks

1 cup water

1/4 cup reduced-fat creamy peanut butter

2 large eggs

1 teaspoon pure vanilla extract

1/2 cup milk or 1/2 cup unsweetened soymilk

1 teaspoon lemon juice

PEANUT BUTTER CHOCOLATE GLAZE

4 ounces good-quality semisweet chocolate, chopped

1/4 cup creamy peanut butter, can be reduced-fat

5 tablespoons water, divided

1 1/2 cups confectioner's sugar

PEANUT BUTTER BUNDT CAKE WITH CHOCOLATE GLAZE

Moist, peanutty cake enrobed in thick, decadent chocolate glaze, this one is perfect just the way it is. However, to really throw it over the top, for dairy use, freeze mini Reese's Peanut Butter cups for about an hour, then cut each in half. Right after glazing the cake, stick the peanut butter cup halves all over the cake.

1. Preheat oven to 350°F. Heavily spray a 10-inch bundt pan with nonstick baking spray. If yours doesn't have flour in the can, shake a little flour into the pan and coat. Hold it over the sink, tapping the sides to get the flour into the crevices.

2. In a large bowl, whisk the flour, sugar, salt, and baking soda. Set aside.

3. In a medium pot, over medium heat, bring the butter, water, and peanut butter to a boil, stirring until smooth. Add to the flour mixture, stirring well with a silicone spatula, about 50-60 strokes, until well mixed and smooth.

4. In a small bowl, whisk the eggs, vanilla, milk, and lemon juice. Stir this into the peanut butter mixture until you have a smooth batter. Pour into prepared pan. Bake for 40-45 minutes, until toothpick inserted in center comes out clean or with moist crumbs attached. Remove from oven to cool. After 10 minutes, slide a small offset spatula around the sides of the cake to loosen it, as well as around the center of the pan. Hold a serving plate over the pan and invert the cake, shaking to loosen it. Set aside to cool.

5. Prepare the glaze: Melt the chocolate, peanut butter, and 2 tablespoons water in a medium pot over medium heat. Stir until smooth. Remove from heat and stir in remaining 3 tablespoons water. Sift in the confectioner's sugar. Keep stirring until a smooth glaze forms. Pour over the cake, allowing the glaze to run down the sides; use a spatula to spread it nicely.

RASPBERRY LEMON BARS

CRUST

nonstick cooking spray

2 sticks butter or margarine, cut into pieces, at room temperature

$1/2$ cup sugar

2 cups all-purpose flour

$1/2$ teaspoon fine sea salt

FILLING

$2\frac{1}{2}$ cup sugar, divided

1 tablespoon cornstarch

1 cup all-purpose flour

1 teaspoon baking powder

$1/4$ teaspoon fine sea salt

12 ounces frozen raspberries, completely defrosted

5 large eggs

2 tablespoons lemon zest (from 3-5 lemons)

$2/3$ cup lemon juice (from 5-6 lemons)

confectioner's sugar

fresh raspberries, for garnish

If desserts could talk, this one would be shouting things like "Do I look like Spring or what?!!" and "Take me to a bridal shower!" Pretty in pink, this new twist on lemon bars will be a big smash wherever you serve it — and it won't need to talk, your guests will be the ones doing all the raving.

Make sure to use raspberries that were frozen fresh, not raspberries in syrup or sugar.

1. Preheat oven to 350°F.

2. Spray a 9 x 13-inch baking pan with nonstick cooking spray. Line with parchment paper, allowing some to come up over the sides. Spray the paper. This will allow for easy removal and cutting of the bars after they are baked.

3. Prepare the crust: In a stand mixer or with hand mixer, cream the butter and sugar on high speed. Lower the speed and add the flour and salt. Mix until combined and a smooth dough forms. With slightly damp hands, press into prepared pan, coming up $1/2$-inch on all sides. Bake 20 minutes until golden. (Prepare filling while crust is baking so you can pour it while crust is warm.) Remove crust from oven. Leave the oven on.

4. Prepare the filling: In a small bowl, whisk $1/2$ cup sugar, cornstarch, flour, baking powder, and salt. Set aside.

5. Place a fine sieve over a large bowl. Add the raspberries to the sieve. Using a wooden spoon, press the raspberries so that all the juice flows into the bowl, leaving the seeds behind. Stir and mix the berries in the sieve until all that is left is a pulp of seeds. Discard the seeds. To the raspberry juice, whisk in the eggs, remaining 2 cups sugar, lemon zest, and the reserved dry mixture. Whisk in the lemon juice, mixing until all the ingredients are incorporated and there is no trace or clumps of the flour. Pour over the hot crust and bake for 25 minutes, until the filling is set; the top will look a little foamy.

6. Cool completely; store in refrigerator. When ready to serve, use
the parchment to lift the lemon bars out of the pan. Cut into
squares, triangles, or diamonds. Dust with confectioner's sugar.
Garnish with fresh raspberries. Serve cold.

DAIRY OR PARVE
YIELD: 10-12 SERVINGS

WALNUT GRAHAM STRUESEL

- ½ cup graham cracker crumbs
- ½ cup chopped walnuts
- ⅓ cup dark brown sugar
- ½ teaspoon ground cinnamon
- 4 tablespoons butter or margarine, melted

CRUMB TOPPING

- ⅓ cup sugar
- ⅓ cup dark brown sugar
- ¼ cup finely ground walnuts
- 1 teaspoon ground cinnamon
- ¼ teaspoon ground ginger
- ¼ teaspoon fine sea salt
- ½ cup (1 stick) butter or margarine, melted and kept hot
- 1½ cups all-purpose flour

Cake ingredients on facing page

WALNUT STREUSEL COFFEE CAKE

Think of this cake for all-day dining. It is wonderful served warm with a cup of coffee in the morning, is a delightful dessert after lunch, and makes a perfect ending with a cup of tea after dinner. It is moist and has the most incredible streusel crumb topping. On second thought, if you cut into it at breakfast, good luck having any left by dinnertime.

If your tube pan does not have a removable bottom, place a parchment paper round at the bottom of the tube; grease as usual.

1. Preheat oven to 350°F. Grease a 10-inch, nonstick tube pan with removable bottom. Set aside.

2. Prepare the Walnut Graham Streusel: In a medium bowl stir the graham cracker crumbs, walnuts, brown sugar, cinnamon, and melted butter until well mixed. Set aside.

3. Prepare the crumb topping: Place the sugar, brown sugar, ground walnuts, cinnamon, ginger, and salt into a medium bowl. Pour the hot melted butter or margarine into the sugar mixture. Stir to melt the sugars. Add the flour and mix; it will start to form a firm ball. Set aside.

4. Prepare the cake: In a medium bowl whisk the flour, baking powder, and salt. Set aside.

5. In the bowl of a stand mixer fitted with the paddle attachment, on high speed, beat the sugar, butter or margarine, and oil until creamy. Add the eggs. Mix until smooth. Lower the speed and add in the flour mixture. Raise speed and beat until a smooth batter forms, scraping sides as necessary. Lower the speed and beat in the milk or nondairy topping, vanilla extract, and almond extract.

6. Spread half the cake batter into the prepared pan. Use a small offset metal spatula to spread the batter into an even layer. Top with the walnut streusel in an even layer. Top with remaining batter. Use the offset spatula to spread the batter evenly.

7. Break the crumb topping into large crumbs $^1/_2$-$^3/_4$-inch in size (even if they are not uniform, keep them big) and sprinkle over the top of the cake. Bake for 45 minutes until a toothpick inserted into the center of the cake comes out clean or with moist crumbs.

8. Cool completely.

CAKE

3 cups all-purpose flour

1 tablespoon baking powder

$^1/_4$ teaspoon fine sea salt

$1^1/_2$ cups sugar

$^1/_2$ cup (1 stick) butter or margarine

$^1/_3$ cup canola oil

3 large eggs

1 cup milk or nondairy whipped topping, defrosted, ready to pour; I like Rich Whip brand

$^1/_2$ teaspoon pure vanilla extract

$^1/_4$ teaspoon almond extract

DAIRY
YIELD: 8-10 SERVINGS

nonstick baking spray with flour in the can

2 cups all-purpose flour

1 teaspoon baking powder

1 teaspoon baking soda

½ teaspoon fine sea salt

6 tablespoons unsalted butter, softened

½ cup sugar

⅓ cup light brown sugar

1¼ cups mashed very ripe banana (3-4 small)

1 teaspoon pure vanilla extract

2 large eggs

½ cup Nutella

CRUMB TOPPING

2 tablespoons butter, melted

2 tablespoons sugar

2 tablespoons light brown sugar

¼ teaspoon ground cinnamon

⅛ teaspoon fine sea salt

2 tablespoons roughly chopped hazelnuts, use whole hazelnuts (filberts) with skin

¼ cup all-purpose flour

HAZELNUT CRUMB-TOPPED BANANA NUTELLA BREAD

It is easiest to measure the Nutella after it has been microwaved for 30 seconds, which makes it softer. Just make sure all of the foil lid is removed or you will see sparks fly in your microwave.

1. Preheat oven to 350°F. Coat a 9-inch loaf pan with nonstick baking spray.

2. In a medium bowl, sift together flour, baking powder, baking soda, and salt. Set aside.

3. In the bowl of a stand mixer, at medium speed, cream the butter, sugar, and brown sugar until creamy and well combined, about 2 minutes. Mix in the banana and vanilla and beat until creamy. Beat in eggs until well combined, about 2 minutes, scraping down sides as needed. Reduce mixer speed to low and beat in flour mixture until just combined; don't overmix. Place half of the batter into a medium bowl. Stir in Nutella; mix until combined.

4. Alternate spoonfuls of batter into loaf pan until all the batter is used. Swirl batter gently with a knife, 3-4 times.

5. Prepare the crumb topping: In a small bowl mix the melted butter with the sugar, brown sugar, cinnamon, and salt until smooth. Using a wooden spoon or spatula, mix in the hazelnuts and flour. It will look and feel like a soft dough. Using your fingers, break mixture into big crumbs, about ½-inch in size. They do not have to be uniform, but most should be around that size. Sprinkle over the batter.

6. Bake 55 minutes-1 hour or until well risen, deep golden brown, and a toothpick inserted into bread comes out clean or with

moist crumbs attached. Check it at 55 minutes. Do not overbake or the bread will be dry.

7. Allow to cool in the pan for 10 minutes. Run a thin spatula around the perimeter to loosen the bread. Invert the pan and slide the bread out; turn it crumb-side-up. Cool completely on a rack. If not using right away, wrap well in plastic wrap.

WHITE CHOCOLATE CHOCOLATE CAKE

CAKE

nonstick baking spray

- 1/3 cup heavy whipping cream
- 2 teaspoons lemon juice, can be bottled
- 1 teaspoon vanilla extract
- 1 1/4 cup water, at room temperature
- 3 ounces best- quality semisweet chocolate, finely chopped; I like Ghirardelli Brand
- 1/4 cup Dutch-process cocoa powder
- 1 1/2 cups all-purpose flour
- 1 teaspoon baking soda
- 1/4 teaspoon fine sea salt
- 6 tablespoons unsalted butter, very soft
- 1 cup sugar
- 2 tablespoons dark brown sugar
- 2 large eggs, room temperature

Frosting ingredients on facing page

The 4 layers make for a wow presentation but if your frosting skills are weak, make this a 2-layer cake; it will be just as fabulous. Use the fine holes on a box grater or a microplane to finely grate the white chocolate for the garnish.

1. Prepare the cake: Preheat oven to 350°F. Spray the bottoms of 2 (8 x 8-inch) square cake pans with baking spray. Line with parchment paper, then spray the entire inside of pan, being careful to cover all seams well with spray. Set aside.

2. In 1-cup liquid measuring cup, whisk together heavy whipping cream, lemon juice, and vanilla. Set aside.

3. In a medium pot, combine water, chopped semisweet chocolate, and cocoa powder. Whisking often, heat over medium or medium-low just until chocolate is melted and cocoa is dissolved. Do not let simmer. (This can be done in the microwave; just don't allow it to get too hot.) Remove from heat and pour the cream mixture into the pot. Whisk to combine and set aside to cool.

4. In a separate bowl, whisk to combine all-purpose flour, baking soda, and salt. Set aside.

5. In the bowl of a stand mixer, using the paddle attachment, cream together butter, sugar, and dark brown sugar until light and well mixed, about 2 minutes. Add eggs, one at a time, beating well after each addition. Mixture should be light and fluffy. Scrape sides. Lower the speed and add in half the dry ingredients; mix until smooth. Add half of the cooled chocolate liquid; mix until smooth. Repeat, scraping sides as necessary. Beat on medium 30 seconds more. Batter may be thin. Divide evenly into pans and bake for 20-25 minutes or until a toothpick comes out clean. Do not overbake. Cool on a wire rack for 15 minutes, then remove from pan to cool completely.

6. Meanwhile, prepare the frosting: Place the white chocolate and heavy cream into a microwave-safe container. Microwave for 20 seconds, then whisk for 30 seconds. Return to microwave and repeat once or twice until the chocolate is melted. Set aside.

7. In the bowl of a stand mixture fitted with the paddle attachment, cream the butter, cream cheese, and vanilla together. Pour in the melted white chocolate and mix to combine. Lower the speed. Beat in the confectioner's sugar. Raise speed and beat until frosting consistency is reached.

8. Cut each cooled cake in half horizontally. Frost one layer with a thin layer of frosting, just enough to get the next layer to stick; if you use too much, the layers may slide. Stack the next layer on it and repeat until all 4 layers are stacked. Frost. Garnish with grated chocolate.

WHITE CHOCOLATE CREAM CHEESE FROSTING

- 4 ounces white chocolate, finely chopped
- 1/4 cup heavy whipping cream
- 1/2 cup (1 stick) butter
- 1 (8-ounce) block cream cheese
- 1 teaspoon pure vanilla extract
- 2 3/4 cup confectioner's sugar

  additional white chocolate, finely grated, for garnish

ALMOND THUMBPRINT COOKIES

- 1/2 cup (2 ounces) whole raw almonds, not roasted or salted
- 1/4 cup sugar
- 1/2 teaspoon fine sea salt
- 1 teaspoon pure vanilla extract
- 1 teaspoon almond extract
- 12 tablespoons (1½ sticks) butter or margarine, cut into chunks
- 1½ cups all-purpose flour

CHOCOLATE FILLING

- 3 ounces good-quality semisweet chocolate, finely chopped
- 2 tablespoons butter or margarine

>> *Variation – Fill with white chocolate and orange zest filling: When preparing filling, use white chocolate in place of semisweet chocolate and add 1 tablespoon orange zest to the mixture.*

This divine cookie is a grown-up version of a popular Shabbos cookie, affectionately known as the Shtreimel or Swiss Fudge cookie. The chocolate here is rich and fudgy.

1. Preheat oven to 325°F. Cover 1-2 cookie sheets with parchment paper. Set aside.

2. Place the almonds, sugar, and salt into the bowl of a food processor fitted with a metal "S" blade. Pulse until very finely ground.

3. Add the vanilla and almond extracts; pulse 2-3 times. Add the butter or margarine and pulse until evenly mixed. Add the flour and pulse until a smooth dough forms. You will need to scrape down the bowl a few times.

4. Scoop the dough by level tablespoons and roll each into a smooth ball. Place on prepared cookie sheet. Using a rounded teaspoon measure or your thumb, create a depression in each dough ball to flatten the dough and to make a well that will hold the chocolate.

5. Bake for 10 minutes. Remove the tray from the oven and re-press each indentation. Be careful, the pan will be hot. Return tray to oven and bake for an additional 10 minutes. Cool completely.

6. Place the chocolate and 2 tablespoons butter or margarine into a microwave-safe bowl. Microwave on high power, using 20-second intervals, stirring the chocolate between each interval until completely melted. This can also be done in a metal bowl set over a pot of barely simmering water, stirring to melt the chocolate. Using 2 teaspoons, one to hold the chocolate the other to push it off and guide it in, fill the well of each cookie completely with some of the chocolate. Allow to cool and harden slightly. Store the cookies covered tightly in the refrigerator but bring to room temperature before serving.

THAI STICKY RICE AND MANGOES

- 1 cup sweet glutinous sticky rice, soaked in cold water to cover by an inch for 30 minutes, longer if the rice is old, up to overnight
- 1 (13.5-ounce) can coconut milk, NOT cream of coconut, shaken and stirred well, divided

  water
- 1 cup sugar
- ½ teaspoon fine sea salt
- 1 teaspoon cornstarch
- 2-3 ripe mangoes, peeled and sliced

  toasted sesame seeds, for garnish

» *While this rice is prepared in the microwave, remember that microwaves vary in power, so the times given are what work for me. Check the rice after the time is up and see if it is ready. If not, give it an extra minute or so until the rice is completely cooked through.*

In Korea, this dish is known as Khao Niao; it's a popular street food that can be found on almost every corner!

Be sure to use the sweet sticky rice specified in the ingredient list. It is a glutinous rice, unlike Jasmine or other rices that will not work in this recipe, and is not the same as sushi rice, as it is sweet.

You can refrigerate the sauce but not the rice, as it will become hard. The rice can stay out on the counter for a few hours. I was told that the rice is fine without any hashgacha, but double-check the label to be sure that there are no additives.

1. Drain the rice and transfer to a microwave-safe container. Cover with water to come up a bit over the rice (a little more than 1 cup of water). Cover with plastic wrap and microwave at full power for 3 minutes. Stir the rice. You may need to replace the plastic wrap if it won't stretch back over the container. Microwave again for 3 minutes. Stir the rice. It should be translucent and cooked; if not, return to the microwave for 1-minute intervals until it is cooked. It should not be crunchy at all. Allow to steam, covered, for 10 minutes. Be wary of the hot steam when you take off the plastic wrap. Pour ½ cup coconut milk over the rice. Stir it in. Cover and set aside.

2. Pour the remaining coconut milk into a medium pot. Add the sugar and salt. Dissolve the cornstarch in 2 teaspoons water. Add to the coconut milk. Bring to just under a simmer and cook for 2 minutes or until thickened. Do not allow the coconut milk to boil or it will break up.

3. Form the sticky rice into oval shapes using two teaspoons, or mold in small cups or ramekins lined with plastic wrap. Remove plastic wrap after unmolding. Serve with sliced mango. Drizzle the coconut sauce over the top and garnish with toasted sesame seeds.

» Index

This symbol » indicates that this entry is included in the Playbook.

C

G

H

I

J

Q

R

T

U

V

Also available in the
the kosher by design®
cookbook series

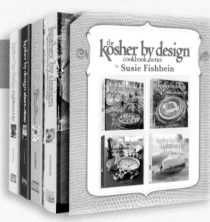

KOSHER BY DESIGN SHORT ON TIME

>> *140 fabulous brand-new recipes*
>> *Large full-color photo featured with every recipe*
>> *Prep time and cooking time*
>> *Innovative ideas for quick and easy table décor*

ISBN: 978-1-57819-072-0

PASSOVER BY DESIGN

>> *Over 30 brand-new recipes, many developed with kosher catering star, Moshe David*
>> *Over 100 Kosher by Design favorites reformulated and retested for Passover*
>> *Over 140 full-color images throughout, with over 40 brand-new photos*
>> *Table décor and entertaining ideas*

isbn: 978-1-57819-073-7

KOSHER BY DESIGN KIDS IN THE KITCHEN

>> *80 kid-friendly recipes*
>> *Large full-color photo featured with every recipe*
>> *Equipment lists*
>> *Ingredient lists*
>> *Helpful tips*
>> *Easy-to-follow* instructions

ISBN: 978-1-57819-071-3

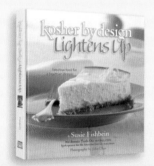

KOSHER BY DESIGN LIGHTENS UP

>> *Over 145 brand-new recipes*
>> *Large full-color photo featured with every recipe*
>> *Creative new entertaining ideas*
>> *Healthy approaches to oils, sweeteners, and grains*
>> *Tips for smarter shopping and more efficient kitchen gadgets*

ISBN: 978-1-57819-117-8

KOSHER BY DESIGN TEENS AND 20-SOMETHINGS

>> *100 delectable brand new recipes*
>> *Over 100 full color photos*
>> *Over 240 pages*
>> *Healthy ingredients for delicious dining in*
>> *Comprehensive cross-reference index*
>> *Inspiring youth-oriented entertaining ideas*

ISBN: 978-1-42260-998-9